On the Law of Nature
A Demonstrative Method

SOURCES IN EARLY MODERN ECONOMICS, ETHICS, AND LAW

Second Series

GENERAL EDITORS

Andrew M. McGinnis
Acton Institute • USA

Wim Decock
KU Leuven • Belgium

Continuing in the line of its predecessor, this series publishes original English translations and editions of early modern religious texts in the disciplines of economics, ethics, and law. Representing a variety of confessional traditions and methodological approaches, these texts uncover the foundations of the development of these and related disciplines.

EDITORIAL BOARD

On the Law of Nature
A Demonstrative Method

Niels Hemmingsen

Translated and edited by E. J. Hutchinson
Introduction by E. J. Hutchinson and Korey D. Maas

CLP Academic

GRAND RAPIDS · MICHIGAN

ISBN 978-1-949011-01-2 (hardcover)
ISBN 978-1-949011-00-5 (paperback)
ISBN 978-1-949011-02-9 (ebook)

CLP ACADEMIC
*An imprint of the Acton Institute
for the Study of Religion & Liberty*

98 E. Fulton
Grand Rapids, Michigan 49503
616.454.3080
www.clpress.com

Interior composition by Judy Schafer
Cover design and image editing by Scaturro Design

Printed in the United States of America

Amicis et fratribus meis ex parte irenica, quae factio nulla est:
et discipulis Philippi Melanthonis per totum orbem terrarum.

CONTENTS

ACKNOWLEDGMENTS

As this project draws to a close, there are several people to whom I owe a debt of gratitude. Peter Escalante and Jordan Ballor were the first to impress upon me the importance of Niels Hemmingsen, and Jordan encouraged the translation of this text. If he hadn't, you wouldn't be holding it in your hands. Drew McGinnis at the Acton Institute was consummately competent throughout the editorial process and provided sure-handed guidance throughout the late stages of the project. Wim Decock provided a number of valuable comments on the translation. As I worked on the translation and tried to refine my ideas about what Hemmingsen was up to, several audiences gave valuable feedback on presentations related to this treatise. I wish to express my thanks to those at Lutheranism and the Classics in Ft. Wayne; the Convivium Irenicum in Landrum, South Carolina; the Classical Association of the Middle West and South in Williamsburg; the Society for Classical Studies in New Orleans; and the Sixteenth International Conference of the International Society for Neo-Latin Studies in Vienna. Jonathan Tomes and Michael Lynch helped me track down citations. David DeMarco, too, was a sleuth extraordinaire of *Quellenforschung*. The staff of Mossey Library at Hillsdale College was invaluable in scaring up hard-to-find books and articles. A generous sabbatical from teaching enabled me to bring this work to completion. Throughout, colleagues at Hillsdale helped me immensely—particularly Korey Maas, with whom I wrote the introduction, and Stephen Naumann, who helped me with some thorny early modern German. I would be remiss if I did not mention the Junius Institute. Without the resources that the institute has made available at the Post-Reformation Digital Library (prdl.org), this undertaking would have been impossible.

On a personal note, I wish to thank my wife, Allison, and our children, Ezra, Isabelle, Silas, Vivian, and Agnes, for their support and good humor. To be honest, I don't think I've talked to them about Hemmingsen nearly as much as I could have. So perhaps they should thank me? (Really, though—if you're reading—thank you.)

Finally, I wish to express profound gratitude for the intellectual friendship and conversation of those friends and colleagues who carry on the irenic spirit of the Philippist tradition. You know who you are, and it is to you that this book is dedicated—fittingly, on the anniversary of Melanchthon's birth.

— E. J. Hutchinson
16 February 2018

Introduction

NIELS HEMMINGSEN AND THE DEVELOPMENT OF LUTHERAN NATURAL LAW TEACHING*

E. J. Hutchinson
Korey D. Maas

Because the Danish Protestant theologian and philosopher Niels Hemmingsen (1513–1600) is today little known outside his homeland, some of the claims made for his initial importance and continuing impact can appear rather extravagant. He is described, for example, not only as having "dominated" the theology of his own country for half a century[1] but more broadly as having been "the greatest builder of systems in his generation."[2] In the light of this indefatigable system building, he has further been credited with (or blamed for) initiating modern trends in critical biblical scholarship,[3] as well as for being "one

---

*This introduction is a revision and expansion of E. J. Hutchinson and Korey D. Maas, "Niels Hemmingsen (1513–1600) and the Development of Lutheran Natural-Law Teaching," *Journal of Markets & Morality* 17, no. 2 (2014): 595–616.

[1] Leif Grane, "Teaching the People—The Education of the Clergy and the Instruction of the People in the Danish Reformation Church," in *The Danish Reformation against Its International Background*, ed. Leif Grane and Kai Hørby (Göttingen: Vandenhoeck & Ruprecht, 1990), 167.

[2] F. J. Billeskov Jansen, "From the Reformation to the Baroque," in *A History of Danish Literature*, ed. Sven Hakon Rossel (Lincoln: University of Nebraska Press, 1992), 79.

[3] Kenneth Hagen, "*De Exegetica Methodo*: Niels Hemmingsen's *De Methodis* (1555)," in *The Bible in the Sixteenth Century*, ed. David C. Steinmetz (Durham: Duke University Press, 1990), 196.

of the founders of modern jurisprudence."[4] Illuminating this last claim especially are the more specific claims for Hemmingsen as having been "an important forerunner for more recent founders of natural law,"[5] most specifically Hugo Grotius, often deemed the "father" of modern natural law.[6] Such attributions rest primarily on the content and influence of Hemmingsen's *De lege naturae apodictica methodus* (*On the Law of Nature: A Demonstrative Method*),[7] which was read widely throughout early modern Europe.[8] The narrative in which the natural law jurisprudence of Grotius and the Enlightenment emanated from that of Hemmingsen is, however, not quite so tidy, as others have also emphasized the great differences between Hemmingsen and Grotius.[9] This confusion with respect to the relationship among Hemmingsen, Grotius, and modernity is perhaps entirely understandable, though, in view of Francis Oakley's droll observation that, among commenta-

---

[4] John Danstrup, *History of Denmark* (Copenhagen: Wivel, 1949), 58.

[5] Jansen, "From the Reformation to the Baroque," 78.

[6] Harold Dexter Hazeltine, introduction to *The Medieval Idea of Law*, by Walter Ullmann (London: Methuen, 1969), xxxn2; and, more expansively, Carl von Kaltenborn, *Die Vorläufer des Hugo Grotius* (Leipzig: Gustav Mayer, 1848), pt. 1, 237–39; pt. 2, 26–44 (excerpts of the Latin text with notes in German).

[7] A selection from *De lege naturae* appeared in English as "On the Law of Nature in the Three States of Life, and the Proofs That This Law Is Summarized in the Decalogue," trans. E. J. Hutchinson, *Journal of Markets & Morality* 17, no. 2 (2014): 619–46. The present work, however, marks its first complete appearance in English. It has been previously translated into Danish: see Niels Hemmingsen, *Om naturens lov 1562*, trans. Richard Mott, 4 vols. (Copenhagen: Øresund, 1991–95).

[8] Lester B. Orfield, *The Growth of Scandinavian Law* (Philadelphia: University of Pennsylvania Press, 1953), 63.

[9] Sebastian Olden-Jørgensen, "Scandinavia," in *European Political Thought, 1450–1700: Religion, Law and Philosophy*, ed. Howell A. Lloyd, Glenn Burgess, and Simon Hodson (New Haven: Yale University Press, 2007), 321. The narrative is, in other words, complex. It is of course plausible that Hemmingsen might be a "forerunner" (cf. the title of Kaltenborn's book) in certain respects, but not in others; see below.

tors, "there appears to be little agreement about the precise nature of the novelty, or 'modernity', or break with scholastic thought patterns they so persistently (if somewhat mystifyingly) ascribe to Grotius."[10]

Those who do find in Hemmingsen an important precursor to the modern natural law theories of the Enlightenment will point to the conclusion of *On the Law of Nature*, where Hemmingsen explains the intention of his work as an attempt to see "how far reason is able to progress without the prophetic and apostolic word."[11] Thus, it is claimed, the result is an ethics that "no longer depend(s) on supernatural authority";[12] therefore, with Hemmingsen "the emancipation of law from theology is complete."[13] Again, however, other commentators have reached the contrary conclusion that Hemmingsen actually finds in the text of divine revelation—most especially in the Decalogue—not only a concise summary of natural law but even its "source."[14] In this view, he is understood simply to be representative

---

[10] Francis Oakley, *Natural Law, Laws of Nature, Natural Rights: Continuity and Discontinuity in the History of Ideas* (New York: Continuum, 2005), 65.

[11] Niels Hemmingsen, *De lege naturae apodictica methodus* (Wittenberg: Rhaw, 1562), Q7r; *On the Law of Nature*, 181.

[12] Harald Høffding, *A History of Modern Philosophy*, vol. 1 (London: Macmillan, 1908), 43.

[13] Roscoe Pound, *The Ideal Element in Law* (Indianapolis: Liberty Fund, 2002), 169.

[14] John Witte Jr., *Law and Protestantism: The Legal Teachings of the Lutheran Reformation* (Cambridge: Cambridge University Press, 2002), 140. It is true that Hemmingsen uses the word "source" (*fons*) to describe the relation between revelation and the law of nature and Witte is therefore correct to say that the Decalogue is for Hemmingsen "a source and summary of natural law." But it is important to note what this does and does not mean: the Decalogue may serve as a proximate "source" of the law of nature in the sense that one can read it republished there; but the ultimate source of the law of nature is God himself. This law was first promulgated in nature or creation, and later in revelation. It is thus accessible through reason and through revelation, both of which ultimately and fundamentally spring from the divine mind; see below. Confusion on this point was once common in the literature. Hence

of contemporary Protestant Reformers, who "saw the natural law exclusively in the words of Scripture."[15]

Natural Law and the Lutheran Reformation

Neither the position of Høffding and Pound nor that of Rommen sketched above is correct, and in fact they present the reader with a false dichotomy: either Hemmingsen must have a purely secular conception of the law of nature or a purely theological one. The confusion is accounted for by inattention to method, which will be taken up more expansively below: in a work of philosophy, Hemmingsen proceeds philosophically, that is, via the findings of reason. In a work of theology (for example, the *Enchiridion theologicum* of 1557), he proceeds theologically. But the conclusions about ethics are in either case the same, because both reason and revelation have God as their author. His use of the Decalogue in *On the Law of Nature* is intended to make just that point.[16]

Christian Friedrich Georg Meister, *Bibliotheca iuris naturae et gentium. Pars prima* (Göttingen: Vandenhoeck, 1749), 59, remarks that Hemmingsen has been criticized, "not undeservedly" (*haud immerito*), for confusing the eternal commands of the natural law with those of the Decalogue. Simliarly, Johann Jacob Schmauss, in his *Neues "Systema" des Rechts der Natur* (Göttingen: Vandenhoeck, 1754), 179, speaks of the "confusion" of reason and revelation ("Vernunft und Offenbarung") at the very foundation of Hemmingsen's project. Even a cursory reading of the treatise shows that this line of critique is not just wrong but absurd. One also notes it is the opposite of the claim that Hemmingsen was a "forerunner" of Grotius, i.e., that he rigidly separated reason and revelation. Both claims spring from a fundamental misreading of Hemmingsen's project.

[15] Heinrich A. Rommen, *The Natural Law: A Study in Legal and Social History and Philosophy* (Indianapolis: Liberty Fund, 1998), 58.

[16] See E. J. Hutchinson, "Divine Law, Naturally: *Lex naturae* and the Decalogue in Two Works of Niels Hemmingsen," in *For Law and for Liberty: Essays on the Trans-Atlantic Legacy of Protestant Political Thought*, ed. W. Bradford Littlejohn (Moscow, ID: Davenant, 2016), 1–19.

The confusion about Hemmingsen's place in the history of natural law is, moreover, rooted in what continues to be a broader confusion concerning natural law in the thought of the Lutheran Reformers, of whom Hemmingsen was indeed a most significant representative throughout the second half of the sixteenth century. Born in relatively humble circumstances on the Danish isle of Lolland and receiving his early humanist education at Roskilde and Lund,[17] Hemmingsen departed for university studies at Wittenberg (he was robbed *en route*)[18] in the very year that Denmark officially adopted the Lutheran reformation.[19] Matriculating in 1537, he lodged with Philip Melanchthon, the architect of Lutheranism's primary confessional document, the Augsburg Confession,[20] and the individual whose thought would most profoundly influence that of Hemmingsen and the broader Danish church. By the time Hemmingsen returned to Denmark in 1542, the

---

[17] On Danish humanism, see Kai Hørby, "Humanist Profiles in the Danish Reform Movement," in *The Danish Reformation against Its International Background*, 28–38.

[18] Melchior Adam, *Decades duae continentes vitas theologorum exterorum principum, qui ecclesiam Christi superiori seculo propagarunt et propugnarunt* (Frankfurt am Main: J. Rosae, 1618), 190.

[19] For background, cf. Ole Peter Grell, "The Emergence of Two Cities: The Reformation in Malmø and Copenhagent," in *The Danish Reformation against its International Background*, 129–45; Martin Schwarz Lausten, "The Early Reformation in Denmark and Norway, 1520–59," in *The Scandinavian Reformation: From Evangelical Movement to Institutionalisation of Reform*, ed. Ole Peter Grell (Cambridge: Cambridge University Press, 1995), 12–41; Thorkild Lyby and Ole Peter Grell, "The Consolidation of Lutheranism in Denmark and Norway," in *The Scandinavian Reformation*, 114–43.

[20] It is worth noting that the Danish government was quite satisfied with the Augsburg Confession as a confessional standard, to such an extent that Frederick II (with the encouragement of Elizabeth I) prevented the adoption of the Formula of Concord and the Book of Concord in Denmark. On Frederick II's rejection of these standards, cf. Lyby and Grell, "Consolidation," in *The Scandinavian Reformation*, 122–23; Eric Lund, "Nordic and Baltic Lutheranism," in *Lutheran Ecclesiastical Culture, 1550–1675*, ed. Robert Kolb (Boston: Brill, 2008), 421–22.

University of Copenhagen—at which he would teach until 1579,[21] when he was removed to the cathedral church in Roskilde for espousing crypto-Calvinist views on the Lord's Supper[22]—had been reestablished along the curricular model of Wittenberg under the guidance of Johannes Bugenhagen. The university, at which Hemmingsen taught Greek, dialectic, Hebrew, and theology, was assigning Melanchthon's own textbooks whenever possible and would for a generation staff its theology and philosophy faculties with professors who had been trained by Melanchthon.[23] Unsurprisingly, those decades encompassing the

---

[21] Hemmingsen also served for a time as pastor of the Church of the Holy Spirit in Copenhagen. For more on Hemmingsen's biography, see the seventeenth-century *Vita* by Melchior Adam, *Decades duae*, 190–92; Holger Frederik Rørdam, *Kjøbenhavns Universitets Historie fra 1537 til 1621*, vol. 2 (Copenhagen: B. Lunos, 1872), 425–55; *Allgemeine Deutsche Biographie*, vol. 11 (Leipzig: Duncker & Humblot, 1880), s.v. "Hemming, Nicolaus"; *Realencyclopädie für protestantische theologie und kirche*, ed. Johann Jakob Herzog, vol. 5 (Stuttgart: R. Besser, 1856), s.v. "Hemming, Nicolaus"; *Realencyclopädie für protestantische theologie und kirche*, ed. Albert Hauck, vol. 7 (Leipzig: J. C. Hinrichs, 1899), s.v. "Hemmingsen, Niels"; *Oxford Encyclopedia of the Reformation*, ed. Hans J. Hillerbrand, vol. 2 (New York: Oxford University Press, 1996), s.v. "Hemmingsen, Niels." These surveys do not agree in all details.

[22] Adam, *Decades duae*, suppresses this controversy entirely. Hemmingsen remained at Roskilde until his death in 1600. For a brief overview of the controversy, see Lund, "Nordic and Baltic Lutheranism," in *Lutheran Ecclesiastical Culture, 1550–1675*, 420–21; Lyby and Grell, "Consolidation," in *The Scandinavian Reformation*, 120–23. Hemmingsen sets out his position in his *Demonstratio indubitatae veritatis de Domino Jesu vero Deo et vero homine unico Christo, Mediatore atque Redemtore nostro unico* (Copenhagen: Balthasar Kaus, 1571) and in his *Syntagma institutionum christianarum perspicuis assertionibus ex doctrina prophetica et apostolica congestis (plerisque propsitis et disputatis in Academia Hafniensi)* (Copenhagen: Vinitor, 1574).

[23] Grane, "Teaching the People," in *The Danish Reformation against Its International Background*, 165.

"Danish Renaissance," and inaugurating Denmark's "golden age,"[24] have also been dubbed its "Melanchthonian era";[25] and Hemmingsen was its central figure. So great was his international standing that he was visited by King James VI of Scotland in 1589. The Danes attributed the bad weather James encountered on his journey home to the malevolent influence of witchcraft, an area in which James' thought (and policy) was influenced by Hemmingsen.[26]

Hemmingsen is best interpreted, then, as firmly situated within this Melanchthonian context, and it is certainly how he was understood by his contemporaries. As works such as his *Enchiridion theologicum* (1557), *Evangeliepostil* (1561), and *Pastor* (1562) were taken up throughout Protestant Europe as popular textbooks (of doctrine and ethics, homiletics, and pastoral theology, respectively), he came to be known as the *Praeceptor Daniae* ("Teacher of Denmark")—a conscious echo by his contemporaries of Melanchthon's own *Praeceptor Germaniae* honorific. His *De methodis libri duo* (1555), an influential work on philosophical and theological method, has similarly been described as a treatise on "Melanchthonian epistemology."[27] Nor were such associations with Melanchthon discouraged by Hemmingsen himself, who urged readers, for example, to understand his own *Enchiridion* as an introduction to Melanchthon's more famous theological handbook, the *Loci communes*.[28]

---

[24] Paul Douglas Lockhart, *Frederick II and the Protestant Cause: Denmark's Role in the Wars of Religion, 1559–1596* (Leiden: Brill, 2004), 13, 17.

[25] Lund, "Nordic and Baltic Lutheranism," in *Lutheran Ecclesiastical Culture, 1550–1675*, 418.

[26] See Lund, "Nordic and Baltic Lutheranism," in *Lutheran Ecclesiastical Culture, 1550–1675*, 426. Cf. Niels Hemmingsen, *Admonitio de supserstitionibus magicis vitandis, in gratiam sincerae religionis amantium* (Copenhagen: Iohannes Stockelman & Andreas Gutterwitz, 1575).

[27] Witte, *Law and Protestantism*, 139. In the *De methodis*, Hemmingsen deals with the different types of argumentative modes appropriate to fields of knowledge in which certainty can be attained as well as those in which only probability is possible.

[28] Niels Hemmingsen, *Enchiridion theologicum* (Wittenberg, 1557), *vv.

For purposes of clarifying some of the confusion respecting Hemmingsen's natural law philosophy, it will thus be much more fruitful to understand him first and foremost as an inheritor and promoter of Melanchthonian Lutheranism, even if aspects of his thought could be taken up and repurposed by later thinkers in the period leading up to and including Grotius. Such clarification will be possible, though, only if certain common errors respecting Melanchthon and Reformation Lutheranism themselves are first addressed. Some degree of misunderstanding—both in particular details and in more general assessments—is most obviously evident where entirely contradictory interpretations are on offer. Beginning most generally, for example, very different conclusions have been put forward in attempts to explain the place of the Reformation in the broader history of law itself. John Witte and Harold Berman speak of its having been a "watershed,"[29] and of its inaugurating a "revolution," ultimately giving birth to the modern nation-state.[30] Paolo Prodi, on the other hand, argues that the legal transformations of the sixteenth century were hardly unique to Protestantism and its territories and goes so far as to suggest that it was actually within Rome that the foundations of the modern state were initially laid.[31] Jan Schröder compares both Protestant and Catholic jurists and theologians of the early modern era and reaches the conclusion that, before the seventeenth century, there remained a "uniformity of the concept of the law."[32] Merio Scattola, while recognizing some sixteenth-century differences in the explication of natural

---

[29] Witte, *Law and Protestantism*, 9.

[30] Harold J. Berman, *Law and Revolution II: The Impact of the Protestant Reformations on the Western Legal Tradition* (Cambridge: Harvard University Press, 2006), 97.

[31] Cf. Paolo Prodi, *The Papal Prince: One Body and Two Souls: The Papal Monarchy in Early Modern Europe* (Cambridge: Cambridge University Press, 1987); and idem, *Eine Geschichte der Gerechtigkeit: Vom Recht Gottes zum modernen Rechtstaat* (Munich: Beck, 2003).

[32] Jan Schröder, "The Concept of (Natural) Law in the Doctrine of Law and Natural Law of the Early Modern Era," in *Natural Law and the Laws of Nature in Early Modern Europe: Jurisprudence, Theology, Moral and Natural*

law especially, suggests that these differences are best understood not as the result of a confessional divide in religion but of the disciplinary divides—especially between law, philosophy, and theology—in Protestant and Catholic universities alike.[33]

In addition to the perplexities introduced by such disparate assessments, others are the result of factors ranging from overlooked context to unwarranted exaggeration and outright caricature. Claims that the Reformation inevitably produced the modern state, for example, are partially predicated on the proposition that Lutheran legal philosophy not only gave rise to "modern" theories of natural law, but also that it was a fundamental source of legal positivism.[34] An example of this view stated most starkly is Roscoe Pound's understanding of Reformation legal theory: "The legal order was to rest on the authority of the divinely ordained state[,] not on an authoritative universal law."[35] Moreover, just as the modern state is believed to be the consequence of the Reformers' nascent positivism, this positivism itself is further traced to what is widely understood to be early Protestantism's inherently nominalist and voluntarist philosophical commitments. James St. Leger, for example, describes the nominalism associated with William of Ockham as "the intellectual framework of Protestant thought."[36] More pointedly, Heinrich Rommen asserts, with reference to natural law, that "the so-called Reformers had drawn the ultimate conclusions from Occamism with respect to theology. Contemptuous of reason,

---

Philosophy, ed. Lorraine Daston and Michael Stolleis (Abingdon: Ashgate, 2008), 63.

[33] Merio Scattola, "Models in History of Natural Law," in *Ius Commune: Zeitschrift für Europäische Rechtsgeschichte* 28 (2001): 96–99.

[34] Berman, *Law and Revolution II*, 97–99.

[35] Pound, *The Ideal Element in Law*, 166–67. This is obviously a false dilemma: natural law is not incompatible with a position that holds the state to be a divine ordinance. This assumption is basic to all premodern and early modern natural law theory.

[36] James St. Leger, *The "Etiamsi Daremus" of Hugo Grotius: A Study in the Origins of International Law* (Rome: Pontificum Athenaeum Internationale "Angelicum," 1962), 35.

they had arrived at a pregnant voluntarism.... Thereby the traditional natural law became speculatively impossible."[37] Even the far more cautious Scattola places the Lutheran Reformers, Melanchthon included, within this "voluntaristic" tradition.[38]

The criterion by which this voluntarism is regularly identified is the Reformers' supposed rejection of eternal law.[39] If Thomas Aquinas is accepted as representative, even definitive, of the "traditional" view, natural law is to be understood as the "participation in the eternal law by rational creatures."[40] This eternal law, in turn, is understood to be that law existing in and proceeding from the immutable nature and intellect of God himself.[41] This "realist" or "intellectualist" account stands in contrast, then, to nominalist or voluntarist accounts, which locate the source of natural law not in the divine nature or intellect but in the divine will alone. Because God, being radically free, *could have* willed and so promulgated a moral law other than that which he did in fact promulgate, this law cannot be understood to reflect an eternal law congruent with God's own unchanging nature and wisdom. Quite obviously, then, if the Reformers did indeed reject the reality of eternal law they would simultaneously have been rejecting natural law as traditionally understood.

In point of fact, however, the early Lutherans—Melanchthon, most relevantly—did not reject the concept of eternal law or embrace the

---

[37] Rommen, *The Natural Law*, 54.

[38] Scattola, "Models in History of Natural Law," 108, 111, 115. That the natural or moral law is for Melanchthon most fundamentally rooted in the divine wisdom or divine mind rather than the divine will is made explicit in, e.g., book 1 of his *Ethicae doctrinae elementorum libri duo*, CR 16:168, 170, 179–81.

[39] Berman, *Law and Revolution II*, 89; Scattola, "Models in History of Natural Law," 115; and the literature reviewed in Antti Raunio, "Divine and Natural Law in Luther and Melanchthon," in *Lutheran Reformation and the Law*, ed. Virpi Mäkinen (Leiden: Brill, 2006), 23–24.

[40] Thomas Aquinas, *Summa theologiae*, I-II, Q. 91, A. 2.

[41] Cf., for example, Thomas Aquinas, *Summa theologiae*, I-II, Q. 91, A. 1; Q. 93, A. 1 and 4; Q. 97, A. 3.

idea that the source of natural law is to be located in the divine will rather than the divine nature or intellect.[42] Melanchthon, for example, confesses the natural law's congruence with "the eternal and immutable rule of the divine mind,"[43] and speaks of that law which "is the eternal and immutable wisdom and justice of God."[44] Similarly, he speaks of the wisdom, justice, and truth eternally existing "in the divine mind," and subsequently "implanted in human minds" by the God who desires men's actions to "conform to the standard of his own mind."[45]

Clarification on this fundamental point allows further clarification respecting the Reformers' understanding of the relationship between natural law and divine revelation. It is on the assumption that they admitted only a voluntarist concept of law that Rommen, for example, asserts that they "saw the natural law exclusively in the words of Scripture." The same assumption, perhaps, informs Witte's and Berman's conclusion that, even for Melanchthon, the Ten Commandments were regarded as "the ultimate source" of natural law.[46] That is, if natural law is not the rational creature's participation in an unchanging eternal law but is only the expression of God's contingent (even arbitrary) will, then its content must be derived from the only unambiguous expression of the divine will—that found in the revelation of Scripture.

Again, though, this conclusion is precisely what one does not find in the Lutheran Reformers. Indeed, even Luther, often understood to lean more toward voluntarism than does Melanchthon, could be so emphatic as to exclaim, with reference to Moses, "Where he gives the

---

[42] It is sometimes allowed that this is true of Melanchthon but not of Luther himself. But even Luther can refer to the reality of eternal law, and speak of natural law being an expression of the divine nature or essence rather than the divine will alone. See Raunio, "Divine and Natural Law in Luther and Melanchthon," in *Lutheran Reformation and the Law*, 22–25, 40, 59.

[43] Melanchthon, *Ethicae doctrinae elementa*, CR 16:228; idem, *Enarratio Symboli Niceni*, CR 23:294.

[44] Philip Melanchthon, *Oratio de Legibus*, CR 11:909.

[45] Philip Melanchthon, *Oratio de Legum Fontibus et Causis*, CR 11:918–19.

[46] Witte, *Law and Protestantism*, 127; Berman, *Law and Revolution II*, 80.

commandments, we are not to follow him except so far as he agrees with the natural law."[47] Yet this does not mean that Luther or his core-ligionists were engaged in an attempt to "throw over the authority of the church,"[48] to "emancipate jurisprudence from theology,"[49] or (à la Grotius) even to defend the possibility of natural law without the necessity of positing God's existence.[50] Given the previously noted criticism of the Reformers for purportedly making natural law wholly dependent on Scripture, it is in fact rather strange that they should also be criticized for allegedly divorcing the two entirely. They do neither, however. Instead, in the same treatise in which Luther gives natural law priority to Moses, he emphasizes that "Moses agrees exactly with nature."[51] Elsewhere, he similarly states that "the natural laws were never so orderly and well written as by Moses."[52] The very same conclusion is reached by Melanchthon, who, like Luther, understands the Ten Commandments to be a summary of natural law, a republication made necessary on account of the noetic effects of sin militating against a clear and consistent recognition of the law divinely "implanted in human minds."[53] That is to say, the Decalogue is not the source of natural law; natural law is the source of the Decalogue.

Especially worth emphasizing at this point is, again, the continuity here evident between the "traditional" understanding and that of the Wittenberg Reformers. This emphasis is needed on account of

---

[47] Martin Luther, *How Christians Should Regard Moses*, in *Luther's Works* [hereinafter *LW*], ed. Jaroslav Pelikan, Helmut Lehman, and Christopher Brown, 75 vols. (Philadelphia: Fortress; St. Louis: Concordia, 1955–), 35:173.

[48] Pound, *The Ideal Element in Law*, 166.

[49] Hazeltine, introduction to *The Medieval Idea of Law*, xxxn2.

[50] See Hugo Grotius, "Prolegomena to the First Edition," in *The Rights of War and Peace*, ed. Richard Tuck, 3 vols. (Indianapolis: Liberty Fund, 2005), 3:1748.

[51] Luther, *How Christians Should Regard Moses*, in *LW* 35:168.

[52] Luther, *Against the Heavenly Prophets*, in *LW* 40:98.

[53] See, for example, Philip Melanchthon, *Loci Theologici Germanice*, *CR* 22:257.

misunderstandings such as that expressed by Johann Erdmann, who judges Melanchthon's association of natural law with the Decalogue to be a novel departure from tradition.[54] In fact, it is precisely the same association—and explanation—that one finds in Aquinas. He, too, equates the content of the Decalogue with that of natural law, stating that "[t]he Old Law showed forth the precepts of the natural law,"[55] and that "such precepts belong to the natural law absolutely."[56] At the same time, Aquinas also gives logical and chronological priority to the natural law, explaining that, "as to those precepts of the natural law contained in the Old Law, all were bound to observe the Old Law; not because they belonged to the Old Law, but because they belonged to the natural law."[57] Despite this priority, however, Aquinas also recognizes the necessity of natural law's summary and republication in Scripture. This was required on account of "the uncertainty of human judgment,"[58] and because the effects of sin have made man "subject to the impulses of his sense appetites" and deprived him of the "full force of reason."[59]

Date and Context of *On the Law of Nature*

Having briefly clarified some common misconceptions concerning the natural law philosophy of those most immediately and influentially informing Hemmingsen's own thought, we are now better situated to understand the date and context of *On the Law of Nature*, what Hemmingsen was and was not attempting to do in the text, and its method and structure. The date and context of the treatise are taken up here; his purpose and method will be treated in the following sections.

---

[54] Johann Eduard Erdmann, *A History of Philosophy*, vol. 1 (New York: Macmillan, 1890), 686.

[55] Thomas Aquinas, *Summa theologiae*, I-II, Q. 98, A. 5.

[56] Thomas Aquinas, *Summa theologiae*, I-II, Q. 100, A. 1.

[57] Thomas Aquinas, *Summa theologiae*, I-II, Q. 98, A. 5.

[58] Thomas Aquinas, *Summa theologiae*, I-II, Q. 91, A. 4.

[59] Thomas Aquinas, *Summa theologiae*, I-II, Q. 91, A. 6.

Hemmingsen's *On the Law of Nature* was first published in Wittenberg in 1562 and subsequently went through several more printings. Hemmingsen himself tells us, in his dedicatory epistle to Lord Erik Krabbe, where the genesis of this work is to be found. The idea occurred to him "last year" (and so presumably in 1560 or 1561)[60] when he was giving lectures on the apostle Paul's letter to the Romans. After noting that he might need to defend himself for venturing across disciplinary boundaries and thus giving offense to specialized gatekeepers, he writes:

> Furthermore, lest anyone accuse me of being a man who, according to the proverb, puts his own scythe into another's harvest, this is my defense. Last year I had to expound Paul's Letter to the Romans, in which, because the apostle declares that the law of nature is the truth and that the law of God is known to the gentiles, which they themselves display by their works while their conscience bears witness at the same time—because of this, I say, I thought that it was worth the trouble to explain what the force of that law is; and, in order not to interrupt my lecturing on Paul with an extended disquisition, I began to put together this method concerning the law of nature in a separate place with, I hope, as much fruit as there has been toil.[61]

Let us follow Hemmingsen's train of thought here: Paul affirms the existence of the law of God among the gentiles (that is, among all non-Jews); this "law of God" for them is called the "law of nature"; Paul indicates *that* this law exists, but he is brief and does not explain *what* this law is in any detail; Hemmingsen therefore wishes to do so, clarifying what its "force" is, but he wishes to accomplish this task without interrupting his lectures on Scripture—hence the need for a separate treatise.

---

[60] The dedicatory epistle to the treatise is dated May 1562, indicating that he had finished the work by that point.

[61] Hemmingsen, *De lege naturae*, B1v; *On the Law of Nature*, 16.

If the gentiles are subject to the law of God, their law must be the same in substance as the law revealed specially to God's chosen people in the Old Testament. For if there is only one God and he is a God of truth, there can be only one law in substance; God cannot contradict himself. Therefore, Hemmingsen argues, the law of nature is, and must be, harmonious with the Decalogue. Hemmingsen explains that he will demonstrate this harmony once he has given a definition of the law of nature and analyzed it:

> I shall undertake an analysis of the ... members ... of the definition; in this analysis, we shall observe the force of nature, and ... what the end of man is and what the first principles and hypotheses of the law of nature are.... In addition to these things, I shall set forth what the rewards of the preservation of the norm of nature are, and the penalties for its violation. *When these things have been set forth, I shall add how the Ten Laws*[62] *can be constructed and inferred from practical principles, and to what extent the law of nature is harmonious with the divine law, and to what extent it is discordant from it.*[63]

Hemmingsen, then, will demonstrate (that is, prove by syllogism) from the principles of practical reason that the precepts of the Decalogue are necessarily true. Incidentally, from this it follows that there is in fact no discord between the law of nature and the Ten Commandments. As he writes elsewhere, "the law of nature ... is also the law of God."[64]

---

[62] I.e., the Ten Commandments.

[63] Hemmingsen, *De lege naturae*, B6v–B7r; *On the Law of Nature*, 23–24 (emphasis added).

[64] Hemmingsen, *De lege naturae*, A6v; *On the Law of Nature*, 10. Compare this to John Calvin's comment: "It is evident that the law of God which we call moral, is nothing else than the testimony of natural law, and of that conscience which God has engraven on the minds of men.... Hence it alone ought to be the aim, the rule, and the end of all laws" (*Institutes of the Christian Religion*, trans. H. Beveridge [Edinburgh: Calvin Translation Society, 1845], 4.20.16).

These Ten Commandments can be further summarized in the Two Great Commandments regarding love of God and love of neighbor; both of these are, for Hemmingsen, "natural." But love of one's neighbor necessarily takes place in a social context. Hemmingsen is happy to put this point in classical philosophical terms, referring to man as a "social animal" (*animal sociale*),[65] such that he can discuss what Scripture calls love of neighbor in terms of the classical discussion of "virtue" (*virtus*)—for "it is proper to virtue to unite the minds of men with one another and to join them in friendship for their mutual uses."[66] This conclusion leads naturally to a discussion of the four cardinal virtues (prudence, justice, courage, and temperance). For Hemmingsen, then, there is ultimate harmony between God's law revealed in the Ten Commandments, the law of nature, the Two Great Commandments, and the classical virtues.

Of course, it is true that, from the Christian standpoint, a problem enters here in the apprehension and application of the law of nature: sin. If sin has corrupted our understanding and made a life lived perfectly in accordance with the law of nature impossible, then what is the point of a project like Hemmingsen's? Hemmingsen is aware of this difficulty and deals with it in more than one passage. In general, Hemmingsen distinguishes between the ability to discern the principles of the law of nature, on the one hand, and the ability to arrive at the goal or end of this law (a blessed life) with nature alone as guide, on the other. The former is common to man, even to fallen man, while the latter is impossible for fallen man, whom only the saving action of God can bring to blessedness.[67]

---

[65] Hemmingsen, *De lege naturae*, K4v; *On the Law of Nature*, 103.

[66] Hemmingsen, *De lege naturae*, K4v; *On the Law of Nature*, 103.

[67] In other words, Hemmingsen argues for the truth of what the apostle Paul says *both* in Romans 2 *and* in Romans 1. For more on this, see E. J. Hutchinson, "Nature and the Wound of Nature: A Pauline View of the Testimony of the Ancients in Niels Hemmingsen's *De Lege Naturae*," in *Ad Fontes Witebergenses: Select Proceedings of Lutheranism and the Classics III: Lutherans Read History*, ed. James A. Kellerman, E. J. Hutchinson, and Joshua J. Hayes (Minneapolis: Lutheran Press, 2017), 58–75.

The former, though insufficient for the blessed life, is still important for a variety of reasons. Hemmingsen writes,

> But since nature is now corrupted and no one is able come to true wisdom and blessedness with nature as his guide, it seems that one undertakes discussion about this matter in vain; to this point I thus wish to make a reply. First, it is worthy of a studious man to see what that thing is that Paul calls in one place the truth of God, in another the δικαίωμα τοῦ θεοῦ [the ordinance of God],[68] which he declares to be known to the gentiles, and to see how one might understand how far reason is able to progress. Next, it is most beautiful to observe from what principles and what demonstrations moral teaching and the laws of a polity are constructed, which human society can no more be without than fire and air. For whatever is handed down in ethics and laws must be judged by the norm of the law of nature. For, as Cicero correctly says, "Good law is separated from bad by the norm of nature."[69]

These abiding uses are, then, both theoretical and practical. First, the knowledge of nature is a good in itself: it enables us to understand God more fully, and at the same time maps out the terrain in which reason (*ratio*) is effective. This use corresponds to the contemplative life. Second, the knowledge of nature shows us the principles that ought to be used to frame the laws of any given polity, for only laws so framed will be worthy of the name. This use corresponds to the practical life, such that the law of nature is beneficial, even necessary, for civic life.

The law of nature is so practical, in fact, that Hemmingsen believed his own project to be relevant to the project of legal reform that his dedicatee, Lord Erik Krabbe, was undertaking contemporaneously with Hemmingsen's treatise. Thus he writes to Krabbe:

> As to the fact that I wanted to publish this method of the law of nature to the public under your name, most illustrious man,

---

[68] Rom. 1:32.

[69] Hemmingsen, *De lege naturae*, B5v–B6r; *On the Law of Nature*, 22–23.

I have two reasons that are most just, at least as it seems to me. One of these is that I desire to declare by some token the gratitude of my mind toward you: just as you desire to be most well deserving from all and to be of benefit to all and to harm none (an attitude that Cicero says is proper to the good man), so you have embraced me for many years with unparalleled goodwill. The other reason is that you have been occupied now for a long time with a generally similar task. For you are trying to bring our Danish laws (which belong to the law of nature, from which I draw out particular hypotheses), as though they are body-parts that had been driven apart and, as it were, scattered (a state of affairs that has come about not at all because of the fault of the legislators, some of whom have passed laws for other nations, but on account of the variety of the peoples for whom in one instance some laws, in another instance others, have had to be passed) back to a condition of bodily integrity, in order that all of the individual parts may be bound together fittingly.[70]

Krabbe undertakes his task "in order that we may have one system of Danish law, when the individual parts have been referred to the laws' source and proper end, which alone sacred laws look toward and wish for," and Hemmingsen hopes that his treatise will make a useful contribution to that endeavor.[71] Though the theoretical and the practical aspects of the law of nature are distinguishable, in other words, the first informs the second, and the practice of legislation and jurisprudence cannot be carried out correctly without a proper understanding of the law that both underwrites and sits over all positive law.[72]

---

[70] Hemmingsen, *De lege naturae*, B1v–B2r; *On the Law of Nature*, 17.

[71] Hemmingsen, *De lege naturae*, B2v; *On the Law of Nature*, 18.

[72] Ralph Keen, "The Moral World of Philip Melanchthon" (PhD diss., University of Chicago, 1990), 40, notes a similar attempt made by Maximilian I: "The only way around the multifarious conflicts of laws and interests was to go over them—by appeal to that authority to which Roman law itself looked for its legitimation, the semi-Stoic theory of natural law."

Hemmingsen's Purpose in *On the Law of Nature*

Hemmingsen's purpose in writing *On the Law of Nature* cannot be understood without a consideration of his use of sources, and so a few remarks on this matter are necessary. Deserving of first mention, simply on account of its ubiquity, is Hemmingsen's constant reference to and quotation of the authors of pagan antiquity. As a good pupil of Philip Melanchthon, Hemmingsen makes copious use of classical sources in *On the Law of Nature*.[73] These range from the obvious (for example, Cicero and Aristotle) to the more surprising (for example, the poets Lucan and Claudian). Hemmingsen cites poets not only ornamentally but as substantive authorities who bear witness to the truth of what he argues.[74] It is almost certain that he draws very many of his Greek quotations from the (probably) fifth-century *Anthology* compiled by John Stobaeus, though it is also probable that several come from his own reading; there undoubtedly would have been overlap between the two. On the Latin side, some quotations are likely taken from collections of maxims and proverbial expressions (one thinks, for instance, of Erasmus' *Adages*) or perhaps from citations in contemporary sources: some of the quotations he uses are also found in the works of Melanchthon, for instance. Again, however, a great many presumably come from his own reading. In the translation, brief biographical notices for all authors cited and references to the original sources of quotations have been provided.[75]

---

[73] For a very brief overview of Melanchthon and the classics, see John Edwin Sandys, *A History of Classical Scholarship*, vol. 2 (Cambridge: Cambridge University Press, 1908), 265–66 and (on two of Melanchthon's other students) 268–69.

[74] Sophocles' *Antigone* and the collection of maxims attributed to Menander are especially important in this regard. For a consideration of Hemmingsen's use of Sophocles and Ovid, see E. J. Hutchinson, "The Poets as Philosophers of Practical Action," in *Acta Conventus Neo-Latini Vindobonensis*, ed. Astrid Steiner-Weber (Leiden: Brill, forthcoming).

[75] Hemmingsen himself almost never gives a reference for his citations, though he normally at least gives the author. Titles of works available in English for the most part follow those in the Loeb Classical Library where

Hemmingsen's use of Scripture in this work is much more sparing, aside from the obvious instance of the Decalogue. Nevertheless, as suggested above, the scriptural narrative of sin and salvation provides the framework for Hemmingsen's understanding of the knowability of the law of nature and the ends for which it can be applied—that is, it can (and must) serve as a guide for civic life but does not enable human beings actually to attain to their supreme end of eternal beatitude.[76] Thus, while individual quotations from Scripture are rare, his adherence to it underpins and guides his philosophical stance in certain important respects.[77] When we view his scriptural principles in concert with his classical reading, we can see that his (much more frequent) citations of the ancients serve an important purpose in his stated attempt to demonstrate "how far reason is able to progress without the prophetic and apostolic word." If even those who "do not have the law" of Moses (Rom. 2:14) are able to articulate and embrace the precepts expressed in that law, it becomes evident that the Decalogue cannot be understood as the ultimate or exclusive source of the natural law. Reason can advance a good distance with respect to *knowledge* of the law of nature, even if it has its limits when one comes to the question of salvation; thus it is Scripture that announces the remedy

---

available, though some liberty is taken (e.g., the translator refers to Cicero's most famous philosophical work as *On Obligations* rather than using its more common title *On Duties*).

[76] So much sits easily in the classical two-kingdoms schema developed by Martin Luther and Philip Melanchthon. Such a perspective provides a corrective to Scattola's claim in *Das Naturrecht vor dem Naturrecht* (Tübingen: Max Niemeyer, 1999), 84, that, according to Hemmingsen, "men could fulfill, out of their own strength, a part of the [divine] instruction." To say this elides the crucial distinction between what one might call man's "horizontal" and "vertical" orientations. With respect to the latter, man of himself does nothing that is pleasing to God apart from divine grace.

[77] On Hemmingen's use of Christian sources more broadly in the treatise, see E. J. Hutchinson, "Pagans and Theologians: An Examination of the Use of Classical Sources in Niels Hemmingsen's *De lege naturae*," *Perichoresis*, forthcoming.

for human beings' inability to *follow* the law of nature with only nature as their guide, a subject that Hemmingsen treats much more fully in his biblical commentaries and works of theology.

However, while Hemmingsen's facility with the sources of classical antiquity serves to highlight his embrace of the humanism he had not only imbibed in his early education but of which his mentor Melanchthon was Protestant Europe's foremost exemplar, an acknowledgment of his humanist predilections ought not to obscure the manner in which he also maintains continuity with medieval and contemporary scholasticism. This is evident, for example, in his penchant for the probative role of logic[78] and his clearly teleological presuppositions.[79] Less obvious, but also worthy of note, is that a line of argument he introduces against polygamy is the very same one taken up by the contemporary Spanish neo-Thomist Domingo de Soto.[80] Overlapping areas of structure and concern such as those pointed out here and in the notes to the translation should moderate in some respects an evaluation like that of Christian Friedrich Georg Meister, who claims that Hemmingsen "neglected the trifles of the

---

[78] Though one should not downplay the important effects that contemporary developments in logic (e.g., the works of Rudolph Agricola) had on Hemmingsen and his contemporaries. Merio Scattola, e.g., notes "striking similarities" between Hemmingsen's method and Ramism (*Das Naturrecht*, 80).

[79] Contra Brad S. Gregory, *The Unintended Reformation: How a Religious Revolution Secularized Society* (Cambridge: Belknap Press, 2012), 207. Gregory suggests that the Protestant Reformers rejected traditional "teleological Christian morality." The claim is without foundation. In the notes to the translation, an attempt has been made to make clear some structural parallels between Hemmingsen's treatment of the virtues and that found in Thomas Aquinas' *Summa theologiae*.

[80] That is, one may not make impossible vows, which one would be doing by promising to love more than one spouse equally. Hemmingsen's congruence with De Soto on this point is noted by Andreas Roth, "Crimen contra naturam," in *Natural Law and the Laws of Nature in Early Modern Europe*, 95.

Scholastics and philosophized in an eclectic way."[81] Hemmingsen was indeed an eclectic philosopher, and he indeed sets great store by brevity in this work, but such observations do not preclude significant common ground between his own principles, method, and conclusion and those of the Scholastics.

Hemmingsen's indebtedness to the categories of Wittenberg Lutheranism is also clear, however, being revealed, for instance, in his text's organization around what the Reformers typically referred to as the three "estates" or "orders of creation": the domestic, the political, and the ecclesiastical (though Hemmingsen refers to the third "type of life" as "spiritual" rather than "ecclesiastical").[82] More substantially, it is evident in his distinction between philosophy and theology, as well as the scope of each.[83] Again, though, the overwhelmingly traditional nature of Hemmingsen's Lutheranism, at least with respect to natural law, also becomes obvious. Like that of Luther and Melanchthon, Hemmingsen's association of natural law precepts with those of the Decalogue—evident especially in his "demonstrations" of its two tables—is entirely traditional. So, too, is his giving priority to natural law. This priority of natural law even over apparent biblical *exempla* becomes clear in his comments on monogamy and polygamy, the

---

[81] *neglectis Scholasticorum quisquiliis, eclectice philosophatus est.* See Meister, *Bibliotheca*, 358–59.

[82] Hemminsgen, *De lege naturae*, G6v; *On the Law of Nature*, 77.

[83] This is the implication of Hemmingsen's argument that "right reason" progresses so far as a knowledge that God must rightly be worshiped, but that even Socrates, unaided by revelation, "wanders away from the true God." See Hemminsgen, *De lege naturae*, H7v–H8r; *On the Law of Nature*, 87. This distinction between philosophy and theology, entirely typical of the Reformers, along with the primarily *theological* truth it wishes to protect, is also obscured by Gregory's unfortunate mischaracterization, when he writes that the Reformers "denied the free, rational exercise of the virtues in pursuit of the good any place in disciplining the passions and redirecting untutored human desires" (*The Unintended Reformation*, 207). In fact, as is especially evident in Hemmingsen's treatise, the exercise of virtue is extolled for precisely these reasons; it is merely denied any contributory role in salvation.

latter of which he understands to be prohibited by nature, despite the Old Testament example of the patriarchs; "one must judge not by examples," he writes, "but by the law of nature."[84] At the same time, however, he also recognizes that Scripture "repeats" the natural law (in prohibiting incest, for instance, in Leviticus 18) as a condescension to man's postlapsarian weakness and perversity.[85] With respect to human law, he is equally clear that its "source" is to be found in natural law.[86] Thus, rather than sanctioning the development of legal positivism, he reiterates the traditional doctrine that one cannot obey a ruler who legislates in contradiction to natural law.[87] Not only does Hemmingsen's grounding of legitimate human law in natural law serve as a check on the potentially arbitrary rule of princes, but also his clear reference to divine commands being rooted in "the will *and nature* of God" prevents one from reading him as a voluntarist for whom the natural law itself derives from the potentially arbitrary will of God.[88]

In sum, rather than anticipating or even precipitating modernity, Hemmingsen's explication of natural law is entirely consistent with that of the Lutheran reformer Philip Melanchthon. Recognition of this fact is significant not only because it lends some small support to Wilhelm Dilthey's suggestion that Melanchthon was "*the* ethicist of the Reformation,"[89] but especially because, in that capacity, Melanchthon himself largely remained within and reiterated the received natural

---

[84] Hemmingsen, *De lege naturae*, I7v; *On the Law of Nature*, 97.

[85] Hemmingsen, *De lege naturae*, I7r–v; *On the Law of Nature*, 96. Cf. also I2v (p. 90 below), where the Decalogue is described as "a summary of the law of nature."

[86] Hemmingsen, *De lege naturawe*, A7r–v; *On the Law of Nature*, 4.

[87] Hemmingsen, *De lege naturae*, H6r; *On the Law of Nature*, 85.

[88] Hemmingsen, *De lege naturae*, K3r; *On the Law of Nature*, 100 (emphasis added). Cf. also B8v (p. 27 below), where Hemmingsen associates natural law with eternal law.

[89] Quoted in Witte, *Law and Protestantism*, 121 (emphasis added).

law tradition.[90] Thus, even if the frequent republication and wide dissemination of Hemmingsen's *On the Law of Nature* testify to its early modern importance and influence, these cannot be attributed to any novelty of content or conclusion.[91] If any novelty is to be found in Hemmingsen's treatise, it is to be sought not in its conclusions but perhaps—and only—in the method by which such conclusions are demonstrated.

Method and Structure of *On the Law of Nature*

Hemmingsen desires to prove the validity and necessity of the law of nature by what he believes to be a "universal method." All disciplines must be understood by the methods appropriate to them, whether implicitly or explicitly, but they grow in our estimation of their worth when the proper method of treatment has been systematized and made explicit. He is, moreover, happy to borrow a method that has been used in other disciplines.[92] He writes:

> A most worthy admiration of this matter drove me to put something down in writing concerning the source of the laws, which we are accustomed to call the law of nature, and to do so by a certain and philosophical method, by means of which the beginnings, progress, turning points, and way of return may be clearly perceived. We see that all the liberal disciplines are understood by their own methods—such as grammar, dialectic, geometry, arithmetic, music, and the others; and just as any discipline is clearer when its method

---

[90] Again, contra Gregory, *The Unintended Reformation*, 208, who claims that the Protestant Reformers rejected "morality's natural law as traditionally conceived."

[91] If, then, Hemmingsen exerts an impact on seventeenth-century thought, that impact comes from within his thoroughly sixteenth-century context.

[92] This shows that particular methods are not exclusively bound to particular disciplinary contexts, despite what the citation that follows may seem to indicate *prima facie*. Instead, methods—ways of organizing and arguing for various kinds of content—can cross disciplinary boundaries.

has been explicated in writing, so also it gains greater admiration. Although doctors borrow their axioms from natural philosophy, nevertheless they deserve not the lowest praise on account of the method of their discipline. Civil laws too, for which moral philosophy supplies the axioms, have their own method.[93]

While each discipline has a method (or methods) appropriate to it, Hemmingsen notes that often the axioms, or first principles that are held to be self-evidently true, must be borrowed from elsewhere. For law, the axioms come from moral philosophy. If Erik Krabbe, for instance, wishes to reform civil law, he will have to make use of moral philosophy.

Hemmingsen, then, intends to make these axioms clear and to subject them to a kind of Euclidean method of demonstration, for he believes that ethics is just as open to this kind of analysis as are geometrical figures—in spite of the fact that "certain men falsely maintain" that geometry is the only discipline susceptible of this sort of proof.

Moreover, although one must admit that there are clear demonstrations in Euclid, according to all the ways of making a demonstration—for Euclid uses a threefold method for making a demonstration; for he composes some hypotheses by synthesis, others he refers by analysis to their first principles, and by no means rarely does he make use of ἐπαγωγῇ εἰς ἀδύνατον [reductio ad absurdum], in order to deduce the truth from what is absurd—nevertheless I justly contend that there are ways of making a demonstration in this branch of knowledge of ours (that is, the knowledge of nature) that are not less ἐναργεῖς [manifest] and clear than in Euclid or in other noble and distinguished branches of knowledge. I attempt in this book to lay these ways open and to refer the law of nature to the method proper to this discipline, and I do so in

---

[93] Hemmingsen, *De lege naturae*, A7r–v; *On the Law of Nature*, 11–12.

order that this part of philosophy, which ought to be very well known to all men, may in some way be rendered illustrious.[94]

There are numerous examples of this method in the treatise. Because of its brevity, we include here his demonstration of the fifth commandment (in Hemmingsen's numbering), "You shall not murder," as an illustration.

> Whatever disturbs human society, whether in the domestic or the political state, is forbidden by the law of nature. Hatreds, reviling, quarrels, and murders disturb human society. Therefore, hatreds, reviling, and murders are forbidden by natural law. And, on the contrary: since mutual love, friendly conversations, kindness, concord, and the pursuit of the preservation and defense of one another preserve human society, they are therefore required by nature.[95]

Indeed, what Hemmingsen believes to be novel about his project is the fact that he uses this type of method in the realm of moral philosophy. While many others, including Greeks and Romans, poets and philosophers, and even his own teacher, Philip Melanchthon, have given the "principles of morals,"[96] no one has yet subjected them to the kind of investigation Hemmingsen proposes to undertake.[97] Thus he writes:

---

[94] Hemmingsen, *De lege naturae*, B1v; *On the Law of Nature*, 15–16.

[95] Hemmingsen, *De lege naturae*, I5r–v; *On the Law of Nature*, 94.

[96] In connection with Hemmingsen's teacher Melanchthon, Ralph Keen remarks that, for him, "philosophy" does not mean "metaphysics," but *moral philosophy* ("Moral World," 13).

[97] He obviously cannot mean that no one before him has used syllogistic reasoning in the realm of ethics. For example, Melanchthon says, in the *Ethicae doctrinae elementa*, that "moral philosophy" is "an explication of the law of nature" that gathers together "demonstrations in the order that is customary in the liberal disciplines," and that this procedure is used to come to conclusions that are congruent with the Decalogue (*CR* 16:167). Hemmingsen

Moreover, although many—both poets (such as Pythagoras, Theognis, Phocylides, Cato, and several others) and philosophers (such as Plato, Aristotle, Plutarch, and Cicero) have handed down the commandments of morals, and in our own day Philip Melanchthon (and neither the serpentine ingratitude of many, nor the secret treachery of the spiteful, nor the open misrepresentation of his enemies will ever obscure the glory of this most holy man) has written about moral philosophy most wisely and usefully: nevertheless no one yet, as far as I know, has handed down these elements and shown the way of demonstrative progress in this most noble art, so to speak, of nature, a task which really would have been by no means easy for the best men, if they had proposed to treat the first principles of nature, and from there the construction of what follows from these first principles, by the method that we are following.

It was somewhat common in the eighteenth century to criticize Hemmingsen for having failed to carry out his purpose. That is, he says that he will follow a "Euclidean" method, which indicates a kind of "mathematical" procedure. He does not in fact do so, or at least not exclusively—or so say Meister and Jakob Friedrich Reimmann.[98] It is alleged that he must have forgotten what he said in the prefatory sections when he came to write the treatise itself. This line of critique, however, is misplaced. Hemmingsen means no more by claiming to pursue a "Euclidean" method than that he will argue deductively from immovable first principles—and this he does in the treatise.

Nevertheless, the criticism may seem to retain some force because an enormous amount of the treatise is devoted to an issue *apparently* altogether different from the proof of the law of nature, and that is

must mean, then, that no one has rigorously carried this method through from beginning to end.

[98] Meister, *Bibliotheca*, 359; Jakob Friedrich Reimmann, *Versuch einer Einleitung in die Historiam literariam derer Teutschen* (Halle im Magedeburg: Renger, 1713), 36. Meister borrows the criticism wholesale from Reimmann, whom he quotes at length.

the theory of knowledge and its acquisition. Through a brief overview of the way in which the work fits together, however, we can see why Hemmingsen dedicates so much of his discussion to this issue and, moreover, how it forms an integral part of his construal of and argument for the validity and accessibility of the law of nature.

Let us start with the prefatory documents just mentioned and from which much of the previously cited material was drawn. Hemmingsen begins *On the Law of Nature* first with an epistle whose dedicatee has already been noted, Lord Erik Krabbe. Krabbe was a jurist and diplomat who served the Danish crown on eighteen embassies to foreign states and was also himself the author of treatises on Danish law.[99] He had intended to write "a lawbook valid for all of Denmark" with the support of King Christian III—the project to which Hemmingsen seems to refer in passages from the letter cited above—but it was never brought to final form.[100]

The second introductory piece is the Preface to the Reader, in which he explains the connection of his project with the Delphic Oracle ("Know yourself") as interpreted through the Christian narrative of sin and salvation. Pure nature can no longer guide man effectually to blessedness, but it can point out the goal toward which our actions should be directed and can cause the welling-up of doxology to the true God who has made and restored nature.

In the preface, Hemmingsen claims that he will follow Galen's "analytical" method; he will begin with a definition of the law of nature, which he will then unpack.[101] But, as he begins the treatise proper, that is not quite what he does. He first gives a "rational account" of the words *law* and *nature*, for which he cites a number of Greek and

---

[99] See O. Garstein, *Jesuit Educational Strategy, 1553–1622*, vol. 3 of *Rome and the Counter-Reformation in Scandinavia* (Leiden: Brill, 1992), 34–35; further references regarding Krabbe can be found on p. 3n1 in the treatise proper.

[100] J. L. Larson, *Reforming the North: The Kingdoms and Churches of Scandinavia, 1520–1545* (New York: Cambridge University Press, 2010), 450.

[101] In fact, Hemmingsen makes use of both analysis and synthesis. The metaphor of "unpacking" is drawn from Hemmingsen's own: he claims that he will first give the definition as though "rolled up … like a bedroll in a sack."

Roman writers. Only then, after citing Cicero's definition, does he give his own "just and complete definition":

> The law of nature is a certain knowledge, imprinted on the minds of men by God, of the principles of knowing and acting, and of the conclusions proved from these principles that are in agreement with the proper end of man. Reason constructs these conclusions from the principles by necessary consequence for the government of human life, so that man may recognize, want, choose, and do the things that are right, and avoid their opposites; and God has bestowed on men the conscience as the witness and judge of all these things.[102]

Hemmingsen states in the preface that, after defining the law of nature, he will undertake an analysis of each part of the definition, as noted above. Now, because the first element of his definition is that the law of nature is a "certain knowledge [*noticia certa*]," he must include a discussion of epistemology—of how we know in general. Thus, he next discusses "sensitive knowing [*cognitio sensitiva*] and intellectual knowing [*cognitio intellectiva*]", and the relation of knowing to desiring, or of knowledge to appetite, as these two are the "principles of acting."

After a brief treatment of the justification for putting faith in first principles, he moves on to the end of man, which should be referred

---

[102] Hemmingsen, *De lege naturae*, C2r–v; *On the Law of Nature*, 30. There is an echo of Stoic epistemology in this definition through Hemmingsen's reference to an inborn *noticia*, rendered "knowledge" above (for further discussion, see Translator's Note below). Scattola, *Das Naturrecht*, 86, states that one is "disappointed in the systematic expectation" of a Stoic approach in what follows, claiming that Hemmingsen instead pursues an Aristotelian teleology that arises from the nature of man's being. It is better to say that Hemmingsen is philosophically eclectic, as has already been noted: his epistemology shows the influence of Stoicism, Platonism, Aristotelianism, Neo-Platonism, and Johann Reuchlin. Those aspects that come from the Stoic tradition (e.g., the belief in innate knowledge) are situated within an approach to human life that is, at both the individual and corporate levels, teleological in not only an Aristotelian but also a Protestant way: it is ordered to the knowledge and praise of God as its ultimate end.

to the true God, about whom Hemmingsen cites several *testimonia* from pagan writers. In fact, man's domestic, political, and spiritual life all must be referred to the true God. This God is the same one who authored the Decalogue, which "is said to be a summary" of the law of nature. To prove the truth of that claim, Hemmingsen provides a series of syllogistic demonstrations of the commandments that show how they cohere with what he has defined as the law of nature discernible outside of Scripture.

To show further consistency between general and special revelation, Hemmingsen then gives a catalogue of the classical cardinal virtues (prudence, justice, courage, and temperance), in which he offers numerous citations of classical authors. The ethics of the ancient Greeks and Romans, then, as well as the ethics of ancient Israel, have their source in the law of nature. Lastly, he discusses conscience, the final part of his definition.

Conclusion

It is hoped that the foregoing summary of the treatise and its place within Philippist ethical reflection gives some indication as to why it is worth bringing Hemmingsen's work into English at long last—the more so because it comes at a time at which there is both revived interest among Protestants in natural law theory, as works such as those by Stephen Grabill, David VanDrunen, Bradford Littlejohn, and Robert Baker and Roland Ehlke (among others) prove,[103] along with, paradoxically, a revival of the nineteenth-century Roman Catholic

---

[103] Stephen J. Grabill, *Rediscovering the Natural Law in Reformed Theological Ethics* (Grand Rapids, MI: Eerdmans, 2006); David VanDrunen, *Natural Law and the Two Kingdoms: A Study in the Development of Reformed Social Thought* (Grand Rapids, MI: Eerdmans, 2009); idem, *A Biblical Case for Natural Law* (Grand Rapids, MI: Acton Institute, [2006]); idem, *Divine Covenants and Moral Order: A Biblical Theology of Natural Law* (Grand Rapids, MI: Eerdmans, 2014); W. Bradford Littlejohn, *The Peril and Promise of Christian Liberty: Richard Hooker, the Puritans, and Protestant Political Theology* (Grand Rapids, MI: Eerdmans, 2017); Robert C. Baker and Roland Cap Ehlke, eds., *Natural Law: A Lutheran Reappraisal* (St. Louis: Concordia,

polemic that Protestants are responsible for the evacuation of traditional Christian principles of ethical reflection.[104] In Hemmingsen's treatise, we have a clear exposition and development of a position that was, in its basic outline, an ecumenical inheritance of Protestants throughout Europe, as well as an erudite account of one possible epistemology that can undergird it, all bolstered with a dazzling array of classical quotations that place Hemmingsen firmly in a tradition that reaches back for over two millennia. Finally, it has at least one other contribution to make to current debates: like so-called new natural law theorists[105] Hemmingsen argues from shared rational principles, but unlike those same theorists he does so without tabling the "God question." For that reason, he is well positioned to serve as a resource for theists who wish to argue for Christian ethics from the common ground of public reason in an increasingly secularized public square, but who wish to do so while continuing to foreground their theistic commitments and teleology. Because of its historical interest and contemporary relevance, then, *On the Law of Nature: A Demonstrative Method* is presented here in English for the first time.

2011). See also David Haines and Andrew Fulford, *Natural Law: A Brief Introduction and Biblical Defense* (Moscow, ID: Davenant, 2017).

[104] Cf. Gregory, *The Unintended Reformation*; idem, *Rebel in the Ranks: Martin Luther, the Reformation, and the Conflicts That Continue to Shape Our World* (New York: HarperCollins, 2017).

[105] Cf. John Finnis, *Natural Law and Natural Rights*, 2nd ed. (Oxford: Oxford University Press, 2011); idem, *Collected Essays*, 5 vols. (Oxford: Oxford University Press, 2013); Robert P. George, *In Defense of Natural Law* (Oxford: Oxford University Press, 1999); idem, *The Clash of Orthodoxies: Law, Religion, and Morality in Crisis* (Wilmington, DE: Intercollegiate Studies Institute, 2002); Robert P. George, ed., *Natural Law, Liberalism, and Morality: Contemporary Essays* (Oxford: Oxford University Press, 2001).

TRANSLATOR'S NOTE

Hemmingsen's work first appeared in Wittenberg in 1562. Thereafter it went through several printings, though none that I have found are expanded or revised editions. Some do, however, contain typographical errors not present in other printings, such that several of them can be used in concert to establish a reliable text and occasionally to clarify difficulties of interpretation. On the whole, however, each printing I have consulted has been sound. The base text referred to in this introduction and used for this translation is the Wittenberg edition of 1564.[1]

In Englishing *De lege naturae*, I have attempted to keep as closely as possible to Hemmingsen's own style and syntax while retaining readability. The translation is intended to be a window into the Latin text rather than a door standing between the reader and the original. If a Greek term or quotation is followed by a translation in brackets, this indicates that Hemmingsen himself did not translate the term or quotation, but I have; if a nonbracketed translation follows, it is an indication that Hemmingsen translated the term or quotation into Latin for his readers and that I have rendered Hemmingsen's Latin translation into English. Unless otherwise noted, all other translations of classical and early Christian sources are mine.

---

[1] Niels Hemmingsen, *De lege naturae apodictica methodus* (Wittenberg: Crato, 1564).

In most respects Hemmingsen's Latin presents no major obstacles to a serviceable English rendering. In one area in particular, however, a few comments are in order: the various terms he uses for "knowledge" and the corresponding English terms I have employed. Latin has several terms for "knowledge" (e.g., *noticia*, *cognitio*, and *scientia*), and Hemmingsen uses them all. Such terms are frequently treated synonymously,[2] but occasionally they have shades of difference in meaning. My approach to this problem is twofold: I have attempted to be as consistent as possible in using different English terms for Hemmingsen's different Latin terms, and I have provided a note with the Latin term used in each instance.

This issue is most important for Hemmingsen's definition of the law of nature and its subsequent discussion, because he uses two different terms for "knowledge," and they are not quite synonymous:

> Lex naturae est divinitus impressa mentibus hominum **noticia** certa, principiorum **cognitionis** et actionis, atque conclusionum ex istis principiis demonstratarum proprio fini hominis congruentium, quas ex principiis necessaria consequentia ad humanae vitae gubernationem extruit ratio, ut homo ea quae recta sunt cognoscat, velit, eligat, agat, vitetque contraria, quorum omnium et testis et iudex conscientia hominibus divinitus est attributa.

> The law of nature is a certain **knowledge,** imprinted on the minds of men by God, of the principles of **knowing** and of acting, and of the conclusions proved from these principles that are in agreement with the proper end of man. Reason constructs these conclusions from the principles by necessary consequence for the government of human life, so that man may recognize, want, choose, and do the things that are right, and avoid their opposites; and God has bestowed on men the conscience as the witness and judge of all these things.[3]

---

[2] I.e., depending on the context, any of the three can map semantically onto our English term *knowledge.*

[3] Niels Hemmingsen, *De lege naturae,* C2r–v; *On the Law of Nature,* 30.

I have chosen to translate *noticia* as "knowledge,"[4] but the reader should be advised that it has a particular nuance in this case, because the term as used here has its origin in the Stoic doctrine of "innate ideas" or "common notions,"[5] first principles that are present in each and every human being by virtue of God's impressing or inscribing them there.

So much is clear from his use of the term in his discussion of conscience at the end of the work. There he says:

> Nam cum ... συντήρησις sit custos ac conservatrix **noticiarum, quae nobis innatae sunt** de recte factis ac secus, attendit semper quid expediat, quidve non expediat. Atque ea de causa suppeditare propositiones syllogismis practicis dicitur. Quales sunt hae: Honesta facienda sunt. Turpes non sunt facienda.

> For, since ... συντήρησις [synteresis] is the guardian and preserver of the **notions that are innate in us** concerning things done in the correct way and in the opposite way, it always attends to what is advantageous or disadvantageous; and for that reason it is said to supply the propositions for practical syllogisms, which are of the following kind: honorable things must be done; shameful things must not be done.[6]

Again, he writes of the *noticiae*, this time comparing them to "sparks" that are present in every human being by nature:

> Haec de lege naturae annotasse satis est, ut aliquo modo indicarem igniculos quosdam in hominibus adhuc reliquos esse, qui si excitarentur educatione bona et honestis exercitiis, magis conspicerentur. Hi igniculi, hoc est, **noticiae naturales** de rebus honestis et turpibus, sunt fontes omnium legum honestarum, quas ad amussim philosophicam, quae est demonstratio, revocare non erit laboriosum illi, qui ea qusae annotavimus recte noverit.

---

[4] Cf. *OLD*, s.v. "notitia" 2–4; LS, II.B.

[5] Cf. *OLD*, s.v. "notitia" 5; LS, II.B.

[6] Hemmingsen, *De lege naturae*, P2v; *On the Law of Nature*, 167.

It is sufficient to have noted these considerations concerning the law of nature in order to point out in some way that some sparks of it still remain in men, which, if they are aroused by good rearing and honorable training, will be more open to view. These sparks—that is, the **natural notions** about honorable and shameful things—are the sources of all honorable laws. Whoever rightly knows the things that I have noted will not find it toilsome to trace these honorable laws back according to the rule of philosophy, which is demonstration.[7]

That Hemmingsen uses the term in this way should not be surprising, for the generally Stoic idea exerted a strong influence on the eclectic thought of Hemmingsen's teacher Philip Melanchthon,[8] who refers to it regularly.[9] For example, in the "Definitions" appended to the *Loci communes*, Melanchthon begins his discussion of *noticiae* as follows:[10]

---

[7] Hemmingsen, *De lege naturae*, Q6v; *On the Law of Nature*, 180–81.

[8] Though not a Stoic himself, Cicero is presumably the intermediary here. In the Preface to the Reader, Hemmingsen quotes Cicero's *On the Laws* 1.59 to describe an "understanding" that is "sketched, as it were, in outline, in the intellect and mind" (Hemmingsen, *De lege naturae*, B4r; *On the Law of Nature*, 20).

[9] Indeed, John Witte Jr. connects the two in this respect:

> Most important, Hemming developed what he called a "demonstrative method of natural law." Using Melanchthon's notion of the *notitiae* (those inborn natural principles of practical reason), Hemming set out to demonstrate the natural universality and superiority of the Decalogue as a source and summary of natural law.

(*Law and Protestantism: The Legal Teachings of the Lutheran Reformation* [Cambridge: Cambridge University Press, 2002], 140). On the question of the relation between the Decalogue and the natural law in Philippist formulation, see xiv–xxiii above.

[10] On the history of these definitions, see Philip Melanchthon, *The Chief Theological Topics*: Loci Praecipui Theologici *1559*, 2nd ed., trans. J. A. O. Preus (St. Louis: Concordia, 2011), 503n2. The definitions, found in appendix 2, are translated by Benjamin T. G. Mayes. The translation of the definition of *noticiae* above is my own; Mayes renders the term "ideas."

Noticiae sunt actiones mentis et cerebri, quibus formantur imagines, quae sunt lumen, quo res monstrantur, ut Iulius cogitans Pompeium absentem, ea ipsa cogitatione format imaginem eius. Hoc ita fieri manifestum est, quomodo fiat, nondum scimus, sed in illa aeterna Academia discemus. Interea consideremus hoc mirandum opus Dei in hominibus, et discamus, hanc formationem imaginum nobis inditam esse.[11]

Noticiae are actions of the mind and brain by which images are formed. These are the light by which things are shown—for example, when Julius thinks about Pompey when he is absent, by this very thinking he forms his image. *That* this happens in such a way is clear; how it happens we do not yet know, but we shall learn it in that eternal Academy. Meanwhile, we should consider this wondrous work of God in men, and we should learn that the forming of images has been placed in us [by God].

Where Melanchthon speaks here of the formation of images, Hemmingsen speaks of principles; but in each case the subject's activity in making use of certain elements implanted by God in the mind is brought to the fore, and I have tried to reflect that by rendering the term for what is innately perceived as "knowledge." Indeed, Hemmingsen himself elsewhere compares *noticia* to a light imprinted by God.[12] Melanchthon, for his part, sometimes connects the term to knowledge of propositions, as Hemmingsen does in the definition.[13]

---

[11] Philip Melanchthon, *Corpus doctrinae Christianae* (Leipzig: Rhamba, 1572), 790.

[12] See Hemmingsen, *De lege naturae*, F3v; *On the Law of Nature*, 63; where he writes that "the knowledge [*noticia*] of the first principles is the light imprinted by God on the minds of men."

[13] So, e.g., when giving the causes or reasons why one should know the virtues (*virtutum cognitio*) at the beginning of the *Ethicae doctrinae elementa*, Melanchthon gives as the first reason the fact that "knowledge [*notitia*] of them is a testimony that God exists" (*CR* 16:166).

To translate *noticia* in this way, however, means that "knowledge" is no longer available as a translation for *cognitio*. In the definition, *cognitio* is used in parallel with *actio*, and because Latin nouns ending in *-tio* are used for the names of actions, I have normally rendered both terms with English nouns in "-ing": "knowing" and "acting." Though this results in slightly awkward English at times, it accurately reflects the Latin of Hemmingsen's crucially important definition and preserves the etymological connection between the words *noticia* and *cognitio*. Hemmingsen, in keeping with the Aristotelian and scholastic tradition, divides *cognitio* into *cognitio sensitiva* and *cognitio intellectiva*, the standard English renderings of which are "sensitive knowledge" and "intellectual knowledge."[14] In my translation, they are rendered as "sensitive knowing" and "intellectual knowing"; such a translation preserves both their relation to tradition and their role in Hemmingsen's own Stoic-influenced definition. One can thereby see Hemmingsen's indebtedness to a wide variety of philosophical sources.

For all other matters of translation in specific instances, the reader should consult the notes *ad loc.*

—E. J. Hutchinson

---

[14] Cf. Roy J. Deferrari, M. Inviolata Barry, and Ignatius McGuiness, *A Lexicon of St. Thomas Aquinas based on the Summa theologica and Selected Passages of His Other Works* (Washington, D.C.: Catholic University of America Press, 1948–49), s.v. "cognitio" 2.2.e^3 (p. 166).

Abbreviations

CR

Corpus Reformatorum. Edited by C. G.
Bretschneider, H. E. Bindseil et al. 101 vols.
Halle a. Salle and Brunsvigae: Schwetschke,
1834–1959.

OCD

The Oxford Classical Dictionary. Edited by
Simon Hornblower and Anthony Spawforth.
3rd ed. New York: Oxford University Press,
1996.

OLD

Oxford Latin Dictionary. Edited by P. G. W.
Glare. 2nd ed. 2 vols. Oxford: Oxford University
Press, 2012.

Opuscula theologica

Niels Hemmingsen. *D. Nicolai Hemmingii,
sacrarum literarum in Haffniensi schola
professoris celeberrimi opuscula theologica.*
Edited by Simon Goulart. Geneva: Eustathius
Vignon, 1586.

LS

*A Latin Dictionary founded on Andrews' edition
of Freund's Latin Dictionary.* Revised and edited
by Charlton T. Lewis and Charles Short. Oxford:
Clarendon Press, 1879.

LSJ   *A Greek-English Lexicon.* Compiled by Henry G. Liddell, Robert Scott, and Henry Stuart Jones. 9th ed. Oxford: Clarendon Press, 1996.

PG   *Patrologiae cursus completus: Series Graeca.* Edited by J.-P. Migne. 161 vols. Paris: Migne, 1857–1866.

Stobaeus, *Anthology*   *Joannis Stobaei Anthologium.* Edited by Kurt Wachsmuth and Otto Hense. 4 vols. Berlin: Weidmann, 1884.

ON THE LAW OF NATURE

A Demonstrative Method

DEDICATORY EPISTLE

For a man most illustrious in the dignity of his birth, in learning, and in virtue, Lord Erik Krabbe,[1] Golden Knight[2] and most wise Senator of the Realm of Denmark, Bustrup's Lord,[3] as well as this author's Patron and Lord, who is especially worthy of esteem, Niels Hemmingsen prays grace and peace.

There is an old saying, most illustrious man, to which Plutarch[4] bears witness, that without justice not even Jove can act as prince. By

---

[1] Krabbe was an important jurist and diplomat; see Oskar Garstein, *Jesuit Educational Strategy, 1553–1622*, vol. 3 of *Rome and the Counter-Reformation in Scandinavia* (Leiden: Brill, 1992), 34; Ove Malling, *Great and Good Deeds of Danes, Norwegians, and Holstenians* (London: C. and R. Butler, 1807), 304. Both his portrait and Hemmingsen's hung at the northern end of a long corridor on the ground floor of King Christian IV's Rosenborg Palace: see Carl Christian Thorwald Andersen, *The Chronological Collection of the Kings of Denmark* (Copenhagen: Forlagsbureauet, 1878), 5–6.

[2] *Eques auratus* ("Golden Knight") was the "common term for knighthood in Denmark"; see Janus Møller Jensen, *Denmark and the Crusades: 1400–1650* (Leiden: Brill, 2007), 326n261.

[3] German *Busdorf* in Schleswig-Holstein.

[4] Plutarch, a Greek who achieved high position in the administration of the Roman Empire, was born before AD 50 and died after 120. Among his many works are the famous *Parallel Lives* and many treatises on moral philosophy. (Unless otherwise noted, all biographical information for classical authors is taken from *OCD*.)

this saying it is doubtless signified both that the office of the prince is especially difficult and that the power of justice is great; without it no commonwealth,[5] no house, and, in short, no association can be preserved. For as law, which is the bond of human society, prescribes the rule of justice, so it belongs to the magistrate (whom the best philosophers call νομοφύλακα, that is, the "guardian of the laws") to devote himself to this task with all his powers, in order that he may hold the body of the commonwealth together by the bond of laws, that is, by justice. And, indeed, just as our bodies without the mind are not able to make use of their parts and sinews and blood and limbs, so the body politic[6] without law, the norm of justice, is not able to make use of its parts and sinews and blood and limbs, as Cicero says.[7] For this reason, the framers of laws deservedly ought to be praised as justice's most holy priests and servants, who, seeking the very sources of laws in nature, have wished to preserve men's union with one another in a sound condition. For no association, unless it is just, will remain stable and in a sound condition for long, and therefore the laws (those that justly deserve this name) look to this and intend this: that men unite together with one another by means of justice, in order that their association with one another may be holy and enduring.

---

[5] Unless otherwise noted, *respublica* will be translated herein as "commonwealth," though I render the title of Cicero's *De re publica* with its commonly accepted English title *On the Republic*.

[6] Unless otherwise noted, *civitas* will be translated herein as "body politic" or "state."

[7] Marcus Tullius Cicero was born in 106 BC and died in 44 BC and was among the most important statesmen, orators, and philosophers of his or any period of Roman history. A great number of his works survive, including letters, speeches, and works on rhetoric and various types of philosophy (especially political philosophy and moral philosophy). Hemmingsen here refers to Cicero, *For Aulus Cluentius* 146, with slight differences from modern editions of Cicero. The passage is also quoted in, e.g., Quintilian, *The Orator's Education* 5.11.25 and Johann Gerhard, *Loci theologici*, ed. F. Frank, vol. 6 (Leipzig: J. C. Hinrichs, 1885), 375, in the article *De legibus politicis*.

There are, moreover, certain sinews, as it were, of this justice: religion or divine worship, our common nature, the ordering of superiors and inferiors, the natural family, marriage, contracts, and the various duties involved in human association, whereby it comes about that some have need of the service of others. The law itself, or the magistrate, who is, as it were, a living law, ought to establish, preserve, and guide these sinews and watch out lest, when these sinews have either been too much relaxed or entirely ruptured, the body of the commonwealth be weakened[8] and gradually fall apart. For this reason, in fact, the magistrate is made overseer of the law as its guardian, so that, just as the soul is the director in the body, so he himself may be the director in the commonwealth of the sinews of its justice.[9] Parts of the body, however, which do not wish themselves to be guided by these sinews the magistrate should either correct or, if they do not allow themselves to be corrected, should cast away, cut off from the body, and should imitate wise doctors, who, convinced by good reasoning and other laws that look to the preservation of health, preserve the parts of a man's body that are healthy; moreover, when these parts are affected by disease, they heal them if they are able. But those parts that are not made better by medical attention, but waste away the more, they cut away, lest by their own disease they little by little infect the healthy parts, until the whole body, once it has been infected, collapses. The poet had this in view when he said:

---

[8] Hemmingsen's Latin includes a wordplay regarding these "sinews" and the "body" of the commonwealth: *cavebitque ne his nervis, aut nimium laxatis, aut omnino ruptis, corpus reipublicae enervetur.*

[9] John Calvin uses a similar metaphor in his *Institutes of the Christian Religion*, but note that, where Calvin calls the laws the "soul" of the commonwealth, Hemmingsen applies that designation to the magistrate himself: "Next to the magistrate in polities are the laws, the strongest sinews [*nervi*] of commonwealths, or the soul [*animae*] (as Cicero calls them, following Plato), without which the magistrate is not able to exist, just as the laws themselves in turn have no force without the magistrate" (*Institutio Christianae Religionis* [1559], in *Ioannis Calvini opera quae supersunt omnia*, ed. G. Baum, E. Cunitz, and E. Reuss, vol. 2 [Brunsvigae: C. A. Schwetschke, 1864], 4.20.14).

> But the incurable wound
> must be cut away with the sword, lest the healthy part be
> dragged down with it.[10]

And the following refers to the same thing:

> An animal, when it has become sick, brings the whole
> sheepfold to ruin;
> it must be separated from the flock, lest it infect the
> others.[11]

The Romans, when they were unable to calm the strife that had arisen between the common people and the aristocrats by means of the laws put in place by Romulus, sent three ambassadors to Greece under orders to copy down the laws of Solon and familiarize themselves with the customs and institutions of the rest of Greece, in order that at least in this way, by the example of the Greeks, the condition of the Roman body politic might be able to be calmed. And after the business had been conducted diligently by the ambassadors, in the next year they returned, and a Board of Ten[12] was created for passing laws. They first wrote the Ten Tables of Roman civil law. Then they added two more, and all were approved by the Centuriate Assembly; and these laws, which are called the Twelve Tables, are most noble. Indeed, the

---

[10] Ovid, *Metamorphoses* 1.190–91. Publius Ovidius Naso (43 BC–17 AD) was the author of several works of poetry in elegiac couplets (e.g., the *Amores* ["Loves"], the *Heroides* ["Heroines"], and the *Letters from Pontus*), as well as the *Metamorphoses*, his only epic work.

[11] This seems to have been a common adage without literary provenance (as is often the case with proverbs). The first line is quoted in Wilhelm Binder, *Novus Thesaurus Adagiorum Latinorum* (Stuttgart: Eduard Fischhaber, 1861), 207 (no. 1885), who in turn gives as his source Johann Georg Seybold, *Selectiora Adagia Latino-Germanica*, first published, as far as I can discover, in 1669; Seybold, in his turn, gives no further source. Interestingly, Seybold has high praise in his preface for Hemmingsen's own teacher, Philip Melanchthon. The sentiment is found in antiquity in Juvenal, *Satires* 2.78–81.

[12] *Decemviri*.

Romans wisely judged that the concord of citizens is nourished and supported not so much by power as by good laws, which are the norms of good morals,[13] and that thus the body politic itself is protected not so much by walls as by morals.

A most pleasing saying of Plautus[14] pertains to this. The slave Sagaristio questions a young woman in the following words: "How does the town seem to you to be fortified?" She responds, "If the inhabitants are of good morals, I judge that it has been fortified beautifully: if treachery, embezzlement, and greed are exiled from the city, along with, fourth, envy; fifth, ambition; sixth, disparagement; seventh, perjury; eighth, carelessness; ninth, injustice;[15] and tenth, crime, whose attack is most terrible. Unless these things are absent from a town, a hundredfold wall is too little for preserving its property."[16] Consequently, laws pertain to this matter: they exist in order that men may be held in check in their duty by the norm of justice, and may be united together with each other by the sinews, as it were, of justice. For this reason Scipio admirably says that there is a commonwealth—that is, the property of the people—when things are conducted well and justly;[17] moreover, things are conducted well and justly only when

---

[13] Or "character," as *mos* in the plural often means. Throughout, *mores* is translated as "morals."

[14] Titus Maccius Plautus, active between around 205 and 184 BC, is one of two Roman comic poets from whom we have entire plays extant (the other is Terence). His plays include *The Persian*, *The Braggart Soldier*, *The Haunted House*, and the *The Two Menaechmuses*, the inspiration for Shakespeare's *Comedy of Errors*.

[15] Reading *iniuria* with the 1577 ed. and with Hemmingsen's *Opuscula theologica* rather than *iuiuria* with the 1564 ed.; the latter must be a typographical error.

[16] Plautus, *The Persian* 553–60. Hemmingsen's text differs slightly from modern editions.

[17] This passage comes from Augustine, *City of God* 2.21, where he is discussing (the mostly lost) book 3 of Cicero's *On the Republic*.

life is lived according to the norms of justice, that is, the laws. The following remark of Ennius also pertains to this matter:

> By ancient manners and men the Roman state stands firm.[18]

For this most profound poet perceives that by uprightness of morals in accordance with the prescribed law and by bravery of spirit the security of the commonwealth stands firm.

Although, moreover, all men of sound mind admit with us that there is only one justice, which preserves homes, cities, provinces, and realms (for I judge that we ought to scorn Carneades,[19] who for the sake of engaging in disputation affirmed that a commonwealth was preserved by injustice, along with those Romans who perverted that ancient statement that we cited from Plutarch above and said that without injustice a commonwealth was not able to be governed; for the former was seeking praise for his cleverness in defending contrary opinions, and the latter looked back to the beginning of the Roman commonwealth, for by this remark they were falsely intimating that if the Romans wanted to be just, that is, if they restored the things that did not belong to them, they would have to return to their huts and waste away in miseries);[20] nevertheless, there have been those who

---

[18] Ennius, *Annals* 165 (Skutsch). Quintus Ennius (239–169 BC) was an important early writer of Roman epic, as well as of comedies and tragedies. The *Annals*, a poem about the history of the Romans, was his most important work but survives only in fragments. The famous tag used by Hemmingsen here is quoted in Cicero, *On the Republic* 5.1, and in Augustine, *City of God* 2.21, the same passage he has just used above. Given that for several centuries, up to and including the time of Hemmingsen, knowledge of Cicero's *On the Republic* depended on Augustine's citations and discussion, it is likely that it is Augustine who mediates the quotation of Ennius (whose work is also lost except for fragments) to Hemmingsen; cf. previous note.

[19] The Cyrenian Academic philosopher Carneades (214/3–129/8 BC) caused a stir in Rome in 155 by arguing on consecutive days for and against justice.

[20] Again, this view, as well as that of Carneades, are treated in book 3 of Cicero's *On the Republic*, summarized by Augustine in *City of God* 2.

have differed in their judgments as to the origin of justice. For as is well known from Plato's writings,[21] some have contended that the just man is such by nature, others that that he is just only by the opinion of men; and the latter seemed to confirm their opinion above all from the fact that the law, which I have frequently testified to be the norm of justice, is not the same everywhere and among everyone—for the fact that some people live by some laws, others by other laws, is without controversy. Minos, in Plato's dialogue,[22] in order to confirm that the just man is just by opinion and not by nature, recounts the following examples of laws that contradict each other: the Carthaginians establish by law that it is lawful and pious to sacrifice their own children to Saturn; the Lycians, compelled by the law of the land, bury the bodies of their dead in their own homes. But the Athenians rightly abhor each of these things as unlawful and impious—nay, rather, by a contradictory law they watch out lest anyone either sacrifice his own children to Saturn or bury a dead man in his house. Many other examples of impiety (albeit an impiety that does not go so far as barbarism)[23] could have been added from the contradictory laws of different peoples—examples that seem to confirm the opinion of those who say that the just man is such not by nature but by opinion.

But Plato's Socrates wisely contends that the opinion of these people is most false. For he affirms that just things are just and that honorable things are honorable; and, on the other hand, that unjust things are unjust and shameful things are shameful—and that this holds everywhere and among all people. And he defines law as being, not the opinion of men, but τοῦ ὄντος εὕρησιν, that is, the discovery of reality. For the name of *law* is rightly given only to that law which not only is

---

[21] Plato (around 429–347 BC) is, along with Aristotle and Socrates himself (the latter of whom Plato immortalized), the most significant philosopher of ancient Greece. Plato wrote in the form of dialogues. He himself never appears as a character, though Socrates figures prominently in many of Plato's dialogues. His most well-known works include the *Apology*, the *Republic*, the *Symposium*, and the *Phaedrus*.

[22] Hemmingsen refers to the pseudo-Platonic dialogue *Minos* 315b6–d6.

[23] I.e., in contrast to the examples he has just given.

9

supported by the authority of princes and magistrates, but also (and this is much more important) relies on reason[24] firm and immovable.

This reason ought not to be sought from anywhere else than from two sources, namely, from nature itself and from the end[25] of the law. In nature itself are certain seeds of the just and the honorable; in addition, there is the faculty of judgment, so that by its use one may prefer just and honorable things to unjust and shameful ones. From these seeds arise laws that are intended for the soundness of a commonwealth that does not deviate from its ultimate end—the end to which all things should be referred. Only those laws that have been constructed in this way deserve to be called *laws*, and not just any decrees whatsoever of tyrants or prescriptions of the powerful.

A certain ruler passed a law by which he ordained that it was licit for one husband to have two wives at the same time.[26] Many men were embracing this law, little worried about whether the law that was passed was in accordance with just reason; but, because this law does not remain within just limits, that is, because it does not proceed from nature and tend to the soundness of a commonwealth that does not deviate from its ultimate end, it should in no way be considered worthy of the name of *law*, but rather should be called the filth of foulest lust. Nor indeed did that ruler pass this law for any other reason than to conceal his own lust by the pretext of law. Whoever, therefore, has obeyed that foul decree is not excused by the authority of the ruler, but is condemned by the law of nature, which is also the law of God. For, as ingrates, they have both departed from nature and scorned God, who is the maker of nature.

Therefore, in considering any law whatsoever, one must look carefully to reason, as I have said. When a law passed by a lawful magistrate is in accordance with this reason, whatever is in keeping with the law that has been passed will be reckoned just; on the other hand, what is undertaken against the law will be reckoned unjust; nor ought one to

---

[24] *ratio.*

[25] Or "goal"; the Latin term is *finis.*

[26] This is presumably a reference to the bigamy of Philip I, Landgrave of Hesse.

judge a thing just or unjust by opinion, but by nature and the truth. But I will speak more expansively about this subject in its own place.

This call to refer the laws according to which it befits us to live in human society back to their origin and proper end is particularly worthy of good men. For regard for this matter not only rouses in peaceful natures a love for the laws, but it also has another most pleasant fruit. For what, I ask, can be more pleasant than to see the most beautiful method that the wise men of antiquity followed in constructing their own laws? So that I may say no more for the time being, I say that it is sufficient to perceive where they turned aside even the smallest amount from the just reason that is proper to laws.

Paul acknowledges that the gentiles, by the guidance of this method, came as far as discerning the same things that God proposes in his own law, although they afterwards deviated from this knowledge[27] they had discerned because they had been overcome by natural vice and the habitual practice of evils. Therefore this light must be discerned and thanks must be given to God, because he himself has adorned human nature with this light and even after the fall has left behind in nature certain little sparks; when these are kindled in one's thinking, a most beautiful harmony of the virtues and the laws and, as it were, their structure is discerned.[28]

A most worthy admiration of this matter drove me to put something down in writing concerning the source of the laws, which we are accustomed to call the law of nature, and to do so by a certain and philosophical method,[29] by means of which the beginnings, progress,

---

[27] *noticia.*

[28] Hemmingsen returns to this point in the closing sentences of the treatise.

[29] Proper method was of great concern for Hemmingsen, who devoted an entire treatise to it (indeed, the first of its kind), the *De methodis libri duo* (1555), on which see Kenneth Hagen, "*De Exegetico Methodo*: Niels Hemmingsen's *De Methodis* (1555)," in *The Bible in the Sixteenth Century*, ed. David C. Steinmetz (Durham, NC: Duke University Press, 1990), 181–96. Reflection on proper method was a preoccupation in the Renaissance, and Galen, whom Hemmingsen will soon mention, was a particularly important ancient source: see *On the Constitution of the Art of Medicine* 6.245K1–16. On

turning points, and way of return may be clearly perceived.[30] We see that all the liberal disciplines[31] are understood by their own methods, such as grammar, dialectic, geometry, arithmetic, music, and the others; and just as any discipline is clearer when its method has been explicated in writing, so also it gains greater admiration. Although doctors borrow their axioms from natural philosophy,[32] nevertheless they deserve not the lowest praise on account of the method of their discipline. Civil laws too, for which moral philosophy supplies the axioms, have their own method.

Moreover, although many—both poets (such as Pythagoras, Theognis, Phocylides, Cato, and several others)[33] and philosophers (such

---

the issue in general, see Neal Ward Gilbert, *Renaissance Concepts of Method* (New York: Columbia University Press, 1960).

[30] Hemmingsen uses a metaphor ultimately deriving from Roman circus races—the same metaphor, in fact, that he uses at the beginning of the *De methodis* (see previous note).

[31] *artes.*

[32] I.e., what we would today call natural or physical science.

[33] The Presocratic philosopher Pythagoras, born in Samos sometime in the mid-sixth century BC, was an important influence on Plato and the founder of a long-enduring philosophical tradition, though its real origins are shrouded in uncertainty. Theognis was a Greek elegiac poet of the sixth century BC, according to ancient sources. A large body of 1,400 verses, the *Theognidea*, survives under his name, but much of it is not by Theognis. Theognis was often linked with Phocylides, the purported name of another sixth-century poet of moralizing maxims. The Cato referred to here is possibly Marcus Porcius Cato, or "Cato the Censor" (234–149 BC), famous for his stern moral disposition and his pithy moral sayings. The only work of his that is extant as a whole is his *On Agriculture*, though he also wrote a *Poem on Morals*. More likely, Hemmingsen is referring to "Dionysius Cato," to whose authorship is attributed the *Distichs of Cato* (third or fourth century AD), though the name is a fabrication of S. Bosius, a work of proverbial verse-couplets that was long believed to be by Cato the Elder and was a standard moral handbook in the Middle Ages. It is likely that Hemmingsen accepted this attribution, as it was not disproven until Joseph Scaliger did so in 1598. See Hubert Cancik, Helmuth Schneider, Christine F. Salazar et al., eds., *Brill's*

as Plato, Aristotle, Plutarch, and Cicero)[34]—have handed down the commandments of morals, and in our own day Philip Melanchthon (and neither the serpentine ingratitude of many, nor the secret treachery of the spiteful, nor the open misrepresentation of his enemies will ever obscure the glory of this most holy man) has written about moral philosophy most wisely and usefully:[35] nevertheless, no one yet, as far as I know, has handed down these elements and shown the way of demonstrative progress in this most noble discipline, so to speak, of nature, a task which really would have been by no means easy for the best men, if they had proposed to treat the first principles[36] of nature, and from there the construction of what follows from these first principles, by the method that we are following.[37]

There are perhaps those who will say that there was no need to refer these things that everyone is said to know by nature back to the straight paths of this discipline. I wish to make no other reply to these people than that, by the same reasoning, they can reject the effort of the greatest men who have referred dialectic back to the standard of a sure method, for this too is a part of the law of nature.

New Pauly, vol. 4 (Leiden: Brill, 2004), s.v. "Dicta Catonis"; and Manfred Landfester with Brigitte Egger, eds., and Tina Jerke and Volker Dallman, trans. and eds., *Brill's New Pauly: Supplements*, vol. 2 (Leiden: Brill, 2009), s.v. "Catonis Dicta/Dicta Catonis."

[34] Aristotle was born in 384 BC and died in 322. In addition to being tutor to Alexander the Great, he wrote works such as the *Nicomachean Ethics*, the *Politics*, the *Poetics*, and the *Rhetoric*, as well as works on logic, metaphysics, and the natural sciences. For Plato, Plutarch, and Cicero, see notes above.

[35] For Hemmingsen's relationship with Melanchthon, see the introduction, pp. xiv–xxiii; for some parallels in Hemmingsen's treatise to Melanchthon's ethical works, consult the notes throughout.

[36] *principia*. The term is translated as "principles" or (as here) "first principles" throughout, unless otherwise noted.

[37] There is an architectural image at work in Hemmingsen's Latin, though it is perhaps a dead metaphor by Hemmingsen's day: *principia* can also mean "foundations"; something else is then erected (*extructationes*, which I have translated as "constructions"), like a building, on top of them.

Well, don't we (you will say) read many things about this law very clearly in Plato, Aristotle, Xenophon,[38] Plutarch, Cicero, and others? I admit that this indeed is very true, but none of them has referred the things that are found scattered in their writings back to the standard of this sure and just and universal method; I have indeed judged that this must at least be attempted, in the hope that good men will not reject this effort of mine, especially since I desire it to be beneficial to the studies of young people. For I do not doubt that it will be both extremely useful and very pleasant to students of moral philosophy to see the beginnings, progress, and turning points of the law of nature; to consider the foundations[39] and, as it were, the building blocks[40] of the axioms of moral philosophy, out of which innumerable hypotheses, once the method of philosophical proof has been brought to bear,[41] are constructed in laws that pertain to the political and domestic spheres; to observe the syntheses and analyses of the demonstrations;[42] and

---

[38] Xenophon, an Athenian, who was born around 430 BC and died in 354, was the author of numerous works such as the *Anabasis*, the *Cyropaedia*, a Socratic *Apology* and *Symposium*, and the *Oeconomicus*. He, Plato, and Aristophanes are the three most important ancient sources for what we know about Socrates.

[39] *principia.*

[40] *elementa.*

[41] *apodixi.* This is "proof" in the technical sense, akin to geometric proofs, as becomes clear below; Hemmingsen normally uses the Latin *demonstratio* (which I have translated as "demonstration") rather than the transliterated Greek term *apodixis.*

[42] For discussion of these terms, see Hemmingsen's *De methodis libri duo* in *Opuscula theologica*, particularly 9–12, 16–19, 21–22. As Hemmingsen sets it out there, universal "synthesis" is the way of proceeding from the parts to the whole, whereas universal "analysis" is the contrary: a way of proceeding from the whole to the parts. (The third universal method is "diaeresis," which has to do with definition; see 13–16.) The "demonstrative method" of the present work's title is what Hemmingsen refers to as a "particular method"—indeed, the one that is "generally proper for philosophers"—which employs types of both synthesis and analysis (and, as we shall see, definition);

to perceive in what way all judicial pronouncements and all laws can be referred back to their proper sources.

As a result, I also hope that students of ethics and jurisprudence will no longer have to endure the abuse of certain men who deny that the teaching concerning morals and laws is subject to demonstration, for they will see most clearly that the conclusions of the law of nature are not more bereft of clear demonstrations than Euclid's discipline,[43] which certain men falsely maintain is the only one to support itself by demonstrations.

Moreover, although one must admit that there are clear demonstrations in Euclid, according to all the ways of making a demonstration— for Euclid uses a threefold method for making a demonstration; for he composes some hypotheses by synthesis, others he refers by analysis back to their first principles, and by no means rarely does he make use of ἐπαγωγῇ εἰς ἀδύνατον [reductio ad absurdum], in order to deduce the truth from what is absurd—nevertheless I justly contend that there are ways of making a demonstration in this branch of knowledge[44] of ours (that is, the knowledge of nature) that are not less ἐναργεῖς [manifest] and clear than in Euclid or in other noble and distinguished branches of knowledge.[45] I attempt in this book to lay these ways open and to refer the law of nature back to the method proper to this discipline,

---

Hemmingsen treats it in book 1 of De methodis, in Opuscula theologica, 26–27; with particular reference to ethics, 29–30. At the conclusion of On the Law of Nature, Hemmingsen says of the method he has employed:

> For I have not only demonstrated the first axioms and principles of the law of nature, which are immovable and infallible, and how hypotheses ought to be constructed from them κατὰ σύνθεσιν [by synthesis], but I have also pointed out how one can return by analysis from the last hypotheses to the principles, so that the truth and certainty of even the smallest hypotheses may be established. (181)

[43] I.e., geometry.

[44] "Branch of knowledge" is my rendering here of scientia.

[45] scientiae.

and I do so in order that this part of philosophy, which ought to be very well known to all men, may in some way be rendered illustrious.[46]

Furthermore, lest anyone accuse me of being a man who, according to the proverb, puts his own scythe into another's harvest,[47] this is my defense. Last year I had to expound Paul's Letter to the Romans, in which, because the apostle declares that the law of nature is the truth and that the law[48] of God is known to the gentiles, which they themselves display by their works while their conscience bears witness at the same time—because of this, I say, I thought that it was worth the trouble to explain what the force of that law[49] is; and, in order not to interrupt my lecturing on Paul with an extended disquisition, I began to put together this method concerning the law of nature in a separate place with, I hope, as much fruit as there has been toil.

For the rest, as to the fact that I wanted to publish this method of the law of nature to the public under your name, most illustrious man,

---

[46] Or "illuminated." It is not impossible that there is an intentional ambiguity here: he seeks to "illuminate" the proper method of approaching the law of nature so that, in so doing, it may receive its proper due of fame and notoriety.

[47] This phrase serves as the title of an essay by Ditlev Tamm, "*Nolo falcem in alienam messem mittere*: Der dänische Theologe Niels Hemmingsen (1513–1600) aus juristischer Sicht," in *Gerichtslauben-Vorträge: Freiburger Festkolloquium zum fünfundsiebzigsten Geburtstag von Hans Thieme*, ed. Karl Kroeschell (Sigmaringen: Jan Thorbecke), 47–56, though the essay is about Hemmingsen's work in broad terms, not about the metaphor itself.

[48] Hemmingsen here uses *ius* instead of *lex*. On the range of meanings of *ius* and *lex* see Henry Nettleship, *Contributions to Latin Lexicography* (Oxford: Clarendon Press, 1889), 497–500, 515–17. Nettleship contrasts the two as follows: "*Ius* is either a law, or rule, or power, or right existing prior to a *lex*; or a decision, or power, or right, granted in accordance with a *lex*; or a provision or ordinance included in a *lex*. The two main meanings of *lex* are (1) a stated or written condition or understanding proposed and accepted; (2) a written law" (515). On the other hand, Hemmingsen does not always observe a rigorous distinction between the two (the present instance serves as a good example), and *ius* is regularly used by Roman jurists and their successors for a code of written law.

[49] He now reverts to *lex*.

I have two reasons that are most just, at least as it seems to me. One of these is that I desire to declare by some token the gratitude of my mind toward you who, just as you desire to be most well deserving from all, also desire to be of benefit to all and to harm none (an attitude that Cicero says is proper to the good man), so you have embraced me for many years with unparalleled goodwill. The other reason is that you have been occupied now for a long time with a generally similar task. For you are trying to bring our Danish laws (which belong to the law of nature, from which I draw out particular hypotheses),[50] as though they are body parts that had been driven apart and, as it were, scattered (a state of affairs that has come about not at all due to the fault of the legislators, some of whom have passed laws for other nations, but on account of the variety of the peoples for whom in one instance some laws, in another instance others, have had to be passed) back to a condition bodily integrity,[51] in order that all of the individual parts may be bound together fittingly.[52] Only the prudent understand how difficult this is. For here there is required not so much the labor of transcription, which indeed is very small in this matter, as there is needed an unparalleled prudence in the comparison of laws of diverse nations, so that the more obscure laws may be elucidated by the clearer; and so that those that seem mutilated on account of their brevity may be filled out by those that are more complete; and so that those that up to this point seemed to be in an order that is not very fitting may be restored to their own places. All of this should be

---

[50] I.e., in this treatise. Hemmingsen's point is that the law of nature serves as the foundation both for his own work and for that of Krabbe. On "hypotheses," see p. 23 in the Preface to the Reader below.

[51] *ad iustum corpus.*

[52] James L. Larson, *Reforming the North: The Kingdoms and Churches of Scandinavia, 1520–1545* (Cambridge: Cambridge University Press, 2010), 450, notes that "Erik Krabbe … wrote a number of treatises on Danish law, and he planned a lawbook valid for all Denmark. In spite of King Christian's encouragement, Krabbe completed only a first draft. The alien element of Roman Law, borrowed from the prevailing legal tendency in the Reich, may have scotched the project."

done in order that we may have one system[53] of Danish law, once the individual parts have been referred back to the laws' source and proper end, which alone sacred laws[54] look toward and intend. I beseech God the Father of our Lord Jesus Christ that he support you in this difficult and most useful labor, and that he give you strength, so that you may finally place a happy ending on the work you have begun. Fare you well, best Maecenas,[55] sound in soul, body, and spirit.

Copenhagen, May 1562

---

[53] *systema*: the word refers to "a whole consisting of several parts" (see LS, s.v. "systema" I).

[54] *sanctae leges.* The semantic range of *sanctus* includes "venerable, morally pure, inviolable, pious, holy," and the like; see LS s.v. "sancio" II.

[55] Maecenas, a close associate of Rome's first emperor, Augustus, was a great patron of the arts; those who received his support included the most important poets of his day, such as Vergil and Horace.

PREFACE TO THE READER

Cicero wisely and rightly says that nothing is more excellent than to clearly understand that we were born for justice, and that what is just has been established not by opinion, but by nature.[1] For the wise man sees that man was not created for bestial pleasures, as the Epicurean school impiously and shamelessly blathered,[2] but rather that he should seek after those things whose sparks men of sound mind have noticed to have been hidden in themselves.

For since man excels the rest of the animate world in mind and understanding, and is gifted in the ability to differentiate between the honorable and the shameful, so that he seeks after the former but avoids the latter (and this by the instinct of nature), it is necessary to admit that a different end has been designed for man from that designed for all other animate beings, which are destitute of mind and understanding and deliberate choice.

In order, moreover, to rouse their students to the contemplation and love of this end, which is proper to man, the ancient philosophers commended to them that saying of the Delphic Oracle (which the Amphictyonic League wrote above the doors of the temple of Delphic

---

[1] Cicero, *On the Laws* 1.28.

[2] Epicureanism was a regular target of Protestant polemic; critics frequently compared its adherents to pigs, as Hemmingsen does in this work.

19

Apollo),[3] γνῶθι σεαυτὸν ["Know yourself"]; by this sound saying they wished for each person to be reminded of his duty. Menander[4] expressed this in the following verses: γνῶθι σεαυτόν ἐστιν ἂν τὰ πράγματα ἴδῃς τὰ σαυτού καὶ τί σοι ποιητέον: "to 'know yourself' is to look to your own affairs and to what you ought to do."[5] "For he who knows himself well," as Cicero says,

> will first of all perceive that he possesses something divine, and that his inborn nature has been inscribed upon him as though an image dedicated in a temple;[6] because of so great a gift of the gods he will always both do and perceive something worthy, and, when he has examined and tested himself as a whole, he will understand how he has entered into life equipped by nature, and how great the tools are that he has for obtaining and acquiring wisdom, since at the beginning of all things he will have conceived understanding, sketched, as it were, in outline, in the intellect and mind; illuminated by this understanding, with wisdom as his guide, he may discern that he will be a good man, and, for this very reason, a happy one.[7]

Therefore, the famous oracular pronouncement of Delphi, "Know yourself," must be interpreted in reference to the following three things: so that a man may ponder with what gifts he has been adorned by God,

---

[3] Amphictionies ("dwellers around") were leagues that took on the responsibility for the care of sanctuaries and their associated cults.

[4] Menander (344/3?–292/1 BC) was an Athenian writer of New Comedy. He wrote over one hundred plays, of which none survives complete (though the *Dyskolos* is nearly so). Hundreds of maxims are attributed to Menander in a collection called the *Sentences*, though most are not actually by him.

[5] This fragment is preserved in Stobaeus, *Anthology* 3.21.2. Hemmingsen's citations from Stobaeus' *Anthology* come from books 3 and 4, which are found in volumes 3–5 of the Wachsmuth and Hense edition.

[6] *simulacrum*.

[7] Cicero, *On the Laws* 1.59. Hemmingsen's text differs slightly from modern editions of Cicero.

what he should do and think, and the fact that blessedness is offered to the one who has followed nature as his guide. For everyone ought to be persuaded that the Lord and governor of all things is God; and that whatever things are done are done by his authority and power; and that he is most worthy of all praise from the human race; and that he observes what sort of person each man is, what he does, what he is guilty of, and with what intention and piety he attends to religion; and that he keeps an account of the pious and the impious in order that he may bestow a blessed immortality on the former but deserved punishments on the latter—as Cicero and Plato in many passages discuss with more cleverness, really, than usefulness. For they understood neither the wound of nature, nor did they find its remedy; God revealed both of these things to the church with his own voice.[8]

For although Cicero saw by the light of nature that man had been endowed with the natural faculties of choosing the good and seeking after the true—faculties that were to act as his guides to blessedness—and nevertheless perceived in the whole human race a dreadful ἀταξίαν [disorder], to such an extent that nearly all men, against the judgment of the mind, rush headlong into dreadful crimes, he attributed so great an evil as this to habit, exclaiming in the following words: "So great is the corruption of habit, that by it the sparks (as it were) given by nature are extinguished and the opposite vices arise and are strengthened."[9] The poets refer this evil to an evil deity whom they call ἄτην [Delusion], because she is accustomed to cast harm and confusion into the affairs of mortal men. Pindar,[10] in his *Olympian Odes*, ascribes this evil to Prometheus when he says: "Prometheus

---

[8] See E. J. Hutchinson, "Nature and the Wound of Nature: A Pauline View of the Testimony of the Ancients in Niels Hemmingsen's *De lege naturae*," in *Ad Fontes Witebergenses: Select Proceedings of Lutheranism and the Classics III: Lutherans Read History*, ed. James A. Kellerman, E. J. Hutchinson, and Joshua J. Hayes (Minneapolis: Lutheran Press, 2017), 58–75.

[9] Cicero, *On the Laws* 1.33. Hemmingsen's text differs slightly from modern editions of Cicero.

[10] Pindar was a Greek lyric poet, probably born in 518 BC. Pindar wrote numerous types of poetry, but all that is extant in non-fragmentary form

brings virtue and happiness to men, but nevertheless the dark cloud of forgetfulness is added and takes the right course of conducting one's affairs away from their minds."[11] In the *Pythian Odes* he refers this evil to the gods as its authors, saying: "Together with one good the gods bestow on men two troubles."[12] But the word of God imputes this evil not to habit, nor to forgetfulness, nor to the gods, nor to fortune, but to Adam transgressing the commandment of God, in response to which the seed of the woman was promised and provided as the saving remedy. Therefore, let us give thanks to God, who shows us the wound of nature and where it comes from, and graciously offers a saving remedy.[13]

But since nature is now corrupted and no one is able come to true wisdom and blessedness with nature as his guide,[14] it seems that one undertakes discussion about this matter in vain; to this point I thus wish to make a reply. First, it is worthy of a studious man to see what that thing is that Paul calls in one place the truth of God, in another the δικαίωμα τοῦ θεοῦ [the ordinance of God],[15] which he declares to be known to the gentiles, and to see how one might understand how far reason is able to progress. Next, it is most beautiful to observe from what principles and what demonstrations moral teaching and the laws of a polity are constructed, which human society can no more be without than fire and air. For whatever is handed down in ethics

---

are his victory odes (the *Olympian Odes, Pythian Odes, Nemean Odes,* and *Isthmian Odes*).

[11] Pindar, *Olympian Odes* 7.44–47. Hemmingsen quotes these lines again in the final section of the work, in that instance including the Greek as well. In his poem, Pindar is not referring to the god Prometheus, but rather to "forethought," which is what his name means. Hemmingsen, however, takes it as the proper name each time he cites it.

[12] Cf. Pindar, *Pythian Odes* 3.103–9.

[13] The foregoing passage closely echoes Philip Melanchthon's preface to his first commentary on Aristotle's *Nicomachean Ethics* (*In Ethica Aristotelis Commentarius* [Wittenberg: Josef Klug, 1529], A5v–6v).

[14] This directly contradicts what Cicero asserts in *On the Laws.*

[15] Rom. 1:32.

and laws must be judged by the norm of the law of nature. For, as Cicero correctly says, "Good law is separated from bad by the norm of nature."[16]

I have therefore resolved to gather together a few remarks concerning the law of nature, not only so that we may be roused to thankfulness toward the creator of nature and may understand, as nature points the way, to what end all our actions and, indeed, our whole life ought to be referred; but also so that there may be a more correct understanding of the apostle, who says that the gentiles display the work of the law written on their hearts.

In order, moreover, to follow a sure method of teaching in the exposition of this matter, it seemed to me most advantageous to follow the one that Galen called analysis.

For, first, I shall put forward the whole matter contained and rolled up in a definition like a bedroll in a sack.

Next, in order to explain the definition, I shall undertake an analysis of those members that are joined together briefly in the body (as it were) of the definition; in this analysis, we shall observe the force of nature, and, in addition to many other things, what the end of man is and what the first principles and hypotheses of the law of nature are. From these, moral philosophy and the knowledge of the right[17] are drawn out[18] as if from a fountain, once the rule[19] of philosophy, which is demonstration, has been applied. In addition to these things, I shall set forth what the rewards of the preservation of the norm of nature are, and the penalties for its violation. When these things have

---

[16] Hemmingsen is paraphrasing Cicero, *On the Laws* 1.44.

[17] *iuris scientia.*

[18] Hemmingsen uses the verb *deducitur.* It could be translated "drawn out," as I have done here to preserve the metaphor of the "fountain" or "source," or as "deduced," to signify its logical meaning vis-à-vis "demonstration." Both meanings are in play.

[19] The word translated "rule" is the relatively rare noun *amussis,* which at its most basic is the rule or level used by carpenters and masons. Hemmingsen uses the same illustration in his discussion of the demonstrative method in book 1 of *De methodis,* in *Opuscula theologica,* 26.

been set forth, I shall add how the Ten Laws[20] can be constructed and inferred from practical principles, and to what extent the law of nature is harmonious with the divine law, and to what extent it is discordant from it.

To this I shall also add a catalogue of the virtues, together with maxims chosen from the best authors, and I shall demonstrate how they flow from the law of nature. In all of these things, we shall perceive the end and use of the law of nature. Finally, because the conscience is the witness of the law of nature, I shall say something about it as well. By this method I hope to make the law of nature, which seems in some degree to lie hidden, to present itself more clearly for contemplation. May God, the author of nature, assist me by his grace.

---

[20] I.e., the Ten Commandments.

1

THE LAW OF NATURE DEFINED

Before, however, I give a complete definition of the law of nature, there seem to be some things that I should say first; it will be evident that they pertain to a rational account of the name. For often the true exposition of a name sheds much light on the entirety of the discussion that has been undertaken about some matter.[1]

---

[1] It was customary in the classical philosophical tradition to begin with a definition; cf. Cicero, *On the Republic* 1.38, where Scipio says: "I begin by observing a rule which all speakers, I fancy, must adhere to if confusion is to be avoided: that is, if the name of the subject under discussion is accepted (whatever it is), the meaning of the name should be explained. Only when that has been agreed can the discussion begin. For the scope of the subject under investigation will never be understood unless people first understand what it is" (*The Republic* and *The Laws*, trans. Niall Rudd [Oxford: Oxford University Press, 1998]). For the method of definition, see Hemmingsen's *De methodis*, in *Opuscula theologica*, 13–14, 16–21.

As, therefore, *law* in Greek terminology (as Plato and Cicero like to explain it) is named from a principle of rendering to each his own,[2] so in Latin *lex* ["law"] receives its name from the verb *eligere* ["to choose"], the former term referring to the end of the law, namely, justice, the latter to the faculty of deliberation and the power of choosing. The result is that it is the law that not only teaches what ought to be rendered to each individual, but also gives the norm for choosing the things that are just and avoiding their opposites. Every law, therefore, ought to be an advocate of virtues and a corrector of vices.

The phrase *of nature* stands for an adjective; by it the kind of law we are speaking about is indicated. For when this law is called the "law of nature," it is signified that it is different from the law that is written, so that the former is prior in order, the latter later; the former has the relation of a source, the latter of tributaries; the former is the cause of the latter; and the latter exists as the effect of the former. Next, by the word *nature* is indicated a certain power that is present in every man, that is, a common understanding that places the virtues among honorable things and shameful things among the vices.

He who denies that this law of nature has been imprinted[3] by God upon the minds of men must necessarily disagree with himself. For the conscience of all men, together with the chief philosophers and the apostle Paul, bears witness to the opposite. More must be said about this matter later in its own place.

The philosophers call the law of nature by various names that they fashion for understanding its power. Cicero calls it in one place the law of nature,[4] because it is imprinted on the minds of men by nature; in another place the law of nations,[5] because, although all men have been scattered far and wide throughout the world, it is the same for

---

[2] I.e. νόμος (though Hemmingsen does not give the Greek term), derived from νέμω, νέμειν ("to deal out, dispense, distribute").

[3] This verb (*imprimere*) could also be translated as "to engrave."

[4] *ius naturae.*

[5] *ius gentium.* For the ancient origins of this phrase, cf. Henry Nettleship, *Contributions to Latin Lexicography* (Oxford: Clarendon Press, 1889), 500–10.

all, for reason does not vary among men as language does;[6] in another place divine law,[7] because God is the author of this law. For this reason Paul also calls the law of nature[8] the truth and the law of God,[9] as I noted above. Sometimes it is called the eternal law[10] because its norm is unchanging and permanent. Cicero discusses this in his speech on behalf of Milo as well: "For this law[11] is," he says, "not written, but inborn—a law that we have not learned, received, or read, but that we have seized, drunk in, and pressed out[12] from the breast of nature herself, a law that we are not taught, but for which we are made, a law in which we are not educated, but into which we are initiated."[13]

---

[6] Hemmingsen here makes use of a common Latin play on words based on the similarity of sound in the terms "reason" (*ratio*) and "language" or "speech" (*oratio*). Cf., e.g., Johannes Scharpius, *Cursus theologicus* (Geneva: Chouet, 1620), 1: "λόγος is twofold: internal, which is called reason (*ratio*), and external, which called speech (*oratio*)."

[7] *ius divinum*.

[8] *naturae lex*.

[9] *ius Dei*.

[10] *ius aeternum*.

[11] *lex*.

[12] *exprimere* is a forceful verb, often meaning "to squeeze or wring out." It can also have the sense of "to imitate, copy." Hemmingsen has earlier used the verb *imprimere* for the way in which the law of nature is given to us, and he now cites Cicero using *exprimere* for the way in which we retrieve it.

[13] Cicero, *On Behalf of Titus Annius Milo* 10. The last verb, *imbuere*, which I have translated as "we have been initiated" (*imbuti sumus*), means most basically "to wet, moisten, dip." This passage was regularly used in discussions of natural law. For instance, Cicero himself uses it in *The Orator* 49.165, and Francis Turretin cites the passage from Cicero's *Milo* in *Institutes of Elenctic Theology*. Immediately afterwards, Turretin also uses both of the Greek expressions used by Hemmingsen in the following sentences, with only slight differences in wording (*Institutio theologiae elencticae* [Geneva: S. de Tournes, 1688–89], 11.1.14).

Sophocles confirms this very thing when he calls the laws of nature ἄγραπτα καὶ ἀσφαλῆ θεῶν νόμιμα,[14] that is, the unwritten but nevertheless steadfast and solid precepts of the gods—such that it is never lawful for a mortal to violate them.

Aristotle calls this same law at one place δίκαιον ἔμψυχον [justice personified],[15] from which every written law derives its force, at another place λόγον [reason], at another νοῦν [understanding]; Cicero, joining together these two words, says: "That law, which the gods have given to the human race, is the reason and understanding of the wise man,"[16] namely, the measuring rod of divine justice shining in the mind—a thing that Euripides[17] expressed elegantly in the following words: "So great a light," he says, "has shone on us from heaven that it is brighter than the evening star or the morning star";[18] but the things that oppose this light have risen from deep darkness.

---

[14] Sophocles, *Antigone* 454–55; Hemmingsen's text differs slightly from modern editions of Sophocles. The Athenian tragedian Sophocles was born in the 490s BC and died in late 406 or early 405. A frequent victor at the City Dionysia, he wrote more than 120 plays, of which seven survive, including *Antigone* and *Oedipus the King*.

[15] See Aristotle, *Nicomachean Ethics* 5.4 (1132a22). But Aristotle is here speaking of a judge rather than the law: "This is why, when people dispute, they take refuge in the judge; and to go to the judge is to go to justice; for the nature of the judge is to be a sort of animate justice" (*The Nicomachean Ethics of Aristotle*, trans. David Ross [Oxford: Oxford University Press, 1954]).

[16] Cicero, *On the Laws* 2.8. Hemmingsen has compressed his source, which reads: *Ex quo illa lex, quam di humano generi dederunt, recte est laudata: est enim ratio mensque sapientis ad iubendum et ad deterrendum idonea.*

[17] The Athenian tragedian Euripides was probably born in the 480s and died in 407/6 BC. Of his ninety plays, eighteen survive, including such works as the *Medea*, the *Hippolytus*, and the *Bacchae*.

[18] Hemmingsen cites a fragment of Euripides also cited by Aristotle in *Nicomachean Ethics* 5.1 (1129b28–9), though Aristotle does not name Euripides, indicating that Aristotle is not Hemmingsen's source (or, at least, not his only source) for the quotation. A scholiast on Aristotle claims that it comes from Euripides' lost play *Melanippe* (frag. 490 Dindorf): see Horace

Demosthenes calls the law a εὕρικα καὶ δῶρον θεῶν,[19] a discovery and gift of the gods, which we can only say reasonably about written law when written law relies on the law of nature as a foundation. What I have said so far sufficiently sets forth for us a rational account of the name. Now, in order to spread ourselves a path toward a suitable definition, I shall add certain brief ἀποδόσεις [explanations] and outlines of the law of nature.

First of all, then, the following remark of Cicero comes to mind: "The law of nature is the highest reason implanted in nature, which commands those things that must be done and forbids their opposites."[20] It is called the "highest reason" because, having gone forth from the divine mind, it is the norm of commanding and forbidding, that is, it is the reasoning about acting rightly that shines in the human mind. Because, therefore, it commands and forbids, it is called "law," and because it is implanted in nature, it is called "natural."

Another writer defines it thus: "The law of nature is the sure and undoubted will[21] of God, imprinted on the minds of men, by which we are taught the things that it is right to do, and the things that it is right to avoid"[22]—that is, it is the knowledge of the distinction between

Rackham, ed. and trans., *Aristotle: The Nicomachean Ethics* (Cambridge, MA: Harvard University Press, 1934), 258na. See also John Burnet, ed., *The Ethics of Aristotle* (New York: Arno Press, 1973), *ad loc.* As Burnet notes, the image is also found in Plotinus, *Enneads* 1.6.4 and 6.6.6.

[19] Demosthenes, *Against Aristogiton* 1.17 (=Demosthenes, *Oration* 25.17). Modern editions of Demosthenes' text differ slightly, which read εὕρημα rather than εὕρικα. The passage is also cited in the *Digest* of Justinian (1.3.2).

[20] Cicero, *On the Laws* 1.18. What Cicero says is slightly different: he writes, "Law is the highest reason."

[21] *sententia*. The word could also be translated in this context as "judgment" or "determination."

[22] I have been unable to locate the source of this definition. Merio Scattola, *Das Naturrecht vor dem Naturrecht* (Tübingen: Max Niemeyer, 1999), 85n196, claims that Hemmingsen's source is Philip Melanchthon, *Loci praecipui theologici* (1559), CR 21:687 (available in English as *The Chief Theological Topics: Loci praecipui theologici 1559*, trans. J. A. O. Preus, 2nd ed. [St. Louis:

honorable and shameful things, so that we seek out the former and guard against the latter.

Now that I have thus briefly noted these things, I shall compose a suitable and complete definition, in the following way:

> The law of nature is a certain knowledge,[23] imprinted on the minds of men by God, of the principles of knowing[24] and of acting, and of the conclusions proved from these principles that[25] are in agreement with the proper end of man. Reason constructs these conclusions from the principles by necessary consequence for the government of human life, so that man may recognize, want, choose, and do the things that are right, and avoid their opposites; and God has bestowed on men the conscience as the witness and judge of all these things.

This fuller definition contains very many elements; when I have set these forth, it will be apparent how widely the force of nature extends itself among men—indeed, how important it is in relation to the things that ought to be sought out and avoided. For it is only

---

Concordia, 2011]), but Melanchthon, though he speaks in a similar way to Hemmingsen both there and at *CR* 21:712, does not say precisely the same thing that Hemmingsen does in this definition.

[23] *noticia.* Hemmingsen uses several different words for "knowledge" in this work (see Translator's Note). *noticia* (classical spelling, *notitia*) means "acquaintance, knowledge, conception, notion"; see LS, s.v. "notitia"; cf. also *OLD*, s.v. "notitia."

[24] *cognitio, actio.* Latin nouns ending in *–tio* give the names of actions, and so I have rendered the terms "knowing" and "acting" in Hemmingsen's definition and discussion of the definition, though *actio* will occasionally be rendered as "action" as well; in the plural, the term will be translated "actions." The term *cognitio* means "a becoming acquainted with, acquiring knowledge, knowledge as a consequence of perception or of the exercise of our mental powers, knowing, acquaintance"; see LS, s.v. "cognitio." Because I translate the term as "knowing" rather than "knowledge," I will not indicate the Latin term in a footnote unless I have translated it differently in that instance.

[25] The antecedent of the pronoun is "conclusions," not "principles."

about these things that I have undertaken my discourse, not about each individual motion and property found in living beings. Therefore, as I have proposed, I shall set forth each individual part of the definition in the order in which the parts were proposed, and I shall provide an anatomy, as it were, by means of which they all may be perceived more distinctly and clearly.

First of all, therefore, my definition calls to mind the origin of the law of nature, and refers it to God as its author, who has imprinted it on the minds of men, such that it is, so to speak, a measuring rod[26] of the divine mind and wisdom. But since I spoke of this several times above, here I shall only point out very briefly the matters that the origin of the law of nature reminds us about.

First, therefore, the origin of the law of nature causes us to remember its authority, worth, and justice. For it cannot but happen that something that has God as its author is preeminent in all those qualities.

Next, its origin will also remind us that, just as whatever is done according to this law is done correctly, so every violation of this law should be understood to conflict not only with nature but also with God himself. For this reason, those who perversely transgress the limits of this law are said by the ancient philosophers to θεομαχεῖν [fight against God]; from this word also those who, having cast this law aside, have lived according to their own lust, are called θεόμαχοι [God-fighters].[27]

Here we must lament the human perversity that followed the fall of our first parents. For it is the outcome of that fall that the obstinacy and rebellion of men against this law of God is so great. Sun, moon, and all the stars obey the divine ordering, and they complete, according to the law imposed upon them, their course in the predetermined amount of time; man, placed in the midst of these things as a sort of investigator, alone is prosecuted unto condemnation for obstinacy, as

---

26 The Latin term is *radius*, the same term Hemmingsen uses above when glossing the law as the reason and mind of the wise man in Cicero, *On the Laws* 2.8; here it is used in reference to the *divine* mind and wisdom.

27 The verb translated as "to conflict" above (*pugnare*) can also be rendered as "to fight."

one who does not wish to be subject to the divine law and ordering. So great is the perversity, so great the obstinacy of men against the creator of nature.

Thus far concerning its origin; the next thing to say is that the law of nature is knowledge,[28] and certain knowledge at that. For the norms of the law of nature are neither doubtful opinions, nor ἀκατάληπτοι [incomprehensible] judgments that cannot be perceived. But they are steadfast perceptions[29] of the things that we ought to seek out and to avoid—perceptions that it is right to embrace with steadfast assent ἄνευ τῆς ἐποχῆς [without the suspension of judgment] of the Academic philosophers.

Before, however, I come to the substance of this knowledge, that is, to its principles, I shall say something about how we come to certainty and apprehension, so that the rest of what I have to say may be better understood.

How, therefore, is the certainty that I am speaking of brought about? What is the reasoning process of apprehension? First of all, it is established from Aristotle—something that common sense itself also clearly shows—that actions have two principles, knowing[30] and appetite,[31] the former perceiving what sort of thing a thing is, the latter either pursuing or avoiding it.[32]

There is, moreover, a twofold knowing, one sensitive, the other intellectual.[33] How each one comes about must be set forth briefly,

---

[28] noticia.

[29] perceptiones.

[30] cognitio, not noticia.

[31] I.e., "desire." Since "appetite" is often used in English translations of philosophical texts for the type of desire under consideration, I maintain it here.

[32] See also Cicero, On Obligations 1.101–2.

[33] cognitio sensitiva and cognitio intellectiva, respectively. The terminology is scholastic; cf. Roy J. Deferrari, M. Inviolata Barry, and Ignatius McGuiness, A Lexicon of St. Thomas Aquinas based on the Summa theologica and Selected Passages of His Other Works (Washington, D.C.: Catholic University of America Press, 1948–49), s.v. "cognitio" 2.2.e³ (p. 166). I have translated

and first I shall speak about sensitive knowing, which comes about in the following way.

First, an object moves a sense that is directed outward, as, for example, beauty moves the sense of sight; what is sweet, the sense of taste; what is aromatic, the sense of smell; what is sonorous, the sense of hearing; what is soft, the sense of touch; and so on.

Next, a common sense, whose seat is in the mind, takes up those things that are presented to the outward-directed senses, and fashions images of them.

Then, if an interval of time is interposed, the memory, which recollection and contemplation reinforce and preserve, retains these same things.

At this point, appetite arises, which seizes upon what is agreeable to it—namely, what is delightful and pleasurable—from which there comes about an impulse to action, or to the enjoyment and use of the object that was sought out.

But here, unless one is obedient to the law of nature, or right reason, he very often commits sin, both in seeking and in avoiding. For, because of the animal appetite that follows sensitive knowing, we often seek out those things that are opposed to the appetite of reason. For as the former follows the irrational judgment of brutes, so the latter follows the judgment that belongs peculiarly to men; and, again, due to animal appetite we often oppose the things that in truth we ought to have sought out.

Accordingly, we must make a distinction among the objects of the senses. For there are some into which animal appetite rushes, others which the same appetite rejects and avoids. Moreover, with the animal sense we desire things that seem agreeable, delightful, and pleasurable, which are called, by one general name, bodily pleasures. For there also exist pleasures of the mind, about which I shall speak in another place.

---

them as "sensitive knowing" and "intellectual knowing" throughout, which keeps close to the standard English rendering of this scholastic terminology ("sensitive knowledge" and "intellectual knowledge"), while preserving the use of *cognitio* as found in Hemmingsen's definition of the law of nature.

There are three different varieties of bodily pleasures: for some are both natural and necessary, others are natural and not necessary, others are neither natural nor necessary.[34] He who is carried off into these three kinds of pleasures without distinction and with a similar impulse must be judged to be a pig rather than a man. Therefore those who prefer to follow reason as their guide, rather than ὁρμήν [impulse] apart from reason, should hold and preserve this distinction.

The natural and necessary pleasure of the body consists in food and drink, as well as clothing. This pleasure is called natural, because it is sought out by nature; necessary, because without it the sound condition of nature cannot be preserved. But the following caution must be added, namely, that we be content with those things that suffice for nature with respect to its preservation and the performance of natural functions.

The pleasure of the body that is natural and not necessary consists in sexual matters. Although this pleasure pertains to the preservation of the whole race, and for that reason is natural, nevertheless it is not necessary, because the wise man can do without it—nay, rather, it must be judged to be wholly illicit unless it is governed by reason and law. For if it is governed by reason, it is approved by natural and divine law;[35] but if it is carried on against reason, it befouls and pollutes nature.

---

[34] The basic distinction goes back at least to Plato, *Republic* 8.558d9–559c13, and Aristotle, *Nicomachean Ethics* 7.4 (1147b20–1148b14), but Hemmingsen's discussion diverges from that of Aristotle, who, for example, includes sexual intercourse among the necessary bodily pleasures. Cf. also Epicurus, *Letter to Menoeceus* (preserved in Diogenes Laertius, *Lives of Eminent Philosophers* 127–29) and *Principal Doctrines* 26, 29–30; Cicero, *On Ends* 1.45 and 2.26–27. The proper categorization of sex is more ambiguous in the Epicurean tradition than one might expect; cf. Lucretius, *On the Nature of Things* 4.1058–1287, but also Diogenes Laertius, *Lives of Eminent Philosophers* 10.6.

[35] *ius*.

Bodily pleasure that is neither natural nor necessary consists in drunkenness, lust, bacchanalian revels,[36] and gluttonous overindulgence that exceeds what is necessary. This pleasure is not natural, because it corrupts nature; it is not necessary, because we can do without it. It is so inconsistent with natural law that even many beasts resist and avoid it. Those, therefore, who pursue this pleasure act most shamefully. For most wretchedly do they lower themselves below the beasts.[37]

Epicurus,[38] therefore, who placed the highest good of man in this type of pleasure, is detestable. The dignity of human nature conflicts with this man's most perverse teaching; the excellence of man's mental abilities conflicts with it; pleasure's subject, object, cheapness, unwholesome accompanying associations, force, and outcome, which the Epicurean longs for, all conflict with it; the appetite of reason and the right judgment in all men of sound mind conflicts with it; conscience

---

[36] *comessationes.* In his 1564 commentary on Galatians, Hemmingsen defines *comessationes* as "nighttime gormandizing, and the wanton incantations of drunks, chanted with railing and abuse." See Hemmingsen, *Commentaria in omnes Epistolas Apostolorum* (Leipzig: Andreas Schneider and Ernst Vögelin, 1572), 363.

[37] Hemmingsen's treatment here is traditional. His discussion is extremely close to, for instance, that of John of Damascus, *Exposition of the Orthodox Faith* 2.13.

[38] Epicurus (341 BC–270 BC) was a Hellenistic philosopher and the progenitor of the Epicurean sect of philosophy and taught that the purpose of philosophy was to obtain a happy life. Happiness consists in pleasure, though Epicurean teaching has often been caricatured in this respect as enjoining a hedonism that amounts to libertinism. In fact, Epicurus subordinated the pleasure of the body to the pleasure of the soul, and both were ordered to *ataraxia* ("freedom from disturbance"). In the wake of the Italian Renaissance a revived Epicureanism became popular once again, and thus it is common to find it attacked in sixteenth century sources for its pursuit of pleasure, but even more so for its practical atheism (for Epicurus taught that if the gods exist at all, they have no interest in our world, thus destroying providence and supernaturalism itself). Though Epicurus wrote voluminously, only three letters and two collections of maxims survive, besides fragments of other works.

conflicts with it; the opinions of all who are truly wise conflict with it; and the praiseworthy examples of all of the most outstanding men and most excellent women conflict with it—in sum, all of nature conflicts with it, so that, for the time being, I need say nothing at all about its conflict with heavenly doctrine. These reasons easily dispel, by their own clarity, the foul smoke that the wretched and insane slaves of Epicurean pleasure belch forth. Therefore, let us leave to the pigs those who are of the herd of Epicurus.[39]

Thus far concerning the objects of the senses that are pleasing, which one may either seek out or not seek out. Now other objects remain that are harsh and troublesome to the senses, and these are not of one kind. For certain of them are hostile to nature and hinder those hastening toward true knowledge[40] and the adornment of virtue—such as disease, imprisonment, exile, poverty, and other things of this kind. If these things cannot be avoided, one must try to let at least a tiny spark of virtue shine through in them.

There are certain things without which the approach to the citadel of Pallas Athena and virtue—that is, to the knowledge[41] of truth and the proper performance of virtue—is open to no one. Things such as these are studies, toilsome labor, and the highest diligence and care in discharging a duty entrusted to oneself. Although these things are difficult, nevertheless they must not be avoided. Hesiod speaks beautifully about these things when he says, τῆς ἀρετῆς ἱδρῶτα θεοὶ προπάροιθεν ἔθηκαν ἀθάνατοι, that is, "The gods established that virtue must be

---

[39] Cf. his remark above: "He who is carried off into these three kinds of pleasure without distinction and with a similar impulse must be judged to be a pig rather than a man."

[40] *scientia*. This term will usually be rendered "true knowledge"; the reader should note that the adjective "true" is mine and is used to express the force of Hemmingsen's customary use of the word in this treatise. It stands in contrast to "opinion" (*opinio*). *Scientia* differs from *noticia* in that the former refers to certain knowledge that comes as a result of reasoning from immovable first principles, whereas the latter refers to knowledge *of* those first principles, even before they have been applied in reasoning to yield *scientia*.

[41] *scientia*.

obtained by sweat."[42] Also relevant is the opinion of Epicharmus[43] found in Xenophon: τῶν πόνων πωλοῦσιν ἡμῖν πάντα τ' ἀγάθὰ οἱ θεοί: "The gods sell us all good things in exchange for toilsome labor."[44] Lucan, too, elegantly says, "Snake, thirst, heat, sand: things sweet to virtue. Endurance rejoices in hard things."[45] This is also most beautifully displayed in the *Tablet of Cebes*.[46]

---

[42] Hesiod, *Works and Days* 289–90. The same passage is cited in Plato, *Republic* 2.364c–d, which may be Hemmingsen's source for it here, though it is also quoted in Stobaeus, *Anthology* 3.1.205b. Hesiod, a native of Cyme and inhabitant of Ascra in Boeotia and the author of the *Theogony* and *Works and Days*, is the oldest Greek poet besides Homer from whom we have entire works extant.

[43] Epicharmus was a Sicilian comic playwright in the first quarter of the fifth century BC. His work survives only in fragments.

[44] Xenophon, *Memorabilia* 2.1.20.

[45] Lucan, *Civil War* 9.402–3. Hemmingsen has *serpens, sitis, ardor, arena, dulcia virtuti, gaudet patientia duris*, which differs slightly from modern editions of Lucan, which read *ardor [h]arenae*, "the heat of sand."

[46] This text, a dialogue, is associated with Cebes of Thebes, a contemporary of Socrates and a character in Plato's *Phaedo*, though in reality the text probably dates from the first century AD. *Cebetis tabula* is the correct reading, as printed in the *Opuscula theologica*, though for *Cebetis* earlier printed versions read *Semetis*. This is not a Latin word, but the misreading is curious. *Semetis* sounds like the Latin word for "path" (*semita*; there is an extremely rare alternate form *semes* with genitive *semitis*) as well as *Samus* (Samos), the birthplace of Pythagoras, who reportedly used the letter *Y* to show the two paths of virtue and vice (cf. Persius, *Satire* 3.56–57; *Latin Anthology* 632, by Maximinus, though at one time attributed to Vergil [Servius' commentary on *Aeneid* 6.136]). Even more interestingly, Cebes was associated with a Pythagorean, Philolaus, though likely not a Pythagorean himself. All of these various strands (the *Tablet of Cebes*, Pythagoras and his *Y*, and Prodicus' account of the choice of Hercules, which Hemmingsen is about to relate) were closely connected with each other in Hemmingsen's day: see George Hugo Tucker, *Homo Viator: Itineraries of Exile, Displacement and Writing in Renaissance Europe* (Geneva: Droz, 2003), 53–151.

Xenophon too bears witness to this same thing through an example he reports from the treatises of Prodicus:[47]

> For Prodicus relates that Hercules, when he was just coming to maturity, thought silently to himself about which way and manner of living he should follow—whether he should pursue pleasure or virtue. For he saw that the way of pleasure was quite easy and exceedingly well-worn, while that of virtue was hard and difficult. As Hercules thought about these things, two women of great stature appeared to him. Of these, one had an elegant and respectable appearance and a noble character, which nature itself had adorned. For her body was lovely, her eyes bashful, her carriage modest, and her clothing resplendent. But the other appeared fleshy and soft; moreover, she was carefully plumed and adorned; indeed, her skin was bright with makeup, so that she seemed more white and more red than she really was; she adjusted the posture of her body so that she appeared taller than she was by nature; she had wandering and wide-open eyes;[48] she wore the kind of clothing that accentuated her sexual allurement; she frequently looked at herself and also took note as to whether anyone else was looking at her; and very frequently she gazed at her own shadow.
>
> When these two women had approached nearer to Hercules, the first one continued on in the same manner in which she had begun, but the other, desiring to get to him first, ran toward Hercules and addressed him with the following words: "I see, Hercules, that you hesitate in deciding which way of living you should direct yourself toward; if, therefore, you should choose me, I shall lead you to the most agreeable and easiest way of life, so that you will abound in those things that are pleasing and will be without those things in life that are

---

[47] Preserved in Xenophon, *Memorabilia* 2.1.21–33. Cicero also summarizes it in *On Obligations* 1.118, but it is the longer version of Xenophon that Hemmingsen uses—or, rather, transcribes.

[48] I.e., in contrast to the bashfulness of the eyes of the other woman.

hard and troublesome. For, first of all, you will not have any care for either wars or business, but you will instead look to how you may find food and drink that are pleasing to you; how you may obtain what is pleasing in sight, smell, and touch; by the enjoyment of what passions you may receive the greatest delight possible; in what way you may sleep as softly as possible; and, further, by what method you may be able to obtain all these things without toilsome labor and trouble. But if you should ever worry that you lack the resources by which to acquire these pleasures, you must not fear lest I lead you to the obtainment of these goods of the body through toilsome labor and trouble; but you will rather use what has been acquired by the toilsome labor of others, holding back from nothing from which you can hope for some profit, since I permit to my friends to seize advantages from any place they wish."

When Hercules had heard these things, he said, "Woman, what is your name?"

In reply, she said, "My friends call me Happiness, but my enemies give me the invidious name of κακίαν [Vice]."

Meanwhile, while she was saying these things, the other woman approached and said, "I too come to you, Hercules; I know your parents, and I have taken note of your character in your boyhood instruction; therefore I hope that you, provided that you direct yourself to the way that leads to me, will be one who pursues and cultivates good and honorable works,[49] and I am confident that you see me to be much more honorable and noble for striving after good things. I shall not deceive you with the reward of pleasure, but I shall tell you truly what sort of nature the gods have bestowed on things. For the gods give to men none of the things that are good and honorable without toilsome labor and exertion. But if you should wish the gods to be well disposed to you, you must by all means worship the gods. If you should desire to be loved

---

[49] *bonorum et honestorum operum fore sectatorem et cultorem.* Cf. Titus 2:14 (Vulg.): *qui dedit semet ipsum pro nobis ut nos redimeret ab omni iniquitate et mundaret sibi populum acceptabilem, sectatorem bonorum operum.*

by your friends, you must confer benefits upon your friends. If you should desire to be honored by a city,[50] you must confer some usefulness upon that city. If you should wish to be held in admiration in all of Greece on account of your virtue, you must try to perform kindnesses for all of Greece. If you should desire that the earth produce fruits for you, you must cultivate the earth. If you have a mind to acquire riches by means of beasts of burden, you must take care of your beasts of burden. If you should desire to be considered glorious in conducting the business of war—by freeing your friends from servitude and reducing your enemies to servitude—you must learn the arts of war from those who know them, and you must be trained in them, in order to know how to use them rightly. If you should wish to be strong in bodily vigor, you must accustom your body to obey the mind's judgment and to be trained in toilsome labors and sweat."

Here, κακία [Vice] interrupted and said, "Do you understand, Hercules, how hard and long the way is toward the pleasures and delights this woman tells you of, and by how easy and short a road *I* would lead you to happiness?"[51]

In response to these words, Virtue said, "Wretched woman, what good do you possess, or what can seem pleasant to you, who are willing to do nothing for the sake of the good or the pleasant? Nor do you wait for any desire for pleasure, but before any desire lays hold of you, you are full of them all, as one who eats before he is hungry and drinks before he is thirsty. Moreover, in order to eat with pleasure, you obtain sought-after cooks; in order to drink with pleasure, you seek varied and expensive wines, and in the summer, traveling around hither and yon, you constantly look for snow;[52] in order to sleep with pleasure, you not only spread out a soft cover, but you also get a frame for your bed. For you seek sleep not

---

[50] *civitas.*

[51] The name given to Vice above.

[52] Snow was used to cool wine; see Josiah Renick Smith, ed., *Memorabilia* (Boston: Ginn & Co., 1903), 2.1.30.

when wearied by toilsome labor, but when you have nothing to do. In order to give your sexual appetite a workout before there is a need, you devise all manner of activities, holding yourself back neither from men nor from women. For you train your friends so that by night they abandon themselves to every kind of shamefulness but waste the most useful part of the day in snoring.

"Moreover, although you are immortal, nevertheless the gods have cast you away and good men scorn you. You have never[53] heard yourself praised—a thing that is, of all things, most pleasant to hear; nor have you looked upon on any illustrious deeds of your own—a thing that is, of all things, the most pleasant sight. Who, therefore, will believe you when you speak? Who could offer aid when you are in need? Or who, maintaining control over his own mind, could endure to be counted among your company? For of those who are in your company, the young are of weak body, and the old are of foolish mind and captive in their judgment. For after they have passed their youth in leisure and luxury, they live out an old age shattered by many toilsome labors and infirmities. As the life they have lived previously ashames them, so, burdened by present evils, they are oppressed. In youth they pursue pleasure, but in old age they lay up trouble for themselves.

"But I have intimate familiarity both with the gods and with good men; a noble and honorable work cannot be done, either by the gods or by men, without me; I am held in the greatest honor both among the gods and among like-minded men. For, indeed, I am the desired fellow-worker of craftsmen, the trustworthy guardian of houses for their masters, a benevolent ally for servants, a good helper in toilsome labors in times of peace, in war a steadfast helper, and friendship's best framer. In addition to these things, my friends enjoy the benefit of a pleasant use of food and drink. For they wait until they desire them.

---

[53] I read *nunquam* ("never") with the text of the *Opuscula theologica* rather than the *unquam* ("ever") of earlier printed editions I have consulted, which must be a typographical error.

More pleasant sleep befalls them than those who are at leisure; if they are bereft of sleep, they meanwhile endure it with no annoyance, nor on its account do they neglect their duty. The younger ones are joyful, while the old are praised. The older ones are happy when they see the younger honored. As they recall the accomplishments of the ancients with the highest pleasure,[54] so, when they themselves do something nobly, they are none too little delighted. On account of me they are dear to the gods, welcome to their friends, and honorable to their country. Besides this, after their end in death has arrived, they do not lie in the grave without honors, consigned to oblivion, but, celebrated in the remembrance of men, they flourish forever.

"In this way, Hercules," she said, "you son of good parents, whoever trains himself by toilsome labor will be able to obtain the most blessed happiness."

I have included this very beautiful dialogue so that students, after they have been instructed by the arguments I have collected from both sides of the case, may prepare themselves for the path of virtue. As no one ever reaches it without toilsome labors, so the pleasure of the body, which in the band of the virtues is as a prostitute in a throng of matrons, diverts a person from the same. It does not befit us, therefore, to rush headlong into those things that seem sweet and pleasant at first sight, due solely to the sense perception that belongs to irrational creatures. For when sensitive knowing, which is necessary for a sentient soul, detains us only in those things that are pleasing to the senses, we ought in opposition to think about the elevation of the soul, by which we stand apart from beasts; for not only do we, like plants, grow and receive life and, like irrational creatures, perceive with our

---

[54] This differs slightly from Xenophon, in whose version the adjective "old" or "ancient" modifies "deeds" and the correlation is that they are pleased by their own both past and present good deeds.

senses, but we also, like angels, are endowed with a mind.[55] For that reason we must look to where the mind calls us.

So much concerning sensitive knowing and the desire that correspondingly answers to it; I shall now add a few words concerning intellectual knowing and the appetite of reason that accompanies it by nature. For these are the two principles of acts of virtue: one of these is called intellect, and it is the principle that directs. The other is called will, and it is the principle that commands; it pertains first to the judgment of things, then to the end of goods. These two are, as Cicero says, the greatest goods in philosophy.[56]

First of all, therefore, we must attend to the differences, in order not to confuse these two kinds of knowing. Sensitive knowing is needed by the sentient soul only; intellectual knowing is needed by the intellect. Sensitive knowing exists both in irrational creatures and in men; intellectual knowing exists only in man. The former always takes its beginning from an external object and from sense perception; the latter takes its beginning from them sometimes, but not always. The end of the former is the use of the thing that was sought out; the end of the latter is true knowledge[57] and prudence regarding those things that we seek out by nature.

---

[55] Cf. Augustine, *City of God* 5.11: "[God] has given to the good and to the evil, being in common with stones, vegetable life in common with trees, sensuous life in common with brutes, intellectual life in common with angels alone" (trans. Marcus Dods, in vol. 2 of *A Select Library of Nicene and Post-Nicene Fathers of the Christian Church*, ed. Philip Schaff, 1st series, 14 vols. [repr., Grand Rapids, MI: Eerdmans, 1952]).

[56] Cicero, *Academics* 2.9.29.

[57] *scientia*.

Before, however, I distinguish the stages[58] entailed in the acquisition of knowledge more precisely, I shall include the words of Cicero, the prince of philosophers among the Romans. He says:

> The mind itself, which is the source of the senses and is also sense itself, has a natural force, which it directs toward the things by which it is moved; and it seizes upon some things, when they have been seen, so as to use them immediately; it stows others away in such a way that memory arises from them; the rest, however, it arranges by means of similarities, from which are brought about notions[59] of things, which the Greeks call sometimes ἐννοίας [notions], sometimes προλήψεις [preconceptions]. When reasoning has been added to it, and syllogistic proof,[60] and a multitude of countless facts, then the perception[61] of all these things becomes clear, and this same reason, perfected by these stages, arrives at wisdom. Since, therefore, the mind of man is most fit for acquaintance[62] with reality and for constancy of life, it especially embraces knowledge,[63] and κατάληψιν itself (which I will call "apprehension,"[64] translating word for word, as I said) it loves both for its own sake—nothing is sweeter to the mind than the light of truth—and also on account of its use. Therefore the mind also uses the senses and creates the disciplines as second senses, as it were, and strengthens philosophy to such

---

[58] Hemmingsen here uses the same word (*gradus*) translated as "elevation" above, in reference to the distinction between the cognitive capacities of irrational creatures and human beings.

[59] *noticiae.* The term could also be rendered "conceptions."

[60] "Syllogistic proof" is a paraphrase of *argumenti conclusio.* Cf. LS, s.v. "conclusio": "the conclusion in a syllogism, the consequence."

[61] Or "comprehension."

[62] *scientia.*

[63] *cognitio.* Cicero uses the two terms (*cognitio* and *scientia*) together also in *On the Orator* 3.29.112.

[64] Or "seizing, grasping." The Latin term is *comprehensio.*

a degree that it creates virtue, from which alone all life is made well-ordered.[65]

See how beautifully and with what learning Cicero here shows by what stages one arrives at virtue! And when this has been acquired, our mind does not progress further. In order, however, that students may be able to understand these things more distinctly, I shall distinguish them by sure stages.

---

[65] Cicero, *Academics* 2.10.30–31. Hemmingsen's text differs slightly from modern editions.

2

The Principles of Knowing and Acting in General

The first stage, therefore, is the conception[1] of simple things, which, as the passible understanding receives them, so, springing into action, it investigates and apprehends; and first it draws out individual forms, and, from there, it then draws out universal forms. The faculty by which these things are accomplished is called simple apprehension. Composition,[2] by which many various conceptions are put together into one whole, accompanies it. Some of these conceptions are affirmed, others are denied. Ὑπόληψις, that is, evaluation, accompanies it. This produces a clear judgment concerning the conceptions that have been proposed, connecting the things that ought to be joined together and separating those that are in opposition to one another—and for that reason the natural philosophers call it division. Afterwards, reasoning[3] is added to it, which, from the conceptions it has judged, at one time infers some things, at another time others, but in different ways.

---

[1] *notio.*

[2] *compositio:* "putting together, compounding, arranging."

[3] *ratiocinatio.*

For if the inference is made from things that are clear, it is called a demonstration; but if it is made only from things that are probable, a conclusion is constructed that is likewise probable.[4] Accordingly, the effect of reasoning is in the one case true knowledge,[5] in the other, opinion. But let us adapt these observations to our purpose.

The conception that I set down in the first place, then, is an act of the mind and the power of perception,[6] by which we contemplate the splendor of the virtues. This conception, drawn out from images of the virtues, becomes the universal norm of integrity of character and this conception of virtue is called simple apprehension.

In the second place, the composition of conceptions is added by the same faculty of the mind. Truth and falsehood belong to this act of composition. There is a simple conception of the honorable, of the just, of seeking out, of the shameful, of the unjust, of avoiding, and so on. But composition, which connects these conceptions, generates propositions: what is honorable must be sought out; what is shameful must be avoided; what is just is honorable; what is shameful is dishonorable; what is just must be reckoned as belonging to virtue; what is unjust must be reckoned as belonging to vice.

In the third place is added the evaluation of the composition, by which the mind produces a clear judgment about the propositions, affirming this as true, pronouncing that to be false, asserting that what is just must be sought out and what is unjust must be avoided, saying that this is good, instructing that that is evil. For example: justice is good; that which comes about in accordance with right reason is not evil.

But, if the things that the mind has thus arranged and judged are so clear that their contraries appear manifestly false, axioms of demonstrations are produced, whereby, once argumentation has been added in the fourth place, very many propositions are inferred.

------

[4] Hemmingsen deals with the differences between demonstrative and probable reasoning in book 1 of *De methodis*; see *Opuscula theologica*, 23–30.

[5] *scientia*.

[6] For this sense of *animus*, see LS, s.v. "animus" II.A.1.

There is, however, a twofold way of argumentation. For there is one that infers a universal theorem from very many particular hypotheses, and it is called induction. There is another that constructs very many particular hypotheses from a universal proposition, and it is called syllogism.[7] For example: Justice must be sought out; similarly prudence, fortitude, temperance. Therefore every virtue must be sought out. From this proposition again: If every virtue must be sought out, surely friendship, gratitude, truth, clemency, and the other particular virtues must be sought out. This result of reasoning is called true knowledge,[8] which naturally is followed either by seeking out or by scorning. For if what is concluded is honorable or useful or pleasant, a man thereupon is carried along by a natural impulse to obtain it; but if the reason discovers that what is concluded is shameful, useless, or unpleasant, then just as the mind judges that that thing ought not to be embraced, so the will turns away from it in disgust. Consequently, one ought to be amazed at the workmanship of God, who created man in such a way that in him are both γνωστικαὶ [cognitive] and ὀρεκτικαὶ [appetitive] faculties, that is, the faculties by which things are perceived and desired. It is fitting to gaze upon and wonder at these, so that we may be grateful to our creator, who has adorned this μικροκόσμον [miniature world]—that is, man—with gifts so wondrous.

Because, however, careful observation of these faculties reveals to us the knowledge[9] of first principles, I shall add a few words about them. The ancient philosophers, then, wrote about these things in the following manner: Ammonius,[10] after Aristotle, supposes that

---

[7] I.e., deduction.

[8] *scientia*. Again, recall that *scientia* ("true knowledge") is the result of reasoning from first principles, while *noticia* ("knowledge"), used below, is knowledge of the first principles used for reasoning.

[9] *noticia*.

[10] Ammonius Saccas was a Platonist philosopher in the first half of the third century AD and the teacher of Plotinus. He did not write any works of his own but is sometimes referred to by later philosophers, e.g., by Nemesius of Emesa, *On the Nature of Man*.

there are five "producers,"[11] which are νοῦς, mind; διάνοια, discursive thought; δόξα, opinion; φαντασία, imagination; and αἴσθησις, sense perception. These five producers serve for both the discovery of things and their perception.

Since, however, enough has been said above about sensitive knowing, here I shall treat only of intellectual knowing, whose progression is twofold.[12]

One is from sense perception, the lowest producer of knowing; the other is from the mind, the highest producer of knowing. When the progression takes its rise from sense perception, from below, a universal proposition, or axiom, is inferred. And this axiom, constructed with the help of διάνοια [discursive thought] through induction, afterwards is taken up as a first principle for proving the particular hypotheses[13] that are contained in it potentially. From here sometimes true knowledge,[14] at other times opinion is generated. When these things have been conceived by reasoning, they are retained in the mind; from this it is easily understood that διάνοια [discursive thought] alone reasons, and the mind alone preserves and retains the things that have been concluded, so that they can again be brought forth from there when the matter demands it.

When the progression takes its rise from the mind, the highest producer of knowing, hypotheses are inferred about which one makes an investigation, and this through a syllogism, whence also sometimes true knowledge,[15] at other times opinion is generated: on the one

---

[11] Or "workers." Hemmingsen uses this noun (*opifex*) elsewhere to refer to God as "maker" or "creator."

[12] On sensitive and intellectual knowledge, cf. Thomas Aquinas, *Summa theologiae*, I, Q. 80, A. 2.

[13] I.e., particular commandments, e.g., "honor your teachers," "honor the magistrate," and so on.

[14] *scientia.*

[15] *scientia.*

hand, true knowledge,[16] when the λήμματα [premises] are necessary; on the other, opinion, when they are only probable.

These things should be shown by examples. Past philosophers noticed that there are some actions belonging particularly to individual things that one does not meet with in things of a different nature. For example: someone found that a particular man had the capacity for learning and was endowed with the faculty of discerning honorable and shameful things. Afterwards this same quality was sought one by one in many men, and because an instance of its opposite did not ever occur in men of sound mind, they[17] inferred the following axiom or proposition: that every man had the capacity for learning and was endowed with the faculty of discerning honorable and shameful things. This progression takes its beginning from sense perception, and through induction infers a universal proposition, which the mind, laying hold of it, stores away and preserves as a faithful guardian, so that it may use it if ever there is need. The first philosophers made use of this method in all the disciplines. For the things that we have received through learning, they perceived by their own discovery. For there are two ways by which we are led to come to know[18] things: μάθησις καὶ εὕρησις [learning and discovery].

Furthermore, if you lay hold of this axiom as a firm first principle and thus infer: Every man is capable of learning and endowed with the faculty of choosing; therefore the Gauls, the Germans, the Danes, the Spaniards, and so on have the capacity for learning and are possessed of the faculty of choosing—if you go by this way, the progression takes its rise from the mind, and it concludes things that are more nearly related to the senses.

And thus it is apparent that intellectual knowing is twofold. Of these two kinds, one takes its beginning from the senses and terminates

[16] *scientia.*

[17] Hemmingsen does not supply a subject; "philosophers" is likely what he has in mind (his reference to "first philosophers" later in this paragraph seems to make this clear). Thus I have included it as the subject of the first sentence of the paragraph.

[18] *cognitio.*

in the mind; the other, in contrast, takes its starting point from the mind and ends either in the senses or in those things that are nearest to the senses.

The doctrines that Plato first handed down, and after him the Platonists, are not inconsistent with the foregoing doctrine of the Peripatetics. I shall ascribe the chief place to the Platonists' position, for it not only elucidates the position of Aristotle, but it also doubtless will be pleasing to those who are of good character and are lovers of the power of nature. For it leads us directly back to admiration for the creator.

The Platonists, then, say that there are four faculties of knowing, which men of sound mind always carry about with themselves. The first of these (if it please the reader to permit me to enumerate them from lowest to highest) is αἴσθησις [sense perception], the one nearest to this is δόξα [opinion], over this rises διάνοια [discursive thought], and the highest of all is νόησις [understanding][19] or νοῦς [mind];[20] Plotinus says that this last has the place of a king, αἴσθησιν [sense perception] that of a servant.[21]

The character Timaeus, in Plato's dialogue of that name, says that there are two συζυγίας [pairs] of these faculties. In the first he joins νόησιν καὶ λόγον or διάνοιαν [understanding and reason or discursive thought]; but he assigns the chief place τῇ νοήσει [to the understanding], to which he adds λόγον ὥσπερ ἐλάττονά τινα νοῦν [reason, as it were a lesser mind] (to put it in the words of Proclus).[22] In the second

---

[19] Or "intellection."

[20] Cf. Plato, *Republic* 6.511d–e and 7.533e–534a, though Plato's terminology is different and his meaning is not the same as Hemmingsen's here.

[21] Or "slave." Plotinus, *Enneads* 5.3.3. Plotinus uses the term ἄγγελος, "messenger."

[22] Proclus was a Neoplatonist philosopher who lived from AD 410/12 to 485; he became head of the Platonic Academy in Athens in 437 and was an important influence in the Middle Ages and Renaissance. His works include philosophical treatises, commentaries on Plato, scientific works, and literary works. Hemmingsen's quotation here comes from Proclus, *In Platonis Timaeum commentaria* 2.77B on Plato, *Timaeus* 28a1–4, though in fact

he places τὴν δόξαν καὶ τὴν αἴσθησιν [opinion and sense perception]. Here, δόξα [opinion], as if a kind of rational sense perception, occupies the first place; αἴσθησις ἄλογος [irrational sense perception] occupies the second.

In the first pair, reason, together with the mind, discerns τὰ νοητά [the things that pertain to the mind], but reason by itself contemplates the intermediate reasons; in the second pair, δόξα [opinion], together with sense perception, sees τὰ γενητά [the things that present themselves], but a particular αἴσθησις [sense perception] by itself considers all the appearances that are in it, and, ἄλογος [irrational], it perceives τὰ αἰσθητά, that is, sensible things. Those sensible things, moreover, are called πάθη [properties],[23] because they exercise influence upon τὰ αἰσθητήρια [the organs of sense]. Because of this, as on the one hand νοῦς [mind] is said to perceive ὁλικῶς [wholly],[24] and on the other λόγος [reason] is said to perceive καθολικῶς [generally or generically],[25] and the φαντασία [imagination] is said to perceive μορφωτικῶς [with images], so αἴσθησις [sense perception], subjected to the senses, is said to perceive παθητικῶς [sensibly]. God alone, however, is said to

---

Hemmingsen draws on Proclus' broader discussion in this section as a whole (for instance, Proclus cites the same words of Plotinus that Hemmingsen has just cited above). The passage from Plato's dialogue that is in the background is worth quoting as the ultimate source of the "pairs" to which Hemmingsen refers: "First then in my judgment this distinction must be made. What is that which is eternally and has no becoming, and again what is that which comes to be but is never? The one is comprehensible by thought with the aid of reason, ever changeless; the other opinable by opinion with the aid of reasonless sensation, becoming and perishing, never truly existent" (Plato, *Timaeus* 27d4–28a3; for the translation, see *The* Timaeus *of Plato*, ed. R. D. Archer-Hind [New York: Arno Press, 1973]).

[23] πάθη is used here in an objective sense rather than a subjective sense—rather, that is, than referring to what is experienced by the subject ("passions"). In this instance, πάθη are what cause the experience of the perceiving subject; see below.

[24] Or "universally, generally."

[25] I.e., not "wholly," but "in accordance with the whole."

discern things ἡνωμένως [as a unity],[26] as the one who, with a simple look, looks upon all things, both present and absent, past and future. But let us speak of the individual matters individually.

Sense perception perceives τὰ πάθη [the properties] of things by means of its seat of sensation.[27] This doubtless comes about in the following way: when a piece of fruit, for example, has been brought before you, you will perceive by means of your vision that it is red or golden-yellow, and this occurs from its influence upon your sensation (for this is what πάθη signifies), which irrupts upon the αἰσθητηρίον [sense organ] of vision, which is the eye. You will perceive by smell that which smells good or bad, and this occurs similarly from the influence upon your sensation that irrupts upon your nose. By taste, therefore, you will comprehend sweetness, by touch, flatness. The things, moreover, that are perceived in this way by the individual senses are called αἰσθητά [sensible things] and are, as it were, accidental properties of the subjects to which they belong; the same things, in respect to the sense organs that are influenced by them, are called πάθη [properties]. But what, pray, is this faculty that declares that the thing that has been brought before you is a piece of fruit?[28] Is it the eye? By no means. For this organ only perceives color. Or is it hearing? Or taste? Or smell? None of these at all. For whichever one you please is busy with its own object. Or is it all the senses together? In no

---

[26] This term is misspelled in all of the editions I have consulted. The relatively rare adverb (though used more than once by Proclus) is derived from the verb ἐνόω, "to make one, unite."

[27] *sensorium.* The "seat of sensation" should be distinguished from "first sense," i.e., a sense organ. Cf. Albert Blaise, *Lexicon Latinitatis Medii Aevi: praesertim ad res ecclesiasticas investigandas pertinens* (Turnhout: Brepols, 1975), s.v. "sensorium": "the central organ where the sensations coming from different senses are united so as to give the representation of an object to the mind."

[28] There is a relative pronoun missing in Hemmingsen's Latin here in all editions I have consulted, which I have supplied in order for the sentence to make syntactical sense.

way. For they do not extend to the essence[29] of the thing, but remain fixed only upon certain common accidental properties.[30] Or perhaps it is the common sense? By no means. For the common sense only distinguishes between the activities of particular senses. From here, therefore, it follows that sense perception perceives neither the οὐσίαν [essence] nor the αἰτίαν [cause], that is, neither τὸ ὅτι [the what] nor τὸ διότι [the why], of things. We are furnished with an account, then, as to how far sense perception is able to progress in the knowing of things, and where it stops once it has performed its duty.

Δόξα, opinion, or τὸ δοξαστικὸν [forming a judgment],[31] that is, the faculty of forming an evaluation of things, once the processes of reason have taken their start from the things that irrupt upon the senses, perceives τὰς τῶν αἰσθητῶν οὐσίας [the essences of sensible things], that is, τὸ ὅτι [the what], of things. This faculty therefore first announces what has been brought before you,[32] which the Platonists call τὸ δοξαστικὸν [forming a judgment]; and thus πᾶν τὸ γενητὸν [everything that exists] is perceivable by means of opinion and sense perception, of which the latter perceives only τὰ πάθη [the properties],[33] while the former observes τὰς οὐσίας [the essences]. Nor does this faculty ascend farther, for it does not extend to the causes of things.

Διάνοια [discursive thought] ascends farther, for it examines both οὐσίας [essences] and causes, that is, it considers not only τὸ ὅτι [the what] but also τὸ διότι [the why], and it takes hold of τὰς τῶν ὄντων ἐννοίας [the conceptions of the things that exist]. From here, it afterwards constructs an extraordinary abundance of hypotheses, and for this reason the Platonists say that λόγον [reason] joined together

---

[29] Or "substance" (*substantia*).

[30] For essential and accidental properties, cf. Teresa Robertson and Philip Atkins, "Essential vs. Accidental Properties," *Stanford Encyclopedia of Philosophy* 2008/2013, http://plato.stanford.edu/entries/essential-accidental/.

[31] Or "conjecturing."

[32] Reading *primum* with the Wittenberg edition of 1577 and the *Opuscula theologica* rather than *pomum* with the Wittenberg editions of 1562 and 1564.

[33] I.e., that cause the sensations.

τῷ νῷ [with the mind] investigates things and the natures of things μεταβατικῶς [discursively]. It looks up, it looks down, it looks to the sides, and thus it gathers together the extraordinary force of its reasonings in order to grasp the truth. Therefore, the following definition is correct: ἡ διάνοια αὐτῆς πρὸς ἑαυτὴν ψυχῆς διάλογος ἄνευ φωνῆς γιγνόμενος [discursive thought is the conversation of the soul with itself, which occurs without sound].[34]

Νόησις [understanding], which holds in itself the conceptions of things ἀμεταβάτως [without interchange],[35] but rather ὁλικῶς [wholly] (as was said above), is the highest producer of knowing in man. For, because νοῦς [mind] has τὸ ἑαυτοῦ νοητὸν [its own purely mental aspect], it is for that reason said to embrace the whole, that is, to perceive things and the ἐννοίας [conceptions] of things ὁλικῶς [wholly].

To these faculties with which God has adorned human nature is added speech, which is also, like reason, called λόγος [speech][36] in Greek, because it is a sort of stream, as it were, of reason;[37] and therefore the Platonists give the following definition of speech: τὸ τῆς διανοίας ῥεῦμα διὰ τοῦ σόματος ἰὸν μετὰ φθόγγου ἢ φωνῆς [the stream of discursive thought through the mouth, which proceeds with sound or voice];[38] by another it is called τοῦ νοήματος ἄγγελος [the messenger of discursive thinking].[39]

---

[34] Plato, *Sophist* 263e4–6. Hemmingsen's version of the definition has some slight verbal differences from Plato's, but these do not affect the sense.

[35] In contrast to the operation of διάνοια, which functions discursively or "conversationally."

[36] The same term used for "reason" above.

[37] Hemmingsen again employs the common wordplay on *oratio/ratio* ("speech"/"reason"), and notes that in Greek the same term (λόγος) refers to both.

[38] Plato, *Sophist* 263e8–9.

[39] Found in a slightly different form in John of Damascus, *Exposition of the Orthodox Faith* 2.21 (cf. also 1.11). The expression is found in exactly the form Hemmingsen gives in the first *Oration* of the twelfth-century Constantinopolitan bishop Nicolaus Methonaeus.

Next, in the matter of words or sounds, three things are observed. First are observed the names, which are chiefly signs τῶν νοημάτων [of the concepts], less chiefly also of the things that are their subjects. Next, in the words are observed τὰ νοήματα [the concepts], which are, so to speak, likenesses and portraits of the things that are their subjects, or, as the Greeks say, ὁμοιώματα καὶ ἐκτυπώματα [likenesses and figures in relief]; from this it comes about that τὰ νοήματα [the concepts] are the same for everyone. For the form impressed by the things that are their subjects is the same for everyone, but the names of the things are not the same, since languages differ in different nations. In the third place, in the words are observed the things that are their subjects, that is, τὰ ὑποκείμενα πράγματα, from which τὰ νοήματα [the concepts] are formed in us—and this by abstraction[40] and comparison, as the most learned Daniele Barbaro elegantly teaches.[41] With regard to this matter, therefore, it is right to make reference to the studies and considerations of the teachers of grammar and dialectic.

Relying up to this point on the judgments of Aristotle, Ammonius, Plato, Proclus, and other Platonists, I have said what and of what sort the producers of knowing are, through which nature brings forth works so wondrous. Now I shall introduce a few items from "Reuchlin's ladder"[42] pertinent to this same matter; for I hope that they too will be welcome to students of philosophy and piety.

---

[40] *abstractio*; etymologically, "separation" (from the verb *abstrahere*).

[41] Daniele Barbaro was a Venetian polymath. Involved in the planning of the botanical garden at Padua, he also served as ambassador to England and Venetian representative at the Council of Trent. He is most well known for his edition and Italian translation of Vitruvius' *On Architecture*; he also wrote on perspective. See Gordon Campbell, ed., *The Oxford Dictionary of the Renaissance* (Oxford: Oxford University Press, 2003), s.v. "Barbaro, Daniele Matteo Alvise."

[42] Johann Reuchlin (1455–1522), German humanist and lifelong Roman Catholic, best known for his Hebrew studies. Reuchlin, who was the first German to achieve proficiency in all three ancient languages (Latin, Greek, and Hebrew), was influenced by the Neoplatonic and kabbalist ideas of Marsilio Ficino and Giovanni Pico della Mirandola, whom he had met during his travels

Reuchlin, Melanchthon's teacher, says that there are ten steps on the ladder of knowing; he says that by these men are able to ascend, from the lowest point to the highest, to the knowing of all things that exist in general, either by sense perception, or by true knowledge,[43] or by faith. The steps, moreover, are these: object, manifestation,[44] external sense perception, internal sense perception, the presentation of a mental image,[45] lower judgment, higher judgment, reason, intellect, and mind itself, by whose received light the lower virtues are directed and governed.

---

to Italy in the 1480s and 1490s. He was great-uncle to Philip Melanchthon and was responsible for his education and his gaining the Greek professorship at Wittenberg in 1518. They had a falling out when Melanchthon would abandon neither Luther's reformation movement (to which Reuchlin's own scholarship and humanism nevertheless contributed) nor the university in Wittenberg for Ingolstadt, where Reuchlin was professor of Greek and Hebrew. For the information in this sketch and further bibliography, see Paul F. Grendler, ed., *Encyclopedia of the Renaissance*, 6 vols. (New York: Scribner's, 1999), s.v. "Reuchlin, Johann"; and Hans J. Hillerbrand, ed., *The Oxford Encyclopedia of the Reformation*, 4 vols. (New York: Oxford University Press, 1996), s.v. "Reuchlin, Johannes." I read *scala* ("ladder") as printed in the 1577 edition and the *Opuscula theologica* rather than the *schola* of the 1562 and 1564 editions. The discussion that follows elucidates what "Reuchlin's ladder" is, and is borrowed to a large extent verbatim from book 1 of Reuchlin's *De arte cabbalistica*. See the facsimile of the text with English translation by Martin and Sarah Goodman, *On the Art of the Kabbalah* (Lincoln: University of Nebraska Press, 1993), 48–51.

[43] *scientia.*

[44] *diaphanon.* Reuchlin describes it as "the light-filled medium" through which a thing's form comes to the "corporeal eye" (*intenditur forma eius per illustre medium quod graeci appellant diaphanon, usque ad oculum corporeum*).

[45] I.e., to the lower judgment that men have in common with irrational creatures. The term rendered by my circumlocution is *phantasia*. Reuchlin glosses it as "the medium of appearance" (*per medium apparentiae*).

Next, the ascent of these steps is ordered in three regions, the lowest, the middle, and the highest. And in each individual region there is one standing-place[46] for abstraction.

In the first region, then, are the following three steps: object, manifestation, and sense perception;[47] and this is the first standing-place for abstraction. For example: I see a very bright fire burning in the distance; its form is extended through the intervening area, through which its light passes all the way to the corporeal eye.[48] This is the first place to stand, where object, manifestation, and sense perception are found.

In the second region are the following three steps: internal sense perception, the presentation of a mental image, and judgment. And this is the second place to stand: internal sense perception receives from the sense of sight the form of fire that has been presented to it; the presentation of a mental image follows, and then the lower judgment. By this activity we render a judgment concerning the fire that is no different from that of irrational creatures.

In the third region is human judgment,[49] reason, and intellect, and the third place to stand. By means of human judgment we perceive the οὐσίαν [essence] of the fire, by means of reason we search out the causes, and by means of intellect we grasp all of these things. The mind is the mistress of them all; with light received from above, it illuminates and perfects man's intellect. For what the eye is in the body, the mind is in the soul.

The names of these three standing-places are sense perception, judgment, and intellect. In the first, the body stands at rest and the

---

[46] Or "platform" (*status*).

[47] This is the sense perception Hemmingsen specifies above as "outward-directed" (*exterior*) (p. 33).

[48] Reuchlin uses the same illustration.

[49] I.e., the judgment that is peculiar to humans in contradistinction to brute animals.

soul[50] begins; from this the name *animal*[51] is taken. In the second, the soul[52] stands at rest and the reason begins; from this the name *man*[53] is taken. In the third, the power of the intellect stands at rest, and the mind begins, which alone comes from without, and for that reason is called *divine*, and is, as it were, a sort of god.[54]

These things are said beautifully and truly, and they commend to us in a wondrous way the wisdom of the creator.

For the rest, because I have spoken about the gifts of nature with which man has been endowed and by which he is led as though by the hand to the knowing of things, I shall now add some remarks on the parts τῆς εὐμαθείας [of readiness in learning], that is, teachableness. There are, then, three parts of teachableness: mental acumen, memory, and shrewdness.

Mental acumen, ὀξύτης, is a quickness of understanding for perceiving both the things that are passed on to us by others and those that we have read ourselves.[55] This acumen is greater in some, less in others; those, however, in whom there is none at all are utterly unfit for learning, worthy of being reckoned as tree trunks rather than as men.

Memory, which the Platonists call τῆς αἰσθήσεως σωτηρία [the savior of sense perception],[56] is the preserver and faithful guardian

---

[50] *anima.*

[51] *animal.*

[52] I read *anima* with Reuchlin's text rather than the *animal* of all editions of Hemmingsen I have consulted. The difference is not a large one. The *anima* in this passage refers to the "soul" that humans share in common with irrational *animalia*. As one moves into the region of the *ratio*, he enters into that which is peculiarly human.

[53] *homo.*

[54] Here ends his adaptation of "Reuchlin's ladder."

[55] Galen mentions this quality as essential for the one who would discover truth; see *Constitution on the Art of Medicine* 6.244K7–9.

[56] This comes from the rhetorical treatise *The Art of Rhetoric* by the third-century-AD rhetorician and philosopher Cassius Longinus; the work survives only in fragmentary form. Hemmingsen's quotation is elliptical.

of the things that you have perceived, both from the instruction of a teacher and from reading. He who is bereft of it, even if he is strong in mental acumen, labors in vain. Hence it comes about that μνημοσύνη [memory] is called a goddess and is given the name "Mother of the Muses" in Plato.[57]

Shrewdness, ἀγχίνοια, is the faculty of swiftly discovering, from the things that we have learned and perceived, things that we have neither learned nor perceived; for those who are strong in this faculty (provided that the others are not absent), the approach to the citadel of Athena and the pinnacle of erudition will be easy.[58] As these three parts of teachableness become dull through laziness and idleness, so they are aroused and grow through diligence and toil.

Thus far concerning intellectual knowing; now I shall add something concerning the appetite that accompanies intellectual knowing.[59] This is the appetite of reason and is called the will.[60] For it is not driven to action without deliberation, as animal appetite is, but by deliberation it chooses this or that thing. Consequently, the will has the power of choosing and the faculty of making a considered determination—a faculty that for that reason is called in Greek προαίρεσις [choosing between alternatives after deliberation], because, when many things have been proposed to it, it chooses some things rather than others once the judgment of reason has been applied. This choosing is followed by effort, in order that we may be able to use the thing we have chosen.

Others use greater subtlety in numbering the steps by which one arrives at the use of the thing he has sought out. For in the first place they put the βούλησις (that is, the will) for the end (that is, for the thing that we want). Next, they append ζήτησιν καὶ σκέψιν, that is, inquiry and reflection. In the third place, if it is possible to obtain the thing

---

[57] The claim that Mnemosyne was the mother of the Muses was much older than Plato and was in fact a standard part of Greek mythic genealogy: see Hesiod, *Theogony*, 53–55.

[58] Cf. Aristotle, *Posterior Analytics* 1.34 (89b10–21).

[59] For Thomas Aquinas' discussion of the intellectual and sensitive appetites, see *Summa theologiae*, I, Q. 80.

[60] Cf. Aristotle, *Nicomachean Ethics* 1.13 (1102a5–1103a11).

we are seeking, βουλὴ (that is, counsel) is applied, for we consider whether it would be pleasing to undertake the thing or not. In the fourth place, if the thing we desire and love has been approved by our judgment, γνώμη (that is, a verdict) is added. To this is joined, in the fifth place, προαίρεσις (that is, choice). Ὁρμή (that is, the impulse to pursue) follows this in the sixth place. By this we are moved to act. In the last place is χρῆσις, use, and thus we reach a state of quietude, or rather we acquiesce in the use of the thing.[61]

Let so much be said concerning intellectual knowing and the appetite of reason, which[62] accompanies such knowing by nature. Now we shall learn about the first principles of knowing and of acting.[63] For I said above that the law of nature is a certain knowledge[64] of the first principles of contemplation and of acting.[65] And because enough was said above about its manner, here I must treat of its matter, in order that the axioms and hypotheses of the law of nature, by which men's morals should be guided, may be able to be discovered.

The contemplating power, or τὸ θεωρητικὸν, considers the condition and disposition of things. The power of acting, or τὸ πρακτικὸν, defines the right reason for doing things. The former power resides in the mind itself, the latter in the reason; the former has theoreti-

---

[61] I attempt to preserve Hemmingsen's wordplay *quiescimus, aut potius … acquiescimus*.

[62] The antecedent is "reason," not "appetite."

[63] Recall how Hemmingsen's definition of the law of nature begins: "The law of nature is a certain knowledge, imprinted on the minds of men by God, of the principles of knowing and of acting, and of the conclusions proved from these principles that are in agreement with the proper end of man" (p. 30). Now that he has finished his discussion of certainty (*certa noticia*), which he claims for our knowledge of the *principia* of knowing and acting, he can move on to those *principia*.

[64] *noticia*.

[65] "Knowing" (*cognitio*) is now equated with "contemplation" (*contemplatio*), a term he did not use in the definition.

cal knowledge[66] as its end, the latter prudence,[67] which guides the actions of virtue.

Consequently, the first principles of contemplation are those from which the theoretical knowledge[68] of things arises. The first principles of acting, which are called πρακτικὰ [having to do with action], are those from which is sought the reasonable basis of morals and of actions that accord with virtue. They are called first principles for two reasons: first, because they do not depend on any prior demonstration; second, because all hypotheses of honorable laws, by which morals should be governed, are derived from them.

The first principles of contemplation that are not complex are simple conceptions, such as: one, true, something, good, being, not being, affirmation, denial, cause, effect. The first principles that are complex are conceptions that are composite, such as: that something exists, that something does not exist, that this thing exists, that another thing exists. Very many axioms are relevant here. The following are of this sort: any whole is greater than any of its parts; nothing happens without a cause; nature does nothing in vain.

The first principles of acting, that is, the practical principles, are also twofold, namely, conceptions that are simple and conceptions that are composite. The simple are conceptions such as: good, honorable, just, useful, seeking, avoiding, evil, shameful, or dishonorable. The composite are conceptions such as: just things ought to be sought out, unjust things ought to be avoided, honorable things ought to be loved, shameful things ought to be shunned, virtue is praiseworthy, vice ought to be censured, and many conceptions of this kind, which are the λήμματα [premises] and the matter of practical syllogisms.

But before I approach the end of man, to whose preservation this whole teaching should be referred, I shall briefly show why it is necessary to put faith in these first principles, although they cannot be concluded from a prior demonstration.

---

[66] *scientia.*

[67] *prudentia*, i.e., practical (not theoretical) wisdom.

[68] *scientia.*

The immovable certainty of the first principles, therefore, is discerned in the following way: first, the knowledge[69] of the first principles is the light imprinted by God on the minds of men. For as all men who are not blind see the sun,[70] and, while they see it, necessarily see (for they do not err in their opinion, but truly look at and perceive the sun), so all men who are of sound mind see by the light of nature, which God kindles in the nature of men, that what is honorable must be sought out and what is shameful must be avoided. He who denies this must with good reason be reckoned to be out of his mind and more foolish than Anaxagoras, who maintained that snow was black, against the universal and shared experience of all men.[71]

Next, the certainty of the first principles is shown by comparison with those that contradict them. All men who are of sound mind understand that two contradictory propositions cannot at the same time be both true and false. For if one is true, the other is necessarily false, and vice versa, just as the following are contradictory: honorable things must be sought out; honorable things must not be sought out. Who is so foolish that he hesitates concerning the first proposition, which is, that honorable things must be sought out, and instead chooses what contradicts it, that honorable things must not be sought out? Here, there is no one, unless he is utterly lacking in mental resources, who will not reject this second proposition as false. From this it follows from the law of contradiction that the first proposition is true and immovable. For if this is false (that is, the proposition "what is

---

[69] *noticia.*

[70] I.e., the physical light of the world, which he compares to man's God-given intellectual light.

[71] See Anaxagoras, fragments A97, B10, and B21 (Hermann Diels, *Die Fragmente der Vorsokratiker*, ed. Walther Kranz [Hamburg: Rowohlt, 1964]), along with Cicero, *Academics* 2.31.100 (also cited in Diels-Kranz), where Cicero writes: "And he will be quicker to approve <the impression that> snow is white than Anaxagoras was! The latter didn't just deny that it was white, but even that he *had* the impression that it was white, because he knew that the water snow comes from is black" (trans. Charles Brittain [Indianapolis: Hackett, 2006]).

honorable must not be sought out"), that which contradicts it will be true, which is, that honorable things must be sought out.

To this is added a comparison of contrary effects. It is posited beyond all controversy that nature seeks those things that preserve nature and rejects those things that are hostile to nature. For what seeks its own destruction? What does not rather exert itself with all its powers for this end, namely, to preserve itself?[72] Accordingly, since the things that are honorable and just preserve nature and their opposites destroy it, it follows that honorable and just things are in accordance with nature, but shameful and unjust things are contrary to nature. Therefore, just as the former things must be sought out, with nature as guide, so the latter must be rejected, with nature again pointing out this fact. This threefold reason gives convincing proof that the certainty of the practical principles is immovable.

But since we understand all these things more correctly once the end of man (to which all the actions of man clearly must be referred) has been pointed out, I shall add a few words concerning the end of man, and I shall propose an axiom from the law of nature from which[73] all other true hypotheses concerning morals are constructed.

There is, then, a threefold end that belongs to each thing. One is seen from the most perfect state of each thing; the second is understood from the actions proper to each thing; the third, which also exists as the end of goods in general, is taken from the order of things in general.

But these matters should be illustrated by definitions and examples. The first end, which does not go beyond the thing, but remains in the thing, is the state of each thing that is most perfect in its own kind, in the following manner: the end of fire is to be especially hot and dry, and the end of water is to be especially wet and cold; the end of man is that there be a sound mind in a sound body. Briefly, in the following way: the end of any thing is to have those most perfect and most complete attributes that the nature of things bestows on it in

---

[72] Cf. Cicero, *On Obligations* 1.11.

[73] The relative pronoun is plural; presumably, then, we are to take the antecedent as both the remarks on the end of man and the axiom he will propose from the law of nature.

its own kind—or rather that God, the creator of nature, bestows. For acquiring and preserving these things, God has appointed the goods in nature that the Greeks call συμφέροντα [useful], so that food, drink, and medicine serve the soundness of the human body. Right reason confers on the soul[74] that it be sound in a sound body.[75]

Next, let us consider these matters in a bit more depth. For the soundness of each of these, therefore—that is, of the body and of the soul, and so of the whole man—the first step is that the body subject itself to the command of the soul. For it has been so ordered by nature that the more perfect ought to command the less perfect, the better the worse, the more worthy the less worthy. When, however, the opposite happens, the order of nature is overturned and there follow great confusions that destroy nature. Now, then, it is evident from the fact that the mind[76] is more perfect and better and more worthy than the body that the former is λογική [rational], the latter ἄλογον [irrational]; the former immortal, the latter perishable; the former spiritual and simple, the latter composed of various bodies, and these corruptible. Therefore, it cannot be doubted that it is in accordance with nature for the soul to command and the body to obey. And assuredly the matter stands in man in just the same way as it does in the commonwealth, in which, when the bad command the better, it must be feared lest it suffer the same fate as a ship when its captain has perished, and in his

---

[74] Hemmingsen had earlier used *mens* in this expression; he now uses *anima*. Though earlier *anima* was distinguished from *mens* as sense was distinguished from intellect, here he seems to use *anima* more broadly as incorporating the rational element.

[75] Hemmingsen follows a Peripatetic rather than a Stoic line here. The former made the honorable the highest good, whereas the latter made it the only good; Hemmingsen clearly acknowledges inferior goods, provided that they are ordered to the higher goods. Cf. Cicero, *On Obligations* 3.11. For a thorough discussion of the topic of the chief or supreme good, see Cicero, *On Ends* 3.

[76] He now uses *animus* for "mind," again with seemingly great overlap between *mens*, *anima*, and *animus*.

place has been substituted a sailor who does not know how to sail.[77] For what else, I ask, can happen in this instance, than that, when a storm has arisen, both the ship be sunk and the things that are in the ship be lost? And this is what Theognis warns about most gravely in the following lines:

φορτηγοὶ δ' ἄρχουσ' ἄνδρες κ' ἀγαθῶν καθύπερθεν,
δειμαίνω μή πως ναῦν κατὰ κῦμα πίῃ.

That is, "When porters are in command of good men, one should fear lest the waves swallow up the ship."[78] In order, therefore, for the state of man to be one of integrity, it is first of all necessary that the body be subject to the command of the soul.

The second step that is necessary for preserving the state of man is that the faculties of the soul look to their own duties and do nothing against the order of nature.

There are, moreover, three faculties that pertain to this ordering of the soul. To these belongs neither a similar dignity nor an equal authority in acting. The faculties, then, are the following: λόγος, θυμός,[79] and ἐπιθυμία—that is, reason, the irascible power,[80] and desire. As these

---

[77] For the image, cf. Plato, *Republic* 6.488a–489c.

[78] Theognis 679–80; Hemmingsen's text differs slightly from modern editions.

[79] θυμός is especially the principle of passion or strong feeling, and can mean "anger" or "wrath" in addition to "spirit" or "courage." Hemmingsen's tripartite division of the soul here corresponds to Plato's in *Republic* 4.434dff., where the soul is divided into τὸ λογιστικόν, τὸ θυμοειδές, and τὸ ἐπιθυμετικόν (the reasoning power, the spirited power, and the desiring power). On the parts of the soul, see also Aristotle, *On the Soul* 3.9 (432a15–432b7). Both Aristotle and Plato will sometimes use the threefold division, sometimes a more general twofold division (rational and irrational). Both also acknowledge the possibility of more parts than three.

[80] *vis irascibilis*. This is the Latin term for θυμός or τὸ θυμοειδές (the spirited power) found in, e.g., Thomas Aquinas, *Summa theologiae*, I, Q. 81–82, where he also treats desire (*concupiscentia*, the same term used by Hemmingsen here).

faculties, taken one by one, are closer or more remote from the mind, so, correspondingly, is their dignity and indignity judged.

Consequently, λόγος [reason], which is closest to the mind, ought to command τῇ ἐπιθυμίᾳ [desire], which is closest to the body and most remote from the mind. If this order is confused, the state of man is shaken at its foundation, and we must fear the destruction of man. For when ἐπιθυμία [desire], once the command of reason has been shaken off, gives commands, it cannot but happen that some great evil follows. For the command of desire is contrary to nature, just as is the command of a woman over a man.

Next, if θυμός [the irascible power] either commands reason or is subject to desire, the laws of nature[81] are violated. For as θυμός [the irascible power][82] is below λόγον [reason] in rank of dignity, so it is above desire. Therefore nature advises that θυμός [the irascible power] obey reason and command desire, but in accordance with the regulation of reason. Hence it follows that λόγος [reason] alone ought to command, desire alone ought to obey, θυμός [the irascible power] alone ought sometimes to obey, sometimes to command. For as it is right for θυμὸν [the irascible power] to obey reason, so it is right for it to command desire. We shall explain this a little more clearly, so that the manner of commanding and obeying may be understood.

Λόγος [reason] possesses the faculty of commanding, or, as the Greeks say, the ἀρετὴν ἀρχιὴν, which is called φρόνησις, that is, prudence. By it reason itself ordains the modes of action both for itself and for the others, namely θυμῷ [for the irascible power] and for desire; and for this reason Plato calls φρόνησις [prudence] the ἡγεμὼν τοῦ ὀρθῶς πράττειν [guide for acting correctly].[83]

Ἐπιθυμία, desire, possesses the virtue according to which it ought to obey reason, and this is called σωφροσύνη, temperance, according to whose regulation it moderates its own longings once it has been turned toward reason, which it obeys in its moderating influence. For temperance preserves moderation in all the dispositions of body and

[81] This is the first time Hemmingsen has used the phrase in the plural.

[82] Equivalent to the "irascible power" in Latin; see above.

[83] Plato, *Meno* 97c1.

mind, lest, overcome by pleasure, or pain, or some other disturbance, we act contrary to right reason.

Θυμὸς [the irascible power] remains in the middle between λόγον [reason] and ἐπιθυμίαν [desire]; when it has reference to desire, it has the faculty of commanding, which is called ἀνδρεία,[84] that is, courage. By means of courage, the irascible power checks desire in accordance with the command of its commander; by courage it also preserves itself, lest it be wounded by itself. But if θυμὸς [the irascible power] has reference to reason, it has the faculty of obeying, which is also called σωφροσύνη [temperance]. By means of temperance, θυμὸς [the irascible power], instructed by reason, moderates its actions. When, however, θυμὸς [the irascible power] rejects the counsels of reason, it becomes that which Medea speaks about in Euripides:

θυμὸς δὲ κρείσσων τῶν ἐμῶν βουλευμάτων,
ὅσπερ μεγίστων αἴτιος κακῶν βροτοῖς.

[The irascible power of my soul, which is the author of the greatest evils for mortals, overcomes the judgments of my mind.[85]]

Furthermore, when these three faculties of the soul act in accordance with the order of nature, as has been said, justice arises, the virtue that is, as it were, a most pleasing symphony of the faculties of the soul in man.

From these remarks it is evident in what circumstances the most perfect state of man was established—namely, the soul was to command, and the body was to be subject to the command of the soul, and, in addition, each of the faculties of the soul was to preserve its own order, such that there be a sound soul in a sound body.

But since man is, as it were, a commonwealth in miniature, the result is that the virtues of the soul by which the soundness of the state of

---

[84] Etymologically, "manliness," like the Latin *virtus*.

[85] Euripides, *Medea* 1079–80; also found in Stobaeus, *Anthology* 3.20.37. Hemmingsen cites this passage again in chapter 6, where he gives a translation, which I have also used for this instance, in which he does not provide one.

man is preserved should be transferred to the society and dominions of men. For by these four virtues—prudence, temperance, courage, and justice[86]—men's societies are preserved, that is, their households and polities. I must say more concerning this matter a little later.

The second end of any given thing is that which I have said must be observed from the actions proper to it, which arise from the faculties properly belonging to each thing. This end varies in proportion to the condition of the faculties that God has conferred on things in nature, in such a way that degrees of actions[87] are judged in proportion to the reason possessed by the faculties. This end, moreover, which is placed in the action of each thing, is inferred in the following way: nature does nothing rashly or in vain, but refers each individual thing to a sure end (the natural philosophers inferred this axiom by induction; the moral philosophers, appropriating it from the natural philosophers, then construct from it the philosophy that concerns morals). Accordingly, the peculiar faculties of each thing are intended for actions peculiar and proper for that thing, something it is possible to see in the individual natures of things. For, as the common faculties of things are intended for common actions that pertain to the common preservation of nature, so the faculties that belong properly to things are intended for actions proper to those things, which look to the proper ends of those things.[88] From this it is demonstrated that since there are peculiar faculties in man that do not exist in other natures, peculiar actions are required of man that belong to his end.

There are, moreover, as I have said several times in the foregoing, faculties or δυνάμεις [powers] in man—γνωστικαὶ, προαιρετικαὶ, καὶ πρακτικαὶ [cognitive, deliberative, and practical]—that do not exist in other natures. Accordingly, the actions of these faculties belong to the end of man, provided that you examine the end that has been placed in the actions about which I am now treating. Now the γνωστικὴ [cogni-

---

[86] I.e., the four cardinal virtues.

[87] In the following section, I have translated *actio* as "doing" when modified (e.g., "the doing of virtue").

[88] I.e., faculties and actions belonging peculiarly to some thing, as opposed to faculties and actions that are common, or shared, with other things.

tive] faculty is intended for the seeking of the truth, the προαιρετικὴ [deliberative] for the choosing of the good, and the πρακτικὴ [practical] for the doing of the virtues. Such a demonstration is deduced in the following way:[89]

The actions proper to man belong to the end of man. The seeking of the true, the choosing of the good, and the doing of virtue are the actions proper to man. Therefore, these actions belong to the end of man.

But because the doing of virtue, to which[90] the seeking of the true and the προαίρεσις [choosing] of the good are in service, occupies the highest degree among these actions, the philosophers correctly located the end of man in the doing of virtue.

From the principle of this demonstration, the dogma of the Epicureans concerning the end of man is overturned, in the following way:

The actions proper to man belong to the end of man. The doing of pleasure is not an action proper to man. For it is common to man together with beasts. Therefore, pleasure does not belong to the end of man. Accordingly, one must employ the measure of pleasure that does not corrupt nature, but that lawfully preserves nature. (But I spoke about pleasure above, when I was treating of the animal appetite.)[91]

The third end is that which is observed from the order of things in general; by this reasoning all lower things are referred to higher things, as to their own ends. For God has so established nature that the worse things serve the better. From this it is shown that God is the ultimate end of all things. For he alone, without any doubt, is most supremely good. Therefore, as he has the most just command over all things, so all things ought to serve him by natural right.[92]

The things, moreover, that are placed in the middle of the chain of nature have the following condition: one is set over another, propor-

---

[89] What follows is the first of many syllogisms found in the treatise.

[90] The antecedent is "doing," not "virtue."

[91] Here I have translated *appetitio* as "appetite" rather than "desire," because he refers to his earlier discussion of the *appetitus animalis*.

[92] *naturale ius.*

tionately as the nature of each one is more or less perfect. Therefore, when we see a multiplicity of degrees of dignity in the things of nature, we ought to know that those that are least are to be referred immediately to those that are nearest to them in respect of degree of dignity. Now, then, whatever things God has made (I speak about visible things) either possess existence only (as the philosophers say)—things such as elements, minerals, and stones; or they possess existence and life only—things such as grass, vegetation, plants, and trees; or they possess existence, life, and sensation only—things such as mules, fish, birds, and every beast; or they possess all these things together, and in addition possess understanding, judgment, and will—such as man.[93] In these degrees of things, proportionately as a particular kind[94] is by nature more perfect and loftier,[95] so the things that are less perfect are ordered to that nature and ought to refer their faculties, actions, and even their whole selves to it. Accordingly, all things belonging to the lower degrees are ordered to man and ought to serve his uses. Now, God is not only above the lowest and middle degrees, but also above man. As, therefore, all the lower degrees are referred immediately to man, so man is referred immediately to God, such that he is established as man's sure and ultimate end when we observe the order of things in general. Hence it is apparent that the opinion of the Stoics is true when they say that all things exist on account of man, and man on account of God. The following verse of Gregory of Nazianzus pertains to this matter as well: ἀρχὴν ἁπάντων καὶ τέλος ποίει θεόν [make God the beginning and end of all things].[96]

---

[93] Cf. Thomas Aquinas, *Summa theologiae*, I, Q. 78, A.1; and Aristotle, *On the Soul* 2.3 (414a29–415a13), which is Thomas' authority.

[94] *forma specifica*.

[95] I read *eminentior* with the 1562 and 1564 editions rather than *eminentiore* with the 1577 edition and the *Opuscula theologica*.

[96] Hemmingsen cites the opening line of Gregory of Nazianzus' *Alphabeticum paraeneticum* (*PG* 37:908–10), an acrostic in which the successive letters of the alphabet begin successive lines. His citation of the Greek differs slightly from modern editions of the text: Hemmingsen gives the active imperative (ποίει) rather than the middle form (ποιοῦ) used by Gregory. The

Therefore, all the actions of man ought to be referred to God, so that just obedience may be rendered to him and the honor that he is owed may be shown. The nature of things as a whole summons us to this; natural sense perception incites us to this; the examples of all peoples, even the most barbaric, exhort us to this. For no one is so savage and void of reason that he does not determine that the things that have been created ought to be subject to the one who made them. No one is so barbaric that he he does not understand that the highest gratitude ought to be rendered to those who are most deserving. Hence it follows that the knowledge[97] of God, and the praising of God once he has become known, holds the first place in human actions.

A demonstration of this fact (even if this will be the only one possible), taken from nature itself, is as follows:

The supreme action of the supreme faculty in man, occupying itself with the supreme and most noble object, is the action proper to man. To know God and to worship him once he has become known is the supreme action of the supreme faculty in man, occupying itself with the supreme and most noble object. Therefore, to know God and to worship him once he has become known is the action most proper to man. Therefore man is rightly happy and blessed when he is occupied in this action; on the other hand, he is rightly wretched and unhappy when he is opposed to it.

That passage of Plato in book 4 of the *Laws* is relevant to this point:

Ἁπάντων κάλλιστον καὶ ἀληθέστατον οἶμαι λόγων, ὡς τῷ μὲν ἀγαθῷ θύειν καὶ προσομιλεῖν δεῖ τοῖς θεοῖς εὐχαῖς καὶ ἀναθήμασιν καὶ συμπάσῃθεραπείᾳ θεῶν κάλλιστον καὶ ἄριστον καὶ ἀνυσιμώτατον πρὸς τὸν εὐδαίμονα βίον.

---

line is also quoted by Melanchthon in his *Philosophiae moralis epitome* (CR 16:29), in the same form as that used by Hemmingsen; Melanchthon may be Hemmingsen's source. For a discussion of how Hemmingsen's use of Gregory (and other Christian writers in the pages that follow) coheres with his claim at the end of the treatise not to have cited any theologians, see E. J. Hutchinson, "Pagans and Theologians: An Examination of the Use of Christian Sources in Niels Hemmingsen's *De lege naturae*," *Perichoresis*, forthcoming.

[97] *agnitio*.

That is:

> I judge the following rule to be the most beautiful and true
> of all: that good men sacrifice to the gods and cling closely
> to them, both with prayers and gifts and all of the religious
> worship that belongs to the gods. For this is most beautiful
> and best and most advantageous for the happy life.[98]

With respect to the conclusion of the present demonstration: Man,
with nature as his guide, is still led astray in this corrupt nature,
because of which, when he has begun to come down to the level of
practice,[99] he soon gropes as a blind man and is deceived by his own
reasonings to such an extent that he both wanders away from the true
God to idols and substitutes monstrous superstitions in place of the
worship of the true God—as also Paul, writing to the Romans, bears
witness.[100] Hence it comes about that, although the philosophers have
handed down noble γνώμας [maxims] concerning God (of which I
shall relate a few farther on), they nevertheless did not arrive by the
right way at God and his worship. Therefore we should give thanks
to God since he kindles the torch of his word, by which he brings[101]
us into saving knowledge[102] of himself and demonstrates the true
system of worshiping him.[103]

---

[98] Plato, *Laws* 4.716d–e (with minor textual differences from modern
editions).

[99] I.e., as opposed to theory.

[100] Rom. 1:18–23.

[101] Hemmingsen uses the same verb (*deducere*), employed earlier in the
paragraph to designate man's turning away from God, now in a positive sense
for God's returning man to himself. The wordplay goes further: *deducere* is
also a scholastic term for making a deduction, i.e., in a syllogism, and thus
is closely related to the "demonstrative method" Hemmingsen employs.

[102] *noticia.*

[103] Again, a play on the technical terminology Hemmingsen has been
using throughout (*demonstrat; rationem,* which here means "system").

3

The Law of Nature in the Three States of Life

Thus far we have inquired in general concerning nature as man's guide in pursuit of the actions proper to himself, and we have laid the firm and immovable foundations on which the remainder of the process depends. But, because the actions of men vary in accordance with different types of life, we must distinguish the types of life, and we must adapt for each one its own proper end, composed from those three ends that I mentioned above.[1] Truly, no matter of contemplation will be more pleasant, none more charming, none more useful in common life, none, in short, more worthy or magnificent than this one.

Therefore the types of life are, in general, twofold, as can be understood from what I have said above, and as Aristotle bears witness in the *Ethics*:[2] the contemplative and the active.

---

[1] See pp. 65–74.

[2] Cf. *Nicomachean Ethics* 1.5 (1095b14–19), though Aristotle there divides life into three types (while admitting that the first type is "fit only for cattle" and thus in a sense subhuman):

> To judge from the lives that men lead, most men, and men of the most vulgar type, seem (not without some ground) to identify the

The contemplative type of life busies itself in contemplation and inquiry. From here come the fields of knowledge[3] and the liberal disciplines, in which life's greatest aid has been placed. Relevant here is that saying of Hipparchus: "For everyone, by far the most precious of all things for living is liberal learning."[4] For, as another poet says, "There is no greater consolation in life for human misfortune than liberal learning; for while the mind is free for its own learning, it sails past misfortune all unknowing."[5] Moreover, as to the fact that the liberal disciplines ought to lead us as if by the hand to God, Plato bears wit-

---

> good, or happiness, with pleasure; which is the reason why they love the life of enjoyment. For there are, we may say, three prominent types of life—that just mentioned, the political, and thirdly the contemplative life. (trans. David Ross [Oxford: Oxford University Press, 1954])

See also 10.7–8 (1177a12–1179a32); and *Eudemian Ethics*, trans. B. Inwood and R. Woolf (Cambridge: Cambridge University Press, 2013), 1.4.2–3 (1215a33–1215b6):

> Since there are three things that rank as conducive to happiness, the ones that were earlier described as the greatest possible human goods, namely virtue, wisdom and pleasure, we see also that there are three lives, chosen by all who have the means to do so—that of politics, that of philosophy, and that of enjoyment. Of these, the life of philosophy tends to be occupied with wisdom and contempla-tion of the truth, the political life with fine actions (these being the products of virtue), and the life of enjoyment with bodily pleasures.

[3] "Fields of knowledge" here renders the term *scientiae*.

[4] A quotation from frag. 2 of Hipparchus Comicus' lost comedy Ζωγράφος ("The Painter"), preserved in Stobaeus, *Anthology* 4.18a.2. Hipparchus flour-ished around 260 BC and wrote New Comedy.

[5] The source of this quotation is uncertain. Hemmingsen attributes it to a "poet," but the Latin is not metrical, and so he must be paraphrasing. It is important to note that by *ars*, sometimes translated as "art," Hemmingsen does not mean what a nineteenth-century Romantic would mean, but rather makes his meaning clear through his citation: "learning." Hence in the sin-gular I have translated *ars* as "liberal learning" and in the plural as "liberal disciplines," as above.

ness, who says that the liberal disciplines contain the sweetest report of the gods.[6] But here we must watch out lest we devote ourselves to idle curiosities and useless things rather than to aids that are useful for life. It is sufficient to have noted these matters concerning the contemplative type of life.

The active type of life looks to actions and busies itself in them on account of some end that is useful in life.

This type of life is, moreover, threefold: the domestic, the political, and the spiritual. This entire type, which we call the active, has an end, which is the preservation of itself through actions proper to itself, which look to God as their ultimate goal.[7] For in every type of life, actions must be so ordered that they do not wander away from the real end of goods, or from the end of ends.

Accordingly, the end of the domestic type of life is the preservation of the family and the household through domestic actions that look to God as the end of goods.

Because the rationale of preserving the whole is the same as that of preserving a part, λόγος [reason] ought to be in charge in this type of life and manage the household by its own prudence. Ἐπιθυμία [desire] ought, by means of a certain moderation and temperance, to be subject to reason, lest the affections attempt anything contrary to right reason. Θυμός [the irascible power] ought to assist reason as a παραστάτης [right-hand man] and check the affections (if there is ever need) by its own courage. To all of these things, justice is added as a moderator that causes husband and wife, master and servant, *paterfamilias* and *materfamilias*, spouses and families, to render the duties owed to one another, in order that the household may thus be preserved sound, united in the sweetest harmony.

In order to better understand the rationale that pertains to preserving the household, let us propose for ourselves the following demonstration, which relies on the foundations propounded above.

---

[6] A (loose) reference, perhaps, to Plato, *Phaedrus* 259d3–7.

[7] The term here is *scopus* rather than *finis*.

Whatever by itself preserves the domestic state[8] in a sound condition is commanded by the law of nature. That spouses embrace one another in mutual love, beget and rear children, protect them, instruct them in honorable morals, guide them with discipline, and provide them with the things that are necessary; and, in turn, that children revere their parents, obey and be grateful to them, and similar comparable duties: these things preserve the domestic state. Therefore, these things are commanded by the law of nature. The major premise is immovable. The minor premise is shown from the contraries and the consequents. When these duties are violated, families fall into ruin, as many sad examples teach. Therefore, we see that by means of these duties households stand fast, flourish, and are preserved sound, especially when these domestic duties are referred to God as their ultimate end, as was said above.

From this demonstration flow the domestic commandments, many of which are found in Xenophon, Aristotle, Plutarch, and other famous philosophers. Many maxims of the philosophers pertain to this matter, all of which fall under the categories denoted by the fourth and sixth commandments.[9] However, we shall rehearse a few for the sake of example.

Concerning the mutual duty of spouses, Clement of Alexandria[10] cites the following verses from an ancient tragedy:

> οὐ χρυσός, οὐ τυραννίς, οὐ πλούτου χλιδή,
> τοσοῦτον εἶχεν διαφόρους τὰς ἡδονάς,
> ὡς ἀνδρὸς ἐσθλοῦ καὶ γυναικὸς εὐσεβοῦς
> γνώμη δικαία, καὶ φρονοῦσα τἀνδρικά.

[8] *status*, used here and in what follows (including in the expression "political state" below) in the general sense of "condition, circumstances."

[9] I.e., the fourth and sixth commandments in the Lutheran numbering, "Honor your father and your mother" and "You shall not commit adultery."

[10] Clement of Alexandria, who was born around AD 150 and died around 215, was a Christian theologian. In addition to the *Paedagogus*, or *The Instructor*, he wrote the hortatory *Protrepticus* (*Exhortation to the Heathen*) and the *Stromateis* (*Miscellanies*). Clement found Christianity to be the fulfillment of both the Old Testament and Greek philosophy.

That is:

> Neither gold nor sovereignty bring such great
> pleasure, no splendor is so delightful,
> as the friendly harmony of dutiful spouses,
> who bravely cherish a mutual love.[11]

And Euripides:

> ὅστις δὲ τοὺς τεκόντας ἐν βίῳ σέβει,
> ὅδ᾽ ἐστὶ καὶ ζῶν καὶ θανὼν θεοῖς φίλος.

That is:

> Whoever reverences his parents in life
> is dear to the gods both alive and dead.[12]

And Menander:

> Βούλου γονεῖς προπαντὸς ἐν τιμαῖς ἔχειν, ἱκανῶς βιώσῃς
> γηροβοσκῶν τοὺς γονεῖς.

That is:

> Whoever shows honor to his parents will live abundantly
> and will be dear to his own.[13]

Homer,[14] who tells of a certain youth killed in the Trojan War
because he did not pay to his parents τὰ θρεπτήρια [the return chil-

---

[11] Clement of Alexandria, *The Instructor* 3.12.84; it is also preserved in
Stobaeus, *Anthology* 4.22a.3, where it is attributed to Apollonides. Hemmingsen's text differs slightly from modern editions of both works.

[12] Euripides, frag. 852[N], preserved in Stobaeus, *Anthology* 4.25.2.

[13] Hemmingsen combines two different lines of Menander, *Sentences* 113
(with a slight textual variant) and 365.

[14] Homer was the most famous, and probably the earliest, of the Greek
epic poets whose works have survived. Two epics are attributed to him, the
Iliad (perhaps around 750 BC) and the *Odyssey* (perhaps around 725).

dren owed to their parents for rearing them], gives the antithesis of this view.[15]

Thus far I have spoken concerning domestic life from the sources of the law of nature. From these the moral philosopher, who undertakes to give instruction concerning the domestic state, ought to seek its principles and demonstrations.

The end of political life is a calm and peaceful state of polities through political actions, all of which ought to be referred to this: that a just harmony of political order be maintained, with proportionate justice preserved among men, and that God be established in human society as the ultimate end of human society. One must watch out, therefore, lest political actions wander away from this end of goods. Because the rationale of preserving the whole is the same as that of preserving the individual parts, insofar as it pertains to the type of actions, the same virtues are required here as we said were required in individual men and then in individual families. For the preservation of polities, therefore, prudence, temperance, courage, and justice are required, and those in the following order, namely, that prudence alone command, but the rest, each in its own place and order, obey, as Plato teaches.[16] For in the harmony of these virtues consists that which is most difficult in life, namely, τὸ εὖ ἄρχειν καὶ τὸ εὖ ἄρχεσθαι, that is, rightly commanding and rightly obeying. Therefore, all of these virtues are required, both in the one who commands and in the one who obeys the command. He who commands has need of courage, by which he may preserve the citizens in their duty and turn harmful things away from the citizens; he has need of temperance in order that he may not destroy the harmony of human society by indulging in vicious affections; he has need of justice by which he may exercise authority in the realm of contracts, distribute honors and services, and confer rewards and decree punishments, with the owed proportion

---

[15] The reference seems to be to Homer, *Iliad* 4.477–9 and/or 17.300–303; in each of these instances death is what *prevents* the young man from returning care to his parents.

[16] Cf. Plato, *Republic* 4.429d7–8, where wisdom or prudence is the preserve of the guardians who rule Socrates' imaginary city.

preserved in each individual instance—that is, in some a geometrical proportion, as in duties and rewards, and in others an arithmetical proportion, as in contracts.[17]

It is necessary to apply prudence to all of these as a moderator. Nor are the virtues mentioned above—courage, temperance, and justice— less requisite for obeying well and lawfully; to these,[18] too, prudence must be applied as a moderator. These virtues, kept unharmed on each side, preserve τὴν ἰσότητα *Geometricam & Arithmeticam* [geometrical and arithmetical proportion],[19] without which commonwealths are not able to stand.

In order, however, that the rationale requisite for preserving a polity may stand out more clearly, let us look to the following demonstration, which relies on the foundations propounded above:

Whatever preserves the political state is commanded by the law of nature. This state, however, is by no means able to be preserved without the ordering of superiors and inferiors, that is, of magistrates and subjects. Accordingly, the ordering of magistrates and subjects is commended to us by the law of nature. For if the rending of human society is contrary to nature, so also ἀναρχία [anarchy], which brings this rending about, will be contrary to nature. Therefore, nature requires the ordering of superiors and inferiors.

Moreover, because the political state cannot be sound unless there is just dealing with allies, courageous dealing with enemies, and moderate and prudent dealing with all, it follows that the law of nature requires those four virtues in political society. Subjoined to these as species to a genus[20] are many others that are required for the soundness of

---

[17] Cf. Aristotle's discussion of justice beginning in *Nicomachean Ethics* 5.1 (1129a1).

[18] I.e., the virtues of courage, temperance, and justice viewed specifically in relation to obedience.

[19] LSJ notes that this Greek noun is often used in political contexts (for instance, in Plato's *Laws* 6.757a and Aristotle's *Politics* 5.1 [1302a7]) in addition to its mathematical and geometrical use; see LSJ, s.v. ἰσότης I.A.2.

[20] Hemmingsen does not say "to a genus," but species/genus ordering is what he has in mind, and so I have made it clear in the translation.

polities. Cicero, having followed nature as his guide, wrote elegantly and wisely on them in his books *On Obligations*, and we later shall rehearse a catalogue of them with the addition of short definitions and the maxims of learned men.

Very many maxims of the ancients pertain to this matter, but I shall note a few for the sake of example. In Homer one finds the most pleasing titles by which the duties of magistrates and subjects are, as it were, painted. These titles, taken one by one, are able to stand for entire statements, such as the following:

Ἤπιος πατὴρ, "kind father"; as by this name the paternal affection of the magistrate toward his subjects is signified, so a similar affection is required in his subjects.

Βασιλεὺς ["king"], as it were βάσις τοῦ λαοῦ, that is, the "support or foundation of the people." For as a building rests upon its foundation and falls to the ground when the foundation has been torn out from under it, so the people supports itself on the laws and power of the magistrate as though on a foundation; when the laws and the magistrate have been taken away, the people is destroyed.

Xenophon, explaining a verse of Homer concerning Agamemnon (Ἀμφότερον βασιλεὺς τ' ἀγαθός, κρατερός τ' αἰχμήτης ["both a noble king and a strong warrior"]),[21] teaches that the good king is not he who has care for his own life but he who renders blessed and happy those whom he commands. He says that a king is chosen for the following reason: οὐχ ἵνα ἑαυτοῦ καλῶς ἐπιμελῆται, ἀλλὰ, ἵνα καὶ οἱ ἑλόμενοι διὰ τοῦτον εὖ πραττῶσι,[22] that is, "not so that he may take care for himself, but so that those who have chosen him may be well and be happy on account of him."

Ἡγεμὼν, "leader": because he leads the people with wisdom and discipline straight on to virtue and happiness.

---

[21] Homer, *Iliad* 3.179, cited in Xenophon, *Memorabilia* 3.2.2; also found in Stobaeus, *Anthology* 4.13.28.

[22] Xenophon, *Memorabilia* 3.2.3; again, also found in Stobaeus, *Anthology* 4.13.28. Hemmingsen's text is slightly different from modern editions of Xenophon and Stobaeus.

Κοσμήτωρ ["commander"]: because he prescribes order for the multitude; no adornment is more beautiful and nothing more useful in the commonwealth than this.[23] Therefore Ischomachus rightly instructs his wife, when he says: ἐστὶ οὐδὲν οὕτως ὦ γύναι οὔτ' εὔχρηστον οὔτε καλὸν ἀνθρώποις, ὡς τάξις, that is, "There is nothing, wife, either so useful or so honorable for human beings as order."[24]

Μέδων ["protector" or "ruler"]: because the magistrate ought to watch over the soundness of his commonwealth with exceeding care and concern.

Ποιμὴν λαῶν, "shepherd of the people": by this image is signified what sort of care the magistrate ought to have for his citizens. As it is necessary for a shepherd to have care for his sheep, so it is necessary for a magistrate to have care for his subjects. Sometimes Plato calls the magistrate ἐπίσκοπος, and Xenophon calls him ἔφορος, that is, "overseer," because the magistrate ought diligently to observe what the individual citizens are doing. He will spur individuals on to performing their duties, and he will summon them to obedience by two things, namely, rewards and punishments. It does not suffice, as Xenophon says, for the citizens to have honorable laws, unless those who are the overseers should also be νομοφύλακες [guardians of the laws],[25] praising those who do what has been commanded and, contrariwise, punishing those who transgress the laws.[26]

Furthermore, a verse of Homer indicates how great a care the magistrate ought to have for the safety of his citizens: οὐ χρὴ παννύχιον εὕδειν βουληφόρον ἄνδρα, that is, "It is not right for a prince, who ought to deliberate about many things, to snore the whole night through."[27]

---

[23] The Greek noun κόσμος, from which this title is derived, means "order" in the first instance and is the source of our word "cosmos."

[24] Xenophon, *Oeconomicus* 8.3.

[25] Hemmingsen uses this term in the dedicatory epistle to Lord Erik Krabbe as well (p. 4).

[26] Paul similarly describes the role of the magistrate in Rom. 13:3–4.

[27] Homer, *Iliad* 2.61; also found in Stobaeus, *Anthology* 4.7.5.

And Sophocles: ὄν πόλις στήσειε, τούτου χρὴ κλύειν,[28] that is, "It is right to obey the one whom the commonwealth has established as magistrate." Sophocles also says: καλῶς μὲν ἄρχειν, εὖ δ᾽ ἂν ἄρχεσθαι θέλειν, that is, "Command well and obey well."[29] The poet adds to this a reason sought from nature. He says that a just command, in which the greater give commands rightly and subjects obey justly, preserves the commonwealth and, contrariwise, that the commonwealth perishes utterly[30] whenever there is ἀναρχία [anarchy]. There are, moreover, the following words of the poet:

> ἀναρχίας δὲ μεῖζον οὐκ ἔστιν κακόν.
> αὕτη πόλεις ὄλλυσιν, ἥδ᾽ ἀναστάτους
> οἴκους τίθησιν, ἥδε ἐν μάχῃ δορὸς
> τροπὰς καταρρήγνυσι, τῶν δ᾽ ὀρθουμένων
> σῴζει τὰ πολλὰ σώματα ἡ πειθαρχία,
> οὕτως ἀμύντε᾽ ἐστὶ τοῖς κοσμουμένοις.

That is:

> There is no greater evil than anarchy:
> it overturns cities, it utterly
> makes families to perish, in time of war
> it turns the lazy to flight. But, by contrast,
> submitting to command is the safety of many,
> and therefore those who are in charge ought
> to watch over obedience.[31]

---

[28] Sophocles, *Antigone* 666; Hemmingsen's text differs slightly from modern editions of Sophocles.

[29] Sophocles, *Antigone* 669.

[30] *Funditus*, "from the very bottom, from the foundation": cf. his discussion above regarding the βασιλεὺς [king] as the βάσις τοῦ λαοῦ [foundation of the people].

[31] Sophocles, *Antigone* 672–77. Hemmingsen's text differs slightly from modern editions of Sophocles. The first line is also found in Stobaeus, *Anthology* 4.1.27.

Here must be observed what I have spoken of above concerning the ultimate end of political life, which is, that all things in human society be referred to God as their ultimate goal.[32] The thought of this end instructs both ruler and subject: him who commands, that he not command his subjects to do anything against God; and him who obeys, that he not obey a prince in illicit things, that is, in those that conflict with natural and divine law. For here Socrates' answer in Plato has a place. This man, when his friends were urging that he yield to the Athenian assembly in order to avoid the punishment of death, answered: Ἐγὼ ὑμᾶς ἄνδρες Ἀθηναῖοι ἀσπάζομαι μὲν καὶ φιλῶ, πείσομαι δὲ τῷ θεῷ μᾶλλον ἢ ὑμῖν. That is, "I indeed respect and love you, men of Athens, but I shall obey God rather than you."[33] Also pertinent to this matter is the remark of the Theban maiden in the same poet referred to above,[34] who, when she was commanded to give preference to the edict of the king over the laws of nature, answered with courageous mind in the following words: "In no way do I judge that your decrees have so much force that you, although you are only a man, are able to violate the unwritten, but nevertheless most firm, laws of the gods. For they thrive and have force not for a brief time, but always."[35] From these remarks it is evident what the sources and the goals[36] of civil laws are, and how it is right to recall all things in civil government to their own principles.

The end of spiritual life is its preservation through actions harmonious with this life. Things of this sort are: to know God, to worship him once he has been known, to fear him, to glorify him, and so forth. The domestic and political states ought to be referred to this spiritual

---

[32] *scopus.*

[33] Plato, *Apology* 29d2–4; also found in Eusebius, *Preparation for the Gospel* 13.10.8.

[34] I.e., Sophocles.

[35] Sophocles, *Antigone* 453–57.

[36] *metae.* On this metaphor from the Roman circus races, see p. 12n30 above.

life as to their ultimate goal. He who wanders away from it turns the order of nature upside down and calls down penalties upon himself.

For the preservation of this life, the virtues mentioned above are required: prudence, courage, temperance, and justice—although the specific differences of these virtues vary to some degree by reason of their object. The following, moreover, is a demonstration:

Whatever preserves the state of the spiritual life is commanded by the law of nature. To know[37] God, and to refer all things to him as to the end of goods, preserves the state of the spiritual life. Accordingly, as these things are commanded by the law of nature, so those things that are contrary to them are forbidden.

The major axiom is dependent on the principles rehearsed previously. The minor is demonstrated in the following way: The supreme action of the supreme virtue, occupying[38] itself with the most noble object, is the end of man.

To worship God, once he has been known,[39] is the supreme action of the supreme virtue of man, occupying itself with the most noble object. Therefore, this is the end of man insofar as the spiritual life is concerned. The philosopher deduces this demonstration of the minor axiom in the following way: The state of the best life resides in happiness. This happiness consists in three things: in the act[40] of the highest power[41] in man, which is the intellect; in the most noble habit, which belongs to virtue; exercised[42] on the most worthy object, namely, God.[43]

---

[37] agnoscere.

[38] The participle modifies "action."

[39] agnitum.

[40] actus, not actio.

[41] Or "potency" (potentia). On the intellective power, cf. Aristotle, On the Soul 3.4–7 (429a10–432a14).

[42] "Exercised" is my addition to make Hemmingsen's meaning clear.

[43] Compare the similar discussion in Philip Melanchthon's Philosophiae moralis epitome (CR 16:30–31).

Man's right reason progresses all the way to this point. But when an attempt is made to construct the actions harmonious with this life from the conclusion of the demonstration I have set out, the path is entirely lost, just as Paul bears witness in Romans 1, as does our experience. Socrates declares that God must be worshiped and refutes his adversary, who thinks otherwise, with many arguments. He further adds that God must not be worshiped with a worship different from that which has been instituted by God himself.[44] But, when Socrates begins to progress from here, he wanders away from the true God as a blind man and becomes entangled in dreadful errors.

Next, many maxims that one reads everywhere in the poets and philosophers are harmonious with our demonstration.

Concerning the oneness of God, I have chosen to note the following few statements out of many. All the Sibyls proclaim that God is one. The Erythraean Sibyl, as Lactantius relates, prophesies thus: Εἷς θεὸς, ὃς μόνος ἐστὶν ὑπερμεγέθης ἀγένητος. That is, "God is one, who is alone greatest and eternal."[45]

This same Sibyl bears witness that God created all things in the following verses:

ἀλλὰ θεὸς μόνος εἷς πανυπέρτατος, ὃς πεποίηκεν,
οὐρανὸν ἠέλιόν τε, καὶ ἀστέρας, ἠδὲ σελήνην,
καρποφόρον γαίαν τε, καὶ ὕδατος οἴδματα πόντου.

That is:

> But there is one God alone over all things, who made the heaven and the sun and the stars and the moon, and, along with these, the fruitful earth and the waves of the sea.[46]

---

[44] See Xenophon, *Memorabilia* 1.4.2–18.

[45] Lactantius, *Divine Institutes* 1.6. The Christian apologist Lactantius (c.250–c.325), at one time a teacher of rhetoric and later tutor to Constantine's son Crispus, is the author, most famously, of *On the Deaths of the Persecutors* and the *Divine Institutes*. The quotation is also found in Pseudo-Justin, *Hortatory Address to the Greeks* 16.

[46] Lactantius, *Divine Institutes* 1.6.

And another Sibyl, speaking in the character of God, prophesies thus:

εἷς μόνος εἰμὶ θεός, καὶ οὐκ ἐστὶν ἄλλος.

[I alone am the one God, and there is no other.][47]

Justin Martyr[48] attributes the following verses on the oneness of God to Pythagoras in his book *On the Sole Government of God*:[49]

Εἴ τις ἐρεῖ θεὸς εἰμὶ, παρὲθ ἑνὸς, οὗτος ὀφέλλει
Κόσμον ἴσον τούτῳ στήσας εἰπεῖν, ἐμὸς οὗτος.

That is:

If anyone except the One should say, "I am God," he ought to display a world that he has created similar to this one and to say, "This is mine."[50]

Many maxims of this type are found in Plato, Xenophon, Sophocles, Euripides, Homer, Menander, and others, which, since I am pursuing brevity, I leave aside.

Concerning the providence of this one God, one finds the following maxims among others: Πάντῃ γὰρ ἐστὶ πάντα καὶ βλέπει θεός, "God is present everywhere and sees all things."[51] Likewise, ὀξὺς

---

[47] Lactantius, *Divine Institutes* 1.6. Hemmingsen's text is slightly different from modern editions of Lactantius.

[48] Justin Martyr, who was born around AD 100 and died around 165 when he was martyred, was an early Christian apologist who, though he wrote in Greek, composed works addressed to the Roman emperor (the *First Apology*) and the Roman Senate (the *Second Apology*). He is also the author of the *Dialogue with Trypho the Jew*.

[49] The conventional Latin title of this Greek work is *De monarchia*. Although traditionally attributed to Justin Martyr, its actual author is unknown.

[50] Pseudo-Justin, *On the Sole Government of God* 2.

[51] Menander, *Sentences* 688.

θεοῦ τ' ὀφθαλμὸς εἰς τὰ πάντα ὁρᾶν, "The eye of God is so keen that it contemplates all things."[52]

Xenophon calls God σοφὸν δημίουργον καὶ φιλόζωον, that is: "the wise and loving creator of living beings."[53] He also says, "Know that God is so great and of such a kind that he sees all things simultaneously, and hears all things simultaneously, and is present everywhere, and simultaneously has care for all things."[54] That this one God must be worshiped he teaches by many other arguments that I do not include here, as well as one that I do—namely, he adds that the form of man, which stands upright toward heaven, signifies that man must worship God. A Latin poet, having imitated him, speaks in the following way:

> He gave to man a face held high, and commanded him
> to see the heaven and to lift his face upright to the stars.[55]

Concerning the worship of God, the very ancient poet Philemon, as Justin relates, speaks thus: θεῷ δὲ θύε διὰ τέλους δίκαιος ὤν, that is, "Sacrifice to God in justice."[56] He also says:r

> If anyone, bringing as a sacrifice, O Pamphilus, a multitude
> of bulls or goats, or, by Jove, of other things of this sort, or
> presenting works of gold and cloaks of crimson, or offering
> animals made of ivory or emerald, should judge that he wins
> over to himself the kindness of God, he errs and has a fickle

---

[52] Menander, *Sentences* 605, though Hemmingsen substitutes a singular form of "God" for the plural of the original. A slightly different version, not attributed to Menander, is found in Stobaeus, *Anthology* 1.3.17. The form in which Hemmingsen quotes the line, along with his attribution, indicates that Stobaeus was not his source.

[53] Xenophon, *Memorabilia* 1.4.7.

[54] Xenophon, *Memorabilia* 1.4.18. Cf. *Cyropaedia* 8.7.22.

[55] Ovid, *Metamorphoses* 1.85–86.

[56] Pseudo-Justin, *On the Sole Government of God* 4. It is also cited in Clement of Alexandria, *Miscellanies* 5.14, where it is attributed to Menander, not Philemon. Eusebius, *Preparation for the Gospel* 13.13.46, also attributes it to Menander.

mind. It is right, rather, that he offer himself as a good man, that he not be a debaucher of virgins or an adulterer, that he not look at and desire another's possessions, or wife, or house, or property, child, maidservant, horses, cattle, and so forth. Nay, rather, my Pamphilus, do not desire one little bit of it.[57] For God, who is present before you, sees—the one who is delighted by just works, not by unjust ones.[58]

It is exceedingly pleasant to know by heart maxims of this kind concerning the oneness of God, and concerning creation, providence, and worship. One finds many maxims of this kind in the philosophers and poets.

I have spoken concerning domestic, political, and spiritual life, and what actions are proper to each one in general, and I have given demonstrative proof of them. Now, because the law of God, which we customarily call the Decalogue, is said to be a summary of the law of nature, I shall briefly show how the commandments of the Decalogue are harmonious with what I have said above.

---

[57] The Latin is *aciculae ... funiculum*, literally, "the cord of a small pin," translating the Greek βελόνης ... ἄμμ'.

[58] Pseudo-Justin, *On the Sole Government of God* 4.

4

An Exposition
of the Decalogue

There is no doubt that the first table, then, pertains immediately to the state of the spiritual life. For it teaches in summary form that God must be worshiped and praised and shows the right way to do this.

Demonstration of the First Table

God must be worshiped by the whole man, as has been demonstrated above. But man consists of soul and body. God, therefore, must be worshiped with mind and body, that is, with the heart,[1] according to the first commandment; with the mouth and tongue, according to the second; and with life and external morals, according to the third.[2]

The manner of the worship of God is disclosed here in the most beautiful order. It takes its beginning from the heart, next makes itself

---

[1] Hemmingsen here uses three different Latin terms for man's internal aspect: *anima*, *animus*, and *cor*.

[2] In Luther's (and Augustine's) numbering the first commandment is "You shall have no other gods before me. You shall not make for yourself a graven image ..."; the second is "You shall not take the name of the Lord your God in vain"; and the third is "Remember the sabbath day, to keep it holy."

known in the mouth and tongue, and afterward declares itself in life and external morals. By the word *heart* all the interior powers of the soul should be understood: the goal is that the illuminated mind correctly understand the things that are of God, the affections burn with the love of God, and the will be so consecrated to God of its own accord that it wishes for nothing except what accrues to the glory of God. This worship of the heart, which the worship of the mouth and of the external life follows by nature, the gentiles also understood by the light of nature,[3] although afterward they wandered away from the true God in their endeavor to perform it.

Bayerische Staatsbibliothek München, 940490 Ph.pr. 629, fol. I2r, urn:nbn:de:bvb:12-bsb00032962-5

General Demonstration of the Second Table

Whatever preserves the domestic and political state is commanded by the law of nature; whatever disturbs and overturns it is prohibited by the same. As, moreover, the works commanded in the second table

---

[3] *naturalis lux.*

preserve the domestic and political state, so those prohibited in it disturb and overturn it. The former things, therefore, are commanded, the latter forbidden.

The major premise is the principle that was made clear above. We shall confirm the minor premise by means of demonstrations of the individual commandments of the second table.

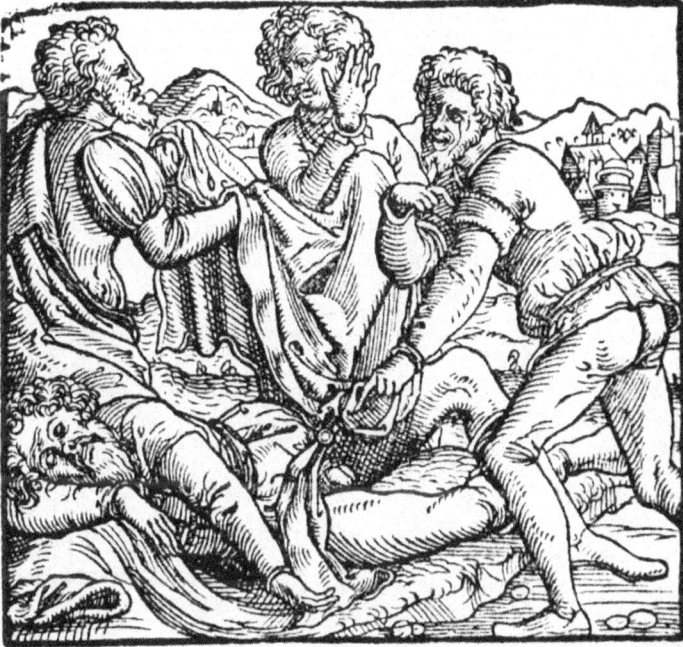

Bayerische Staatsbibliothek München, 940490 Ph.pr. 629, fol. I3v, urn:nbn:de:bvb:12-bsb00032962-5

Demonstration of the Fourth Commandment

Whatever preserves the domestic and political state belongs to natural law,[4] just as those things that are their contraries conflict with nature. The corresponding duties of superiors (as of parents and the magistrate) and of inferiors (as of children and subjects) preserve the domestic and political state. Therefore, these duties are commanded

---

[4] Hemmingsen in this instance employs the phrase *ius naturale* rather than his usual *lex naturae*.

93

by the law of nature, and the things that are contrary to them are prohibited as hostile and harmful to human society.

The order in this table is worth noting. For as in the first table the beginning is made from the foundation of the worship of God, so here it is made from obedience toward superiors, which is the mother of all the duties that are required in the following commandments.

Demonstration of the Fifth Commandment

Whatever disturbs human society, whether in the domestic or the political state, is forbidden by the law of nature. Hatreds, reviling, quarrels, and murders disturb human society. Therefore, hatreds, reviling, and murders are forbidden by natural law.[5] And by contrast: because mutual love, friendly conversations, kindness, concord, and zeal for preserving and defending one another preserve human society, they are therefore required by nature.

Bayerische Staatsbibliothek München, 940490 Ph.pr. 629, fol. I4v, urn:nbn:de:bvb:12-bsb00032962-5

---

[5] *ius naturale.*

Demonstration of the Sixth Commandment

Bayerische Staatsbibliothek München, 940490 Ph.pr. 629, fol. I5r, urn:nbn:de:bvb:12-bsb00032962-5

Whatever conflicts with integrity in the domestic or political state is forbidden by the law of nature. Promiscuous lusts and incest conflict with integrity, which nature demands in every state of life. Therefore, promiscuous lusts and incest are forbidden by the law of nature. And by contrast: the honorable and lawful bond of spouses is the seedbed of human society. Therefore, lawful marriage is commended by the law of nature.

Concerning incest—that is, concerning the bond of persons whom the law of nature prohibits from being joined because of the woman's relationship to the man either by blood or by marriage[6]—the reasoning in our present state of corruption is more obscure.

---

[6] I.e., the marriage of someone else in her family to someone else in his family.

Plutarch writes that it was prohibited for kinsmen to get married, and his reasoning is most honorable and upright—namely, so that just as those joined by blood love each other in turn, thus the chain of kinship might connect more people by means of love when marriages had been spread abroad into many households and did not remain within the same ones. It is clear that in such a way the love of the human race creeps forth and is extended.[7] Cicero, too, teaches this in book 5 of *On Ends*.[8] Therefore, who does not see that marriages of kinsmen—that is, of those related by blood or marriage—is prohibited by the law of nature? To this is added the natural judgment present in all men of sound mind by which all judge that one must abstain from sexual relations with those persons whom relationship either by blood or by marriage has joined together most closely. "There is somehow present in human modesty," says Augustine,[9] "something natural and praiseworthy, so that it keeps back lust (which is still lust, even though it is procreative) from the one to whom modest honor is owed on account of kinship—concerning which lust we see even conjugal chastity itself to blush with shame."[10] In the perversity of human nature the force[11] of this law concerning the illicit union of persons who are kin is rather weak in many people. And so we should give thanks to God who, for this reason, repeats this law in Leviticus 18 and warns that many nations had been exterminated because of the violation of this law.

---

[7] Cf. Plutarch, *Roman Questions* 6 and 108. On the subject of kin-marriage in ancient Rome, see also Tacitus, *Annals* 12.5–7.

[8] See also Cicero, *On Obligations* 1.54–55.

[9] Augustine (354–430) is the most important Western theologian of the ancient Church and was bishop in the North African city of Hippo. Among his most famous and important works are the *Confessions*, *On the Trinity*, and the *City of God*. He also wrote numerous works against the Donatists, Manichaeans, and Pelagians, in addition to a large collection of letters and sermons.

[10] Augustine, *City of God* 15.16.

[11] Hemmingsen has no subject for this sentence; I have supplied *vis*.

Now we can inquire whether, according to the law of nature, only two people ought to be joined in one marriage—namely, one man and one woman—and not one man and many women, especially because we see that certain of the holy patriarchs had two and sometimes more wives at the same time. Because one must judge not by examples but by the law of nature, I declare clearly that whoever has more wives than one at the same time violates the law of nature.[12]

I draw from nature four reasons for this response.

First, conjugal association requires an equal obligation of husband and wife insofar as it pertains to the use of their bodies. However, when one husband has more than one wife, or one woman has more than one husband, equality in obligation cannot be preserved. Because inequality is contrary to nature, it is also contrary to nature if more persons than two, one man and one woman, are joined in one marriage.

Second, right reason dictates that no one ought to obligate himself to something impossible. However, one man cannot be obligated equally to many wives in the same way as he is to only one. The union, therefore, of one man with many women conflicts with nature.

Third, domestic peace cannot be preserved when one husband has more wives than one. It cannot but happen that the women be jealously inflamed against each other. From this circumstance quarrels arise, and from these arises a household disorder that conflicts with nature.

Fourth, it is the justice of nature[13] that no one does to another what he does not wish to be done to himself. Therefore, a husband who does not wish his wife to be married to more men than one ought himself to be content with one. When this ἀνάλογον [proportionate] justice is violated, violence is done to the law of nature, and injustice is done to one of the spouses.

---

[12] Hemmingsen's focus on this question is presumably more than merely theoretical due to the bigamy, at first countenanced by Martin Luther, of Landgrave Philip of Hesse (see the dedicatory letter to Erik Krabbe, where the issue of bigamy is also raised, p. 10n26).

[13] *ius naturae.*

Demonstration of the Seventh Commandment

Bayerische Staatsbibliothek München, 940490 Ph.pr. 629, fol. I8r, urn:nbn:de:bvb:12-bsb00032962-5

Whatever destroys human society and whatever overturns households and polities conflicts with nature. Deceit, thefts, and robberies destroy human society and overturn households and polities. Therefore, these things are forbidden by the law of nature. And in contrast: whatever preserves human society both in the domestic realm and in the political realm belongs to natural law.[14] The distinction of property,[15] faithfulness, and sincerity in contracts preserves human society. Therefore, these things are commanded by the law of nature.

---

[14] *ius naturale.*

[15] I.e., the right to ownership: some property belongs to certain people, other property to others.

Demonstration of the Eighth Commandment

Bayerische Staatsbibliothek München, 940490 Ph.pr. 629, fol. I8v, urn:nbn:de:bvb:12-bsb00032962-5

Whatever contributes to the preservation of human society is required by the law of nature. Trustworthiness in the professions and truth between men makes for the preservation of human society. Therefore, these things are required by the law of nature.

The minor premise is illustrated by the antithesis: it is clear that lies and untrustworthiness in the professions destroy the society of men and that, for that reason, they are forbidden by the law of nature.

Demonstration of the Ninth and Tenth Commandments

No one wants another person to covet his goods unjustly. Therefore, no one ought to desire another's goods unjustly. The consequent is proved by the following rule of nature: That which you do not wish to be done to you, you ought not to do to another.[16]

These are the demonstrations of the commandments of the Decalogue drawn from the principles immediately relevant to the preservation of human society. Just as I have frequently stated that all the states of life must be referred to God as their ultimate end, so also the reasons for the commandments must be sought from the will and nature of God in the following way:

---

[16] The Golden Rule in its negative form (as here) is found in Tobit 4:15, but it is found in classical sources as well.

God is the source and giver of all goods. Therefore, God must be worshiped, and gratitude must be shown to him by his creation.

God is a lover of order and gratitude. For that reason, he gave the fourth commandment.

God does not wish his own image to be destroyed. He therefore prohibits murder.

God is most pure and most chaste. Therefore, he requires purity and chastity from rational creatures.

God is most just. Therefore, he abhors evil deceit, theft, fraud, and murders, and he is delighted by the virtues that contend with these vices.

God is true. Therefore, he is offended by lying and loves the truth.

God is holy and pure. He therefore does not want our minds to be defiled by the impurity of lusts.

Bayerische Staatsbibliothek München, 940490 Ph.pr. 629, fol. K2v, urn:nbn:de:bvb:12-bsb00032962-5

It is also possible to demonstrate the second table from the law of the love of neighbor, which is natural, in the following way:

The person who loves his neighbor, pays the honor owed to him, and renders his corresponding duty according to the fourth commandment is one who does no injustice to him, either in his own person, which is forbidden by the fifth commandment; or in a person joined to him by marriage, according to the proscription of the sixth commandment; or in possessions, as the seventh law demands; or in words, according to the prohibition of the eighth law; nor in his heart does he desire the things that belong to him, which is forbidden by the last two commandments. Thus, the laws of the second table are the effects and duties proper to love.

5

An Exposition of the Virtues

Moreover, since man is a social animal, and it is proper to virtue to unite the minds of men to each other and to join them in friendship for their mutual uses (as Cicero bears witness),[1] I shall append a list of the virtues together with definitions, so that the parts of virtue, which ought to shine in every life, may be clearly seen.

In the exposition of the virtues, moreover, let us principally follow Cicero, both on account of his brevity and on account of his clarity and characteristic facility in handling the material.

Cicero defines virtue, ἀρετὴ, in the following way: "Virtue is a habit of the mind consistent with nature, moderation, and reason."[2] The ancients, moreover, define it thus: "Virtue is the art of living well and

---

[1] Cicero, *On Obligations* 2.17.

[2] Cicero, *On Invention* 2.53.159. The traditional fourfold division of the cardinal virtues of prudence, justice, courage, and temperance (on which see below) follows. The passage is also cited in Augustine, *Responses to Miscellaneous Questions* 31.1.

correctly." To this is opposed vice, κακία,[3] a habit of the mind that, according to the judgment of nature, conflicts with right reason. And just as virtue unites the minds of men to each other and adapts them to one another's mutual uses, as has been said, so vice alienates the minds of men and turns them away from one another's mutual uses. Therefore, as nature dictates that the former must be sought, so she also instructs us that the latter must be avoided.

The commendation of virtue in Menander is relevant to this matter: ὅπλον μέγιστόν ἐστι ἡ ᾽ρετὴ βροτοῖς. That is, "Virtue is the greatest armor for mortals."[4]

Also relevant is the remark of Isocrates to Demonicus: τῆς ἀρετῆς οὐδὲν κτῆμα σεμνότερον, οὐδὲ βεβαιότερον. That is, "No possession is more worthy of respect nor firmer than virtue."[5]

And this expression of Menander is as well: Καρπὸς τῆς ἀρετῆς ἐστὶν εὔτακτος βίος, "The fruit of virtue is a well-ordered life."[6] It can easily be inferred from the contrary effects what one ought to think about vice, which is opposed to virtue.

According to Plato and Cicero, the parts of virtue are four: prudence, justice, courage, and temperance.[7] I remarked above that these four

---

[3] Recall that "Vice" was personified in Hemmingsen's earlier use of Xenophon's account of Prodicus' "Choice of Hercules."

[4] Menander, *Sentences* 582.

[5] Isocrates, *To Demonicus* 5. Isocrates, who lived from 436 BC to 338, was an important Athenian orator and the founder of a rhetorical academy, one very different from Plato's Academy in goals and outlook. Twenty-one of his orations (including his *Panegyric*), as well as nine letters, survive.

[6] Similar to Menander, *Sentences* 418, which reads: καρπὸς δ᾽ ἀρετῆς δίκαιος εὔτακτος βίος.

[7] The first literary reference to the so-called four cardinal virtues, to which Hemmingsen has already referred in chapter 3 above, is found in Plato, *Republic* 4.427e10–11, though the division is presumably traditional and therefore predates Plato. The division is widely influential: Cicero, for example, whom Hemmingsen mentions here, uses it to structure his discussion of the virtues in *On Obligations* 1.15ff. (but see n9 below). In the Christian tradition, these four virtues were frequently supplemented by the so-called theological

parts of virtue are required for the preservation of human nature and for uniting men together in society. I must now speak of them in order.[8]

On Prudence and Its Parts[9]

virtues of faith, hope, and love (cf. Thomas Aquinas, *Summa theologiae*, II-II, Q. 1–170). Hemmingsen does not discuss these in this work, because *On the Law of Nature* is a work of philosophy rather than of theology.

[8] In *De methodis*, Hemmingsen uses the four cardinal virtues as an example illustrating the demonstrative method of argument: see *Opuscula theologica*, 29–30.

[9] Hemmingsen said above that he will chiefly follow Cicero in his discussion of the virtues, and it is true that in book 1 of *On Obligations* Cicero discusses the virtues that are subordinate to the four major categories, and frequently makes note of the vices that are opposed to the virtues. Hemmingsen's discussion is nevertheless much more schematic and clearly organized,

Prudence, φρόνησις, is the knowledge[10] of good things, evil things, and things that are both good and evil. Or, as Aristotle defines it: Prudence is a habit fit by true reason for doing those things that are profitable or harmful to the life of men.[11] To it is opposed ἀφροσύνη, or ignorance, because of which someone is unsuitable for doing the individual things that they ought to do in their proper place and time. That this prudence is required by the law of nature is clear from the fact that nothing can be done correctly without it.

---

and thus bears some similarity to the approach of, e.g., Thomas Aquinas in *Summa theologiae*, II-II, Q. 47–170, though Aquinas' treatment is much more elaborate. Indeed, Hemmingsen's order of topics is often quite close to that of Aquinas (with omissions), as the notes below show. Stobaeus too, in his *Anthology*, pairs the various virtues with their corresponding vices. The search for definitions, of course, has roots ultimately in Plato's philosophy, and the contrast of virtues with their opposed vices is redolent of Aristotle, who construes virtue as the mean between two vicious extremes.

[10] *scientia*. Though the term can mean theoretical or speculative knowledge, as it does elsewhere in this treatise, it clearly does not here, where it is used in connection with "prudence," or practical wisdom. This use of *scientia* parallels Aristotle's use of ἐπιστήμη in the same context in the *Nicomachean Ethics*.

[11] Cf. Aristotle, *Nichomachean Ethics* 6.5 (1140b20–21). Hemmingsen's text is obscure here and Aristotle does not quite say this, that is, he says nothing about harmful actions in the passage in question. Moreover, it makes little sense to say that prudence is useful for doing the things that are harmful to human society. Hemmingsen gives the same supposedly Aristotelian definition with the same wording in *De methodis*, in *Opuscula theologica*, 18, where he argues that prudence can be called neither a science nor an art (oddly, given that he refers to it here as *scientia*), and so it must be a "habit." He concludes that his method of proceeding demonstrates the usefulness of Rudolph Agricola's instructions on definition.

There is great praise for prudence in the poets. Menander says:

ἀγαθὸν μέγιστον ἡ φρόνησίς ἐστι ἀεί.

That is:

Prudence is always the greatest good.[12]

The same poet adds the cause of this praise, when he speaks thus:

ἂν εὐφρονῇς, τὰ πάντα γε εὐδαίμων ἔσῃ.[13]

That is:

If you act wisely, you will be entirely happy.[14]

Cicero enumerates three parts of prudence: memory, understanding, and foresight.[15]

Memory, μνήμη, is the virtue by which the mind revisits the things that have been.[16] This is reckoned part of prudence for the following reason: because the experience of many things is required for deliberating prudently, and one cannot have this without the memory of things past. For experience, as Aristotle says, results from numerous memories, so to speak.[17] Forgetfulness, λήθη, conflicts with memory; memory is aided by recollection, ἀνάμνησις, which is a searching for what has escaped from the memory.

---

[12] Menander, *Sentences* 14.

[13] Menander, *Sentences* 74.

[14] Menander, *Sentences* 74.

[15] Cicero, *On Invention* 2.53.160. This passage is also cited by Thomas Aquinas, *Summa theologiae*, II-II, Q. 48, A. 1.

[16] This sentence, aside from the insertion of the Greek term, is taken word for word from Cicero, *On Invention* 2.53.160.

[17] Aristotle, *Metaphysics* 1.1 (980b.29–981a2). Again, this passage is cited by Thomas Aquinas, *Summa theologiae*, II-II, Q. 49, A. 1. In fact, Hemmingsen's wording in his "quotation" of Aristotle's definition is identical to Thomas'.

Memory receives this praise because it is the storehouse of all things and the guardian of the rest of the parts of character. Order brings the greatest light to it, as Simonides bears witness.[18]

Understanding, νόησις, is the virtue by which the mind perceives the things that are,[19] or it is the perception itself of the mind. Its office is twofold. One is that by which we grasp or perceive simple things absolutely. The other is that by which we compare among themselves the things that have been understood and form a judgment about them, whence we compose some things in making affirmation, we divide others in making denial, and we deduce some from others by reasoning. Mind, sense perception, imagination, and experience, about which I spoke above, are servants to understanding. Without this understanding, prudence is not able to protect its own name. For the substantial part of prudence, so to speak, is understanding, which is occupied with things present, just as memory has to do with things past.

To understanding is opposed dullness, ἀσυνεσία, the privation of mental acumen and sharp-sightedness. Those who are endowed[20] with it are unsuited for all refinement and learning, fit to be reckoned as beasts rather than as men. Hence it is easy to understand why there is great praise for understanding, as that which is the mother of all arts and honorable actions.

---

[18] Hemmingsen refers to Simonides' supposed invention of mnemonics. After having stepped out of a dinner party, the roof of the hall in which the banquet was being held collapsed and killed everyone inside. When the bodies could not be distinguished for burial, Simonides was able to identify them based on his memory of where each one had been reclining. See Cicero, *On the Orator* 2.351–54 (here 354). The story is also found in Quintilian, *The Orator's Education* 11.2.11–19. Cicero mentions Simonides' powers of memory in *Tusculan Disputations* 1.24.59 as well.

[19] Again, the first part of this sentence, aside from the Greek term, is taken word for word from Cicero, *On Invention* 2.53.160.

[20] Hemmingsen seems to be engaging in irony here, as *praeditus* ("endowed") is usually connected with positive or desirable qualities.

Foresight, πρόνοια, is the virtue by which some future thing is seen before it has been done.[21] To it is opposed ἀπρονοησία [improvidence];[22] this causes us not to foresee future things by our planning, which is, according to the expression of Seneca,[23] the eyes of future things.[24] It is the duty of foresight to ponder and form a judgment about future things from things past and present, and to fortify the mind in advance with early planning, before a person arrives at the reality of the future.

To foresight must also be referred diligence, ἐπιμέλεια, which is prudence in foreseeing the end and the means to the end, and the application of the mind in obtaining and maintaining those means. Or, it is the deliberation concerning the end and concerning the means, and a sort of exertion of the will and constancy in maintaining the means.

---

[21] Again, aside from the Greek term and the substitution of *factum sit* for Cicero's *factum est*, this is taken word for word from Cicero, *On Invention* 2.53.160.

[22] Cf. Thomas Aquinas, *Summa theologiae*, II-II, Q. 54, on negligence (to which he says, in Q. 53, that improvidence belongs).

[23] Seneca the Younger, born in Roman Spain between 4 BC and AD 1, was a Roman Stoic philosopher and playwright and was the author of such philosophical treatises as *On Mercy* and *On Providence*, as well as the plays *Phaedra* and *Medea* and the *Epistles* to Lucilius. He committed suicide in 65 at the behest of Nero, having been accused of participation in a conspiracy against him.

[24] Seneca seems nowhere to have said this. The phrase is rather found in the pseudo-Aristotelian *Secret of Secrets*. The work (of which there are more surviving manuscripts than of any other Aristotelian work) claims to be a letter from Aristotle to Alexander the Great and covers an impressive number of fields of knowledge, including statesmanship and ethics. First partially translated into Latin (from Arabic) in the twelfth century, and then translated completely over the course of the next one hundred years, it heavily influenced Roger Bacon. See Steven J. Williams, *The Secret of Secrets: The Scholarly Career of a Pseudo-Aristotelian Text in the Latin Middle Ages* (Ann Arbor: University of Michigan Press, 2003), 1. A cursory search shows that the particular expression cited by Hemmingsen was proverbial and in almost every case was attributed to Aristotle.

To it is opposed idleness and πολυπραγμοσύνη [meddlesomeness].[25] The former makes us neglect our duty; the latter makes us care about duties that belong to others, and about it the following verse is commonly cited: τῆς πολυπραγμοσύνης οὐδὲν χερεώτερον ἄλλο. That is, "Nothing is worse than meddlesomeness."[26] We everywhere meet with many maxims regarding diligence, such as the following remark of Menander:

τῆς ἐπιμελείας δοῦλα πάντα γίγνεται.

That is:

All things are subject to diligence.[27]

The following remark of Demosthenes is relevant as well: "For cautious and circumspect men, there is nothing so terrible that it cannot be guarded against beforehand, nor anything evil that cannot happen to the incautious and the sluggish."[28]

---

[25] On the vice in general, cf. Plutarch, *On Being a Busybody*.

[26] I have been unable to find a source for this quotation, which is a complete line of dactylic hexameter. It is quoted in two eighteenth century texts on the Greek language (though the adjective is different), in both instances without attribution. I have not found an instance prior to Hemmingsen, though such instances surely exist. He quotes it again below with respect to propriety.

[27] Menander, *Sentences* 727 (with a slight variation in word order from modern editions), also preserved in the form quoted here in Stobaeus, *Anthology* 3.29.51, where it is, however, attributed to the Middle Comic poet Antiphanes.

[28] Demosthenes, *Philippic* 1.3.

On Justice and Its Parts[29]

Bayerische Staatsbibliothek München, 940490 Ph.pr. 629, fol. K7v, urn:nbn:de:bvb:12-bsb00032962-5

Justice, δικαιοσύνη, is a habit of the mind bestowing on each his own, while preserving the common welfare;[30] or, as Aristotle defines it, "Justice is that disposition of the mind by which men are fit for carrying out just things, and by which they both do and desire to do just things."[31]

---

[29] Cf. Aristotle, *Nicomachean Ethics* 5; Cicero, *On Obligations* 1.20–60; Thomas Aquinas, *Summa theologiae*, II-II, Q. 57–122. Justice is treated by Melanchthon in, for example, book 2 of his *Philosophiae moralis epitome* (CR 16:63–164); *Ethicae doctrinae elementa* (CR 16:221–76).

[30] Again, taken directly from Cicero, *On Invention* 2.53.160, though Cicero's text reads *suam cuique tribuens dignitatem* ("bestowing on each one what he deserves") rather than Hemmingsen's *suum cuique tribuens* ("bestowing on each his own").

[31] Aristotle, *Nicomachean Ethics* 5.1 (1129a7–9).

To it is opposed injustice,[32] ἀδικία, by which men are unfit for carrying out just things, and by which they neither do nor desire to do just things—nay, rather, they strive after their opposites.

The encomia of justice in Greek and Latin authors are splendid. Theognis says: ἐν δὲ δικαιοσύνῃ συλλήβδην πᾶσ' ἀρετὴ 'στί: "Justice contains all the virtues in itself."[33] And Cicero says: "This one virtue justice is alone mistress and queen of all the virtues."[34] Aristotle proclaims it to be more beautiful than the evening star and the dawn; its foundation is trustworthiness, that is, constancy and truth in words and agreements.[35]

The first duty that belongs to justice is that no one harm anyone. The second is that we render to each and every person what is his own. The third is that we refer all things to the common welfare.

Its fruit is most abundant: happiness and a good reputation. For that reason, Menander says: δίκαιος ἴσθι, ἵνα καὶ δικαίων δὴ τύχοις. That is, "Be just, in order that you may also obtain justice."[36] The same one says: ἀνδρὸς δικαίου καρπὸς οὐκ ἀπόλλυται. That is, "The fruit of virtue does not perish."[37] The parts of justice have a twofold division. For some are called subject parts, others are called cognate parts. The parts subjected to it are: religion, natural affection, gratitude, innocence, punishment, benevolence, liberality, kindness, civility, trustworthiness, respect, and law.[38] The cognate parts are: glory, dignity, distinction,

---

[32] Cf. Thomas Aquinas, *Summa theologiae*, II-II, Q. 59.

[33] Theognis 147, cited (without attribution) in Aristotle, *Nicomachean Ethics* 5.1 (1129b29). Hemmingsen's text differs slightly from modern editions of Theognis and Aristotle.

[34] Cicero, *On Obligations* 3.28. Modern editions of the text differ slightly from Hemmingsen's citation.

[35] Aristotle, *Nicomachean Ethics* 5.1 (1129b28–29), a passage to which Hemmingsen already referred, where he attributed the sentiment to Euripides in accordance with a scholiast on Aristotle (see p. 28n18).

[36] Menander, *Sentences* 179.

[37] Menander, *Sentences* 28.

[38] *ius.*

and friendship. I shall illustrate these parts with definitions in the order in which I have listed them.

Bayerische Staatsbibliothek München, 940490 Ph.pr. 629, fol. L1r, urn:nbn:de:bvb:12-bsb00032962-5

Religion, θρησκεία, is for Cicero the part of justice that bestows care and reverence on the higher nature that they call divine.[39] When this has been taken away, as Cicero also says, trustworthiness, too, as well as the fellowship of the human race and justice, the most excellent virtue, are of necessity destroyed.[40] Moreover, that God must be worshiped religiously has been demonstrated above from the law of nature. But I

---

[39] Cicero, *On Invention* 2.161. Cf. also Thomas Aquinas, *Summa theologiae*, II-II, Q. 81.

[40] Cicero, *On the Nature of the Gods* 1.2.4.

thought that to this ought to be added the laws on the worship of the
gods that Cicero lists in the second book of *On the Laws*:

> Approach the gods with purity.
> Display piety.
> Put away wealth.[41]

He interprets the first law in the following way:

> The law commands us to approach the gods with purity,
> namely, with the mind, under which term everything else is
> included.[42] The commandment does not do away with con-
> cern for the purity of the body, but it ought to be understood
> as follows: since the mind much surpasses the body, and one
> makes sure to approach the gods with a pure body, so much
> the more must this purity be preserved in our minds. For the
> stain of the body is removed by the sprinkling of water or by
> the passage of a set time, but the stain of the mind can neither
> vanish by long duration of time, nor can it be washed away
> by any hands.[43] But as to the fact that the law commands
> that piety be displayed and wealth be put away, it signifies
> that piety is pleasing to God, but that lavish expense should
> have no place. For what are we doing when we wish that even
> among men poverty and riches not disrupt equable relations,
> but, when we employ lavish expense for sacred rites, we keep
> poverty away from approaching the gods?—particularly since
> nothing is less pleasing to God himself than that the way to
> appeasing and worshiping him not be open to all.[44]

---

[41] Cicero, *On the Laws* 2.19.

[42] There is a textual problem in all editions of *De lege naturae* I have consulted: they all print *in qua*, which does not make sense here, for Cicero's *in
quo*. I assume it is a typographical error and translate with Cicero's *in quo*.

[43] Again, there is a difference from Cicero: Cicero has *amnibus*, "rivers,"
whereas, by a transposition (by Hemmingsen or by his source), Hemmingsen
reads *manibus*, "hands."

[44] Cicero, *On the Laws* 2.24–25. Modern editions of the text differ slightly
from Hemmingsen's version.

Superstition,[45] δεισιδαιμονία, and Epicurean ἀθεότης [godlessness] conflict with religion. The former thinks excessively about types of cult, the latter rejects all care for religion, just as the Cyclops does in Euripides,[46] who acknowledges no other divinity than his own stomach, to which alone he professes to perform services. He says that other things are κόμπους καὶ εὐμορφίας λόγων [the ringing and elegance of words]—whom not a few ἄθεοι [godless men] today imitate. Just vengeance will teach them more correctly someday.

Natural affection,[47] στοργὴ, is the part of justice by which duty and diligent attention is bestowed upon those joined to us by blood and upon those who yield willing service to our country.[48] To it is opposed ἀστοργία [want of natural affection], the root of all vices. Therefore natural affection, without which there cannot be any religion at all, cannot be sufficiently praised. For it is for the sake of religion that men are closely bound by natural affection to one another, just as that outstanding man Stigelius elegantly says in the following verses:[49]

---

[45] Cf. Thomas Aquinas, *Summa theologiae*, II-II, Q. 92.

[46] Melanchthon makes the same comparison in book 1 of the *Philosophiae moralis epitome* (CR 16:30).

[47] *pietas*, also used just above, where it was translated as "piety." The Latin term has a wider range than the English term "piety" as customarily used (that is, the Latin term encompasses duties to God or the gods, family, and country), and so my translation in this instance represents more closely what Hemmingsen means by it here.

[48] Again, borrowed from Cicero, *On Invention* 2.53.160.

[49] Johannes Stigelius (Johann Stigel) (1515–62) was a Latin poet and professor in Wittenberg, where he had also been a student, having been drawn there by the renown of Martin Luther and Philip Melanchthon. He was appointed poet laureate by Emperor Charles V, to whom he had dedicated a congratulatory letter in verse in 1541. See Karl Hartfelder, "Stigel, Johann," in *Allgemeine Deutsche Biographie* 36 (1893): 228–30, https://www.deutsche-biographie.de/gnd104318864.html#adbcontent. Cf. also Wilhelm Kühlmann, "Neo-Latin Literature in Early Modern Germany," in *Camden House History of German Literature*, ed. Max Reinhart, vol. 4, *Early Modern German Literature 1350–1700* (Rochester, NY: Camden House, 2007), 288, 295.

In order that some might teach others about religion,
natural affection commanded us to place our houses
near one another.[50]

Gratitude,[51] χάρις, is the part of justice by which the memory of
another's friendship and the services he has done you, along with the
will for repaying him, is retained.

To it is opposed ingratitude,[52] ἀχαριστία. The laws of the Persians
judged no vice more grievous than this one; and, on the other hand,
all the poets and philosophers have extolled gratitude with the greatest
encomia. Hesiod, in the *Theogony*, depicts the parts of gratitude with
a most beautiful prosopopoeia,[53] when he says:

Τρεῖς δέ ἡ Εὐρυνόμη Χάριτας τέχε καλλιπαρήους,
Ἀγλαΐην τε καὶ Εὐφροσύνην Θαλίην τ' ἐρατεινήν.

[And Eurynome bore the three beautiful-cheeked Graces,
Aglaia and Euphrosyne and lovely Thalia.][54]

With these words, Hesiod, just as he makes Jove the father of the
Graces, in the same way makes Eurynome their mother. These words

---

[50] The couplet comes from lines 138–39 of Johann Stigel's poem *Osculamini
Filium*, based on the Second Psalm. See Johann Stigel, *Poematum liber I* (Jena:
Donatus Ritzenhayn and Thomas Rebart, 1566), C2r. Melanchthon quotes the
passage at least four times: in the prefatory material to his commentary on
Romans (*CR* 15:529); in his declamation *De restituendis scholis* (*CR* 11:493);
in the *Postilla Melanthoniana* (*CR* 25:844); and in a letter to Christianus
Egnolphus (*CR* 3:1118).

[51] Cf. Thomas Aquinas, *Summa theologiae*, II-II, Q. 106; Melanchthon,
Philosophiae moralis epitome (*CR* 16:157–58).

[52] Cf. Thomas Aquinas, *Summa theologiae*, II-II, Q. 107.

[53] "A figure of speech by which an inanimate or abstract thing is repre-
sented as a person, or as having personal characteristics." See *Oxford English
Dictionary*, s.v. "prosopopoeia" 2.a.

[54] Hesiod, *Theogony* 905 and 907 (Hemmingsen omits 906, and his 905
reads slightly differently from modern critical editions).

signify that God has implanted a law concerning gratitude in the minds of men.

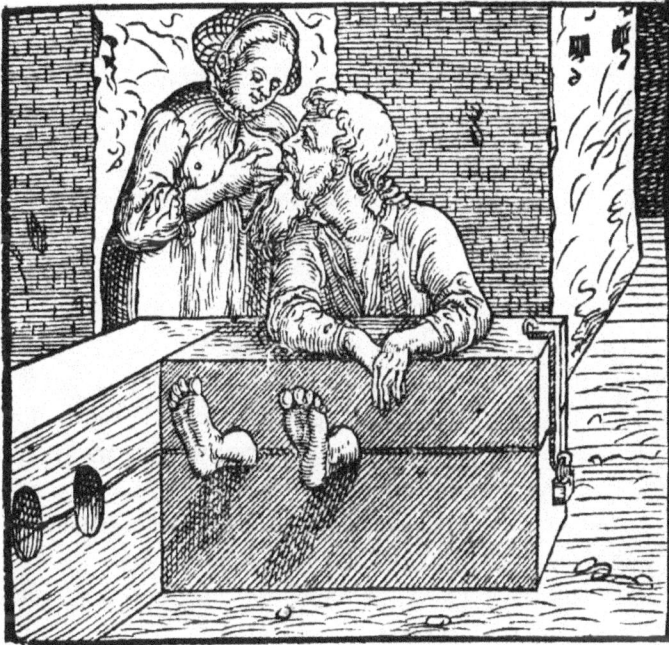

The number of the Charites, that is, of the Graces, signifies three distinct acts in the rendering of kindnesses, which are performed reciprocally—these are to give, to receive, and to repay.

The names of the Charites denote the affections of those who strive reciprocally in the rendering of kindnesses. For ἀγλαία, in Latin "the lustre of excellence" and "dignity,"[55] advises that he who has received a kindness should acknowledge it and make it publicly known. Εὐφροσύνη, "cheerfulness,"[56] advises the giver about cheerfulness, so that he may confer a kindness without moroseness and delay, in accordance the remark of Euripides: "He who quickly shows

---

[55] splendor et dignitas.

[56] hilaritas.

gratitude is the sweetest of mortals."[57] Consider also this saying: "He who gives quickly gives twice."[58] Θαλεῖα, "bounteous,"[59] advises that we not allow the memory of kindnesses received to grow old. To this pertains that remark of Theocritus:

Χρύσειοι πάλαι ἄνδρες ὅτ' ἀντεφίλησ' ὁ φιληθείς.

That is:

Formerly men were golden, when he who had received kindnesses repaid thanks in turn.[60]

These three Graces are virgins according to the poets, and they are depicted as naked and linked together. Nakedness and virginity are symbols of simple integrity, in order that no one may, on the pretext of giving a gift, devise treachery against anyone. For gifts that are so conferred are rarely of benefit to the one receiving them; for that reason, Ajax says in Euripides, ἄδωρα τῶν ἐχθρῶν δῶρα, that is, "the gifts of enemies are not gifts."[61] He who bestows gifts on others with so hostile a mind acts just as one who would cut the tongue out of the mouth of a serpent and offer gifts tinged with poison, as Medea did in Euripides.[62]

---

[57] I have been unable to find a source for this quotation, which Hemmingsen cites only in Latin.

[58] A Latin proverb. Erasmus attributes it (incorrectly, though he qualifies the attribution by adding *ni fallor*, "unless I am mistaken") to Seneca. See Erasmus, *Adagia*, pt. 2, ed. M. L. van Poll-van de Lisdonk and M. Cytowska, in *Opera omnia Desiderii Erasmi Roterodami*, pt. 2, vol. 2, ed. J. H. Waszink (Amsterdam: North Holland, 1998), 791.

[59] *florida*.

[60] Theocritus, *Idyll* 12.16.

[61] This quotation actually comes from Sophocles, *Ajax* 665, not Euripides, and is not quite a quotation. The line in Sophocles reads: ἐχθρῶν ἄδωρα δῶρα κοὺκ ὀνήσιμα.

[62] In Euripides' play, Medea, having been abandoned by her husband Jason for another woman, murders his new wife by means of a poisoned

Innocence, ἀκακία, is a purity of mind that shrinks back from every commission of injustice. Or, it is the part of justice by which integrity of life and morals is preserved. Cicero offers great praise for this part of justice. "Peace of conscience," he says, "and the security of innocence make life happy."[63] To it is opposed the desire to do harm,[64] κακότης, by which someone is prepared to commit injustice and malice—clearly a satanic vice, and one most unworthy of human nature.

Punishment, ἐκδίκησις, is the virtue by which violence and injustice, and absolutely everything that intends harm, is driven back by making defense and taking vengeance.

To it is opposed, on one side, savagery or cruelty, ὠμότης; on the other, indulgence, ἄνεσις.

Benevolence, εὔνοια, is the part of justice by which we wish well[65] for others. To it is opposed malevolence, κακόνοια; hatred, μίσος; and envy, φθόνος, which is grieved at another's goods. Livy, moreover, shows in the following words where envy proceeds from: "No temperaments are so prone to envy as the temperaments of those whose character does not correspond to their birth and fortune, because they hate the virtue and the good qualities of others."[66] The poets have passed down very many celebrated maxims against this vice, but I shall include just a few from the many. There is the following Greek epigram:

---

garment delivered by her and Jason's children, and then murders the children themselves.

[63] This is a fascinating instance of misattribution. Though Cicero wrote a work *On Obligations*, often rendered as *On Duties* (*De officiis*), already referred to several times, so did Ambrose of Milan; his own *De officiis* was modeled on that of Cicero, but was addressed to ministers in the church. This citation is from Ambrose's, not Cicero's, work (*On the Duties of the Clergy* 2.1.1).

[64] The Latin term phrase is *nocendi cupiditas*, which stands in antithetical relationship to *innocentia*.

[65] *bene volumus*.

[66] I.e., their minds are inferior to their rank and fortune in life. Livy, *History of Rome* 35.43. Hemmingsen's text differs slightly from modern editions.

ὁ φθόνος ἐστὶ κάκιστον, ἔχει δὲ τὶ καλὸν ἐν αὐτῷ,
τήκει γὰρ φθονερῶν ὄμματα καὶ κραδίαν.

Envy is the worst thing, but it has something good in itself,
  for it causes the eyes and heart of those who envy to
    waste away.[67]

And the following saying of Horace pertains to this vice: "The Sicilian tyrants did not discover a greater torment than envy."[68] And this one of Ovid:

There is a pallor on her face, her whole body's thin,
her eyes never see straight, her teeth are black with blight,
her chest is green with gall, her tongue suffused with
    poison.
She doesn't laugh, except for the laughter that comes from
    seeing someone's pain.
Nor does she enjoy sleep, kept awake by disturbing
    anxieties,
but she looks at men's successes, unwelcome to her, and
    wastes with envy
at the sight. She gnaws and is gnawed in turn,
herself her own punishment.[69]

And Horace says: "The envious man pines away when another's affairs prosper."[70]

---

[67] The lines seem to be proverbial and their author unknown.

[68] Horace, *Epistles* 1.2.58–59.

[69] Ovid, *Metamorphoses* 2.775–82. Hemmingsen's text differs slightly from modern editions of Ovid's in 778, where he reads *fecere* for Ovid's *movere*.

[70] Horace, *Epistles* 1.2.57; this line thus immediately proceeds the two quoted just above.

Liberality,[71] ἐλευθεριότης, is the part of justice that preserves the mean in conferring kindnesses. Valerius Maximus makes humaneness and mercy—Cicero bears witness that nothing is more worthy of man than these[72]—the companions of liberality.[73] Martial has expressed the fruit of liberality in the following verses:

> Whatever is given to friends is not subject to fortune;
> only the riches that you have given away will you always
> have.[74]

Claudian says the following: "The liberal man denies nothing, and offers himself even to those who do not ask."[75]

To liberality is opposed, on the one hand, prodigality, ἀσωτία, in excess and, on the other, illiberality, ἀνελευθερία, in defect.[76] Of this

---

[71] Cf. Thomas Aquinas, *Summa theologiae*, II-II, Q. 117; Melanchthon, *Philosophiae moralis epitome* (*CR* 16:153–54).

[72] Cicero, *On Obligations* 1.88 (though Cicero uses the term *placabilitas* rather than *humanitas*).

[73] Valerius Maximus, *Memorable Doings and Sayings* 5.1.praef.

[74] Martial, *Epigrams* 5.42.7–8.

[75] Claudian, *Against Eutropius* 1.365. Interestingly, in its original context this remark is made in *criticism* of Eutropius rather than for his praise.

[76] Conceptualizing virtue as a mean between two vicious extremes is Aristotelian (see p. 105n9). Cf. Aristotle, *Nicomachean Ethics* 2.6 (1106a26–29, 1106b5–8):

> In everything that is continuous and divisible it is possible to take more, less, or an equal amount, and that either in terms of the thing itself or relatively to us; and the equal is an intermediate between excess and defect.... Thus a master of any art avoids excess and defect, but seeks the intermediate and chooses this—the intermediate not in the object but relatively to us. (trans. David Ross [Oxford: Oxford University Press, 1954])

On liberality in particular, cf. Aristotle's discussion in 4.1 (1119b22–1122a18), along with his earlier (and more concise) remarks in 2.7 (1107a9–16). Aristotle, however, does not include liberality under the heading of justice

there are three types: shameful profit, niggardliness, and κιμβεία. Shameful profit is αἰσχροκέρδεια,[77] when someone seeks to become rich indiscriminately from any source and counts profit as worth more than decency. Niggardliness is φειδωλία, when someone is sparing of expense and outlay in an honorable matter. Κιμβεία [stinginess] is as it were the parceling of a cucumber; this happens when someone makes an expenditure, but piecemeal and badly, without making any consideration of appropriate timing; from this tactic it comes about that he can make more of his expense.

Kindliness, φιλοφροσύνη, is a humane and distinguished pleasantness of manners,[78] from the verb "I adorn,"[79] which means "I embellish."

This virtue is joined to friendship, for thus Cicero says: "Friendship ought to be more indulgent and sweeter, and readier for every kindness and politeness."[80] For those who are endowed with this virtue serve others kindly and by no means reluctantly. To it is opposed severity on the one side, scurrility on the other. The former decrees that one must not depart from virtue in even the smallest point, the latter, more indulgent than it should be, is delighted by excessively unrestrained trifles.[81] The former is called ἀποτομία in Greek—"pruning," as it were—by which a thing is required with utmost strictness. The latter

---

as Hemmingsen does, following Cicero in *On Obligations* 1.42–60. Thomas Aquinas too includes liberality under justice; he discusses its opposites (covetousness and prodigality) in *Summa theologiae*, II-II, Q. 118–19.

[77] The Greek term means most properly "sordid love of gain" or "base covetousness."

[78] *mores*. Elsewhere in this work I have rendered *mores* as "morals," but "manners" is more serviceable in this context.

[79] Hemmingsen derives the noun "kindliness" (*comitas*) from the verb "I adorn" (*como*).

[80] Cicero, *On Friendship* 18.66; Hemmingsen leaves out two words of the original.

[81] I read *iocis* with the 1564 edition rather than *locis* with the *Opuscula theologica*.

is called εὐτραπελία, which bends itself to the temperaments of men, so that they may be pleased by charm and refined wit.

Courteousness, τὸ πολιτικόν, is a restraint and propriety especially suitable to a man involved in politics. To it is opposed discourteousness, ἀγριότης, which is a rudeness of manners and boorishness, and impudence, ὕβρις, which attacks others through arrogance.

Bayerische Staatsbibliothek München, 940489 Ph.pr. 628, fol. L8v, urn:nbn:de:bvb:12-bsb10191732-4

Trustworthiness, πίστις, is steadfastness and truthfulness in words and agreements,[82] so called because what was said is done. Seneca calls it the most sacred good of the human heart.[83] And it is called the foundation of justice by Cicero.[84] Plautus therefore correctly advises: "Be sure to be trustworthy to one who is trustworthy; beware lest your

[82] Or "compacts," "covenants." The Latin term is *conventus*.

[83] Seneca, *Moral Epistles* 88.29.

[84] Cicero, *On Obligations* 1.23.

trustworthiness be crooked."[85] Moreover, when the sophist Theon says μέμνησο ἀπιστεῖν ["remember to disbelieve"],[86] he wishes no one to be easily persuaded by anyone unless clear reasons are manifest. To it is opposed vanity, ματαιότης, and fickleness, ἀστασία.

Respect,[87] θεράπεια, is the virtue by which we deem those preceding us in some dignity worthy of reverence and honor; or, it is the virtue by which persons placed in a dignified rank are honored. To it is opposed contempt, ὑπεροψία, which consists of an aversion of the mind.

Truthfulness,[88] ἀλήθεια, is the virtue by which the things that are, or have been, or will be, are spoken about without alteration. To this is opposed mendacity, ψευδολογία. The following commendation of truth is found in Philemon:

> Οὐκ ἐστὶν οὔτε ζωγράφος, μὰ τοὺς θεοὺς,
> οὔτε ἀνδριαντοποιὸς, ὅστις ἄν πλάσαι
> κάλλος τοιοῦτον, οἷον ἡ ἀλήθει' ἔχει.

That is:

> There is not a painter, by the gods, or a sculptor, who could make such beauty as the truth has.[89]

---

[85] Plautus, *The Captives* 439. Hemmingsen's text differs from modern editions of Plautus.

[86] The remark is found in Lucian, *Hermotimus, or Concerning the Sects* 47, where it is attributed to a "sophist" or "wise man," but Theon is not named. It should actually be attributed to the fifth-century-BC Sicilian comic poet Epicharmus (frag. 250 [Kaibel]), as it is in the *Suda*, the tenth-century-AD lexicon (s.v. νῆφε and πρόχειρος).

[87] Cf. Thomas Aquinas, *Summa theologiae*, II-II, Q. 102.

[88] Cf. Aristotle, *Nicomachean Ethics* 4.7 (1127a12–1127b23); Thomas Aquinas, *Summa theologiae*, II-II, Q. 109; Melanchthon, *Philosophiae moralis epitome* (CR 16:151–54).

[89] The quotation is preserved in Stobaeus, *Anthology* 4.21a.5.

Law,[90] τὸ δίκαιον, is nothing other than what either nature, or the city, or the people, or the nation, or custom commands. It is divided into natural law,[91] the law of nations,[92] and civil law.[93]

Natural law is that which is common to every nation, because it is everywhere held by the instinct of nature, not by some decision made by man, but by the creator of nature himself—such as the union of male and female, the rearing of offspring, and the children's inheritance of their parents' goods.[94]

The law of nations is that which human nations use; by it we are obedient to God, religion, and country.

Civil law exists when something is either added to or taken away from common law[95]—that is, when a people makes for itself its own, as it were, law of the city. These three types of law must be approved only when they are demonstrated to have flowed from the first axioms of nature.

The fair and the good, equity, ἐπιείκεια, is threefold.[96] For it is either the suitable application of the law[97] to the demands of the situation, in which is seen the law's will and intention, and not τὸ ἀκριβοδίκαιον

---

[90] *ius.* Hemmingsen uses this term throughout the discussion in this section. For a comparison of *ius* and *lex*, see p. 16n48 in the Dedicatory Epistle above.

[91] *ius naturale.* Hemmingsen's usual term elsewhere in the treatise is *lex naturae.*

[92] *ius gentium.*

[93] *ius civile.*

[94] Hemmingsen here, in contrast to the rest of the treatise, uses the term "natural law" in a much more restricted sense to refer to a kind of instinct. Cf. Cicero, *On Obligations* 1.54. The same idea is found (confusingly) in Justinian, *Institutes* 1.2, which he borrows from the jurist Ulpian. It is immediately followed, as here, by a definition of the *ius gentium* or "law of nations" (*Institutes* 1.2.1).

[95] *commune ius.*

[96] Cf. Thomas Aquinas, *Summa theologiae*, II-II, Q. 120.

[97] Hemmingsen reverts to *lex* here.

[the act of being a stickler for one's rights];[98] or it is the moderating and amendment of the law that comes about from the prudence of the judge accommodating himself to the circumstances of the case, and bending the law to the case, not the case to the law.[99] Or it is the just exchange of property, with equality preserved. Or it is the distribution of goods and rewards, and also of penalties, in accordance with the proportion that is owed and the terms of duties.

From here arise the species of justice: distributive and commutative.[100]

---

[98] Aristotle uses the term in *Nicomachean Ethics* 5 (1138a1); I borrow the translation from Ross, trans., *Nicomachean Ethics*, who takes the masculine form of the noun as a "stickler for one's rights in a bad sense," whereas the truly equitable man "tends to take less than his share though he has the law on his side."

[99] This whole sentence forms the first part of the threefold definition of equity.

[100] Cf. Aristotle's discussion in *Nicomachean Ethics* 5.2–5 (1130a14–1134a16); Thomas Aquinas, *Summa theologiae*, II-II, Q. 61; Melanchthon, *Philosophiae moralis epitome* (CR 16:65–69); Melanchthon, *Ethicae doctrinae elementa* (CR 16:223–26). Melanchthon's comments on Aristotle, *Nicomachean Ethics* 5.2, can be found in his *Enarrationes aliquot librorum Ethicorum Aristotelis* (CR 16:370–94).

Bayerische Staatsbibliothek München, 940490 Ph.pr. 629, fol. L8v, urn:nbn:de:bvb:12-bsb00032962-5

Distributive justice is the ordering of persons and duties in all of life, public and private. It bestows on persons the duties that befit them according to geometrical proportion. For just as geometrical proportion (which Aristotle calls διηρημένην [divided], and Cicero calls "divided") does not simply consider numerical intervals, but looks to the equality of the proportions of things and persons, so distributive justice does not distribute functions indifferently according to the number of persons, but attends to the proportion between persons and functions, and bestows on persons their fitting functions. Just as a person who is going to build a house does not lay any wood he happens to stumble upon as the foundation of the house, but chooses what is suitable from a great heap, so in a commonwealth the office of magistrate is not imposed on just anyone, but on one who is sufficient for the task. Where this justice is not preserved, the commonwealth is driven away from a healthy condition.

Commutative justice, συναλλακτικὴ [having to do with exchange], is the ordering of the exchange of property in contracts. This type of justice preserves equality in the exchange of property according to arithmetical proportion. In it, equality of property is sought, without persons being taken into account. For as the arithmetical proportion of numbers considers equal intervals (for example, 3, 6, 9, 12, 15—here, one number is always three distant from the next) so commutative justice, without respect to persons, looks simply to equality in the property that is exchanged so that the number of the buyer is as great as that of the seller, in order that the thing bought and its price may be equal. Without this justice, no house, no city, and no commonwealth can stand.

Next, this commutative justice is adapted to kind[101]—that is, to any kind of valuation or exchange you like, and not only where loss and profit, but also where crime and punishment, are appraised—as, for instance, homicide is punished with death according to the principle of the punishment fitting the crime. Nevertheless, we must carefully observe that, because of the circumstances of persons and occasions, the judge ought sometimes to take geometrical proportion into account, by which he punishes drunkenness in a senator more harshly than in a soldier; thus, too, a *paterfamilias* will punish a son who visits a prostitute more harshly than a servant who does so.

Glory, κλέος, is a common renown,[102] with praise, concerning someone; or, it is the noble and widespread renown that comes from just desserts, belonging to many great men, either among their own citizens, or in their own country, or among every race of men; or, as it is defined elsewhere: it is the unanimous praise of good men, the uncorrupted voice of those who judge well about excellent virtue. It responds to virtue and is as it were its echo.[103]

---

[101] *ad genus.*

[102] "Common" not in the sense of "pedestrian," but in the sense of "widely recognized."

[103] "Responds" should be taken literally here: Hemmingsen is using the metaphor of sound and echo (*imago*). Virtue is the "sound," and glory or reputation is what is repeated back (*resonat*).

Its foundation is virtue or any deed honorably done and worthy of praise, as song is the Muses' glory, as Hesiod bears witness.[104] However, where this foundation is not solid, but rather fictive, glory is empty, as that of the soldier in the comic poet.[105] Nothing, according to the line of Menander,[106] is more wretched than this. The parts of this empty glory are boasting, presumption, and hypocrisy.

Boasting,[107] ἀλαζονεία, is an empty and foolish commendation of oneself, by which someone promises more than he is able to deliver.

Presumption, τόλμημα, is when someone hunts with immodest zeal for glory as a reward for deeds that are deserving of only a more moderate admiration.

Hypocrisy[108] is when someone seeks for glory because of that which he does not possess, but of which, nevertheless, a specter (as it were) appears on the outside, as when an actor who puts on a mask of Hercules in a play soon boasts that he really is Hercules come to life.

Next, as pride is the mother of empty glory and φιλαυτία [self-regard], so it begets indolent offspring: obstinacy, discord, strife, disobedience, and other vices of this kind.

Dignity, ἀξιοπρέπεια [what is becoming], is the worthy authority someone has due to his integrity, refinement, position,[109] and modesty. To it is opposed indignity, ἀναξία, an obscure condition of life.

Grandeur, τὸ πληρωματικὸν, is a great abundance of power, or of majesty, or of resources. To it is opposed lowliness and impoverished obscurity.

Friendship,[110] φιλία, is the will for good things toward someone for the sake of the person you love, together with a corresponding will

---

104 Cf. Hesiod, *Theogony* 1–21, 36–55, 98–105.

105 The reference is to Plautus' play *The Braggart Soldier*.

106 Menander, *Sentences* 408.

107 Cf. Thomas Aquinas, *Summa theologiae*, II-II, Q. 112.

108 Cf. Thomas Aquinas, *Summa theologiae*, II-II, Q. 111.

109 Or "grace, beauty, charm" (*honore*). There seems to be a play on words with *honesto* (translated above as "integrity").

110 Cf. Melanchthon, *Philosophiae moralis epitome* (CR 16:157–64).

on his part. It is proper to it to keep and nourish good will, kindness, and συμπάθειαν [sympathy], by which you suffer together with one who is afflicted: ἡ γὰρ συμπάθεια ἐστὶ πάθος τινὸς διὰ πάθος ἑτέρου [for sympathy is the suffering of one person through the suffering of another].[111]

The philosophers recognize three kinds of friendship.

They say that the first and best kind belongs to those whom virtue has joined together. For solid is the love that comes from reason.

The second and middle kind is found in a relation of doing favors. For this kind of friendship consists of mutual repayment, quite useful in all of life; for common is the friendship that comes from doing favors.

The third and last kind takes its rise from familiar habit. The Pythagorean Hippodamus[112] teaches the kinds of friendship quite beautifully in the following words:

ἃ μὲν ἐξ ἐπιστήμας θεῶν, ἃ δὲ ἐκ παροχάς ἀνθρώπων, ἃ δὲ ἐξ ἀδονᾶς ζώων.

That is:

One kind of friendship comes from the knowledge of the gods, another from the generosity of men, another from the pleasure of animals.

And he adds that "the first kind of friendship belongs to the philosopher, the middle to man, the last to animals."[113]

---

[111] Clement of Alexandria, *Excerpta ex Theodoto* 30.

[112] That is, Hippodamus of Miletus, a well-known Greek town planner, born probably around 500 BC. He planned, for example, the Piraeus, the port of Athens.

[113] Quoted in Clement of Alexandria, *Miscellanies* 2.19.

On Courage and Its Parts[114]

Bayerische Staatsbibliothek München, 940490 Ph.pr. 629, fol. M4v, urn:nbn:de:bvb:12-bsb00032962-5

Courage, ἀνδρεία [manliness], is a reflective undertaking of dangers and the endurance of toil. This virtue is a protectress of justice, which has as its end the preservation of human society or the defense of the adornments of all the virtues. It strives against all vices: unconquerable in the face of toils, brave in the face of dangers, altogether inflexible when confronted with pleasures, so as to avoid greed (which makes virtue effeminate)[115] as though it were destruction. Cicero also approves of the following definition of the Stoics: "Courage is

---

[114] Cf. Aristotle, *Nicomachean Ethics* 3.6–9 (1115a6–1117b22); Cicero, *On Obligations* 1.61–92; Thomas Aquinas, *Summa theologiae*, II-II, Q. 123–40.

[115] There is a play on words here: etymologically, *virtus* means "manliness." Hemmingsen writes: *quam virtutem effoeminat.*

the virtue that fights for the right."[116] For that reason, he proclaims that it is not those who do injustice, but those who drive it back, that should be considered brave and great-hearted.

We should, moreover, observe that just as "virtue" is named from the virile sex in Latin,[117] as Cicero bears witness, so "courage" in Greek is named from the word "man,"[118] because courage is especially proper to men. Its two greatest duties are contempt for death and for pain. We must make use of courage, then—as Cicero also says—if we wish to have a share in virtue, or rather if we wish to be men verily,[119] since this virtue derives its name from the word "men." Courage, moreover, stays between two extremes, audacity and timidity.[120]

Audacity, θάρσος, is an unreflective confidence in undertaking hard things. Nevertheless, Cicero says that sometimes it is connected to courage.

Timidity, δειλία, is a constriction of the mind, because of which someone, faced with the smallness of his mind, is afraid to undertake hard things. Those who suffer from this vice are called effeminate.[121]

Laziness and worthlessness are also opposed to courage. Laziness, ῥαθυμία, is that which dissuades someone from undertaking what reason persuades him to undertake with courage.

---

[116] *aequitas.* Hemmingsen refers to Cicero, *On Obligations* 1.62: "So courage is splendidly defined by the Stoics when they term it 'the virtue which champions the right'" (trans. P. G. Walsh [Oxford: Oxford University Press, 2000]). Walsh, 139, notes that there is no attestation for this Stoic definition outside of this passage. Hemmingsen's wording differs slightly from modern editions of *On Obligations.*

[117] I attempt to preserve the wordplay: *virtus a viro ... dicitur.*

[118] That is, ἀνδρεία (courage), used at the beginning of this section, is derived from ἀνήρ (man).

[119] Once again, I attempt to preserve Hemmingsen's wordplay: *virtus ... viri.*

[120] Most of this paragraph comes from Cicero, *Tusculan Disputations* 2.42.

[121] Again, because they lack *virtus,* "courage" or "manliness."

Worthlessness, ἀχρειότης, is that which is opposed not only to courage, but even to all the virtues. It takes its name from "nothing,"[122] that is, from sterility, since it does nothing right or good, but obstinately does whatever evil it can. And for that reason those who suffer from it are called lost,[123] and day by day they hasten to their own ruin. Opposed to them are the frugal, so called from "fruit,"[124] that is, from fertility.

The parts subjected to courage are magnificence, confidence, endurance, and perseverance.

Magnificence,[125] μεγαλοπρέπεια, is the doing and managing of great and lofty things with a strong and noble resolution of the mind.

It stays between two extremes, βαναυσίαν [servility][126] and parvanimity.[127]

Βαναυσία [servility] pursues servile and contemptible trades on account of smallness of mind.

Parvanimity, μικροπρέπεια, is a smallness of mind and despondency unworthy of a man.

Confidence, παρρησία, is the virtue by which, in great and honorable affairs, the mind itself has placed much trust, along with sure hope, in itself. Or, as Cicero defines it elsewhere, it is the firm assurance of the mind.[128]

Opposed to it on one side is θάρση [recklessness], on the other, diffidence, which because of a dread of evil dares to undertake nothing that seems threatening.

---

[122] The Latin term for "worthlessness," *nequitia*, is derived from a compound meaning "not able."

[123] That is, "corrupt, flagitious, incorrigible."

[124] The Latin term is *frux, frugis*.

[125] Cf. Thomas Aquinas, *Summa theologiae*, II-II, Q. 134.

[126] The primary meaning of the term is "handicraft."

[127] Whereas "magnanimity" refers to the quality of being great-souled, "parvanimity" refers to the quality of being small-souled.

[128] Cicero, *Tusculan Disputations* 4.80.

Bayerische Staatsbibliothek München, 940490 Ph.pr. 629, fol. M6v, urn:nbn:de:bvb:12-bsb00032962-5

Endurance,[129] ἀνεξικακία, is the voluntary and long-lasting endur-ing[130] of hard and difficult things for the sake of honor and utility. Here it is pleasant to include the reasons for endurance from the first book of Ovid's *Fasti*, where Nicostrata exhorts her exiled son Evander to endurance with the following words:

> Remember to bear your exile bravely.
> So it was fated, nor has your fault put you to flight,
> But God; you have been driven from the city by an offended
>   God.
> You are not enduring deserved punishment, but the wrath of
>   divine power.

---

[129] Cf. Thomas Aquinas, *Summa theologiae*, II-II, Q. 136.

[130] The definition of "endurance" as a "long-lasting enduring" sounds redundant, of course, but Hemmingsen uses two related words (*patientia* and *perpessio*).

It is some consolation, at least, that you are innocent of
    crimes while in the midst of great evils.
As is the state of each man's conscience, so it conceives in
the heart either hope or dread in keeping with his deed.
Nor, still, should you grieve as though you were the first to
    endure such evils;
that gale has overwhelmed mighty men.
Cadmus endured the same thing, who once driven from
Tyrian shores settled, an exile, in Aonia.
Tydeus endured the same thing, and Pagasean Jason too,
and others as well, whose stories would take long to relate.
For the brave all soil is his homeland, as water is to the fish,
as whatever place lies open in the empty world is to the bird.
But the savage storm does not rouse fear the whole year
    through,
and there will be for you—believe me—seasons of spring.[131]

Here the poet enumerates the reasons for endurance: the providence
of God, innocence, a good conscience, examples of others who have
endured, courage, and hope for better fortune. Next, endurance stays
between extremes: an unwillingness to endure and insensibility. The
former avoids all toil and pain, the latter casts off all feeling of toil
and pain; in Greek it is called ἀπάθεια, just as the former, which by
chance does not have a proper name,[132] is called by the general name
φόβος [fear].

Perseverance,[133] καρτερία, is a stable and perpetual persistance, well
established in the reason. Moreover, it stays between two extremes:
stubbornness and fickleness.

---

[131] Ovid, *Fasti* 1.481–96. Hemmingsen's text differs slightly from modern
editions, and his first line (*Fortiter exilium ferre memento tuum*) is not found
in Ovid. An expression in Seneca, *Moral Epistles* 3.24.4, contains much of
the same vocabulary (*exilium Metellus fortiter tulit*).

[132] Wordplay again: the word for "by chance" is *forte*, related to *fortitudo*.

[133] Cf. Thomas Aquinas, *Summa theologiae*, II-II, Q. 137.

Stubbornness, αὐθάδεια, is that which is extremely hostile to deliberation, for it stands too fixedly in its own opinions. It arises, moreover, from love of oneself and an honorable belief about oneself. Those who labor under this vice are too pleasing to themselves, and think too highly of their own qualities, and for that reason are generally ἰδιογνώμονες [attached to their own opinions], for they do not allow for the judgments and opinions of others.

Aeschylus opposes αὐθάδεια [stubbornness] to εὐβουλία [prudent deliberation], for he speaks thus:

μήδ' αὐθάδειαν εὐβουλίᾳ ἀμείνον' ἡγήσῃ ποτέ.

That is:

> Nor should you ever judge stubbornness to be better than prudent deliberation.[134]

Fickleness, κουφότης, by which a person is rashly carried now into this, now into that opinion, behaves no differently from a feather, which is very easily driven now here, now there by the slightest breeze.

---

[134] Aeschylus, *Prometheus Bound* 1034–35. Modern editions of Aeschylus differ slightly.

On Temperance and Its Parts[135]

Bayerische Staatsbibliothek München, 940490 Ph.pr. 629, fol. M8v, urn:nbn:de:bvb:12-bsb00032962-5

Temperance, σωφροσύνη, is reason's firm and restrained rule over the mind against lust and other wrongful impulses. The Latin word[136] is derived from "moderating,"[137] that is, from "restraining"[138]—clearly because this virtue restrains the affections and actions and gestures, in order that a certain charm and, as it were, a pleasing harmony may appear in them. In Greek, the word σωφροσύνη is used, as if,

---

[135] Cf. Aristotle, *Nicomachean Ethics* 3.10–12 (1117b23–1119b17); Cicero, *On Invention* 2.54.164–65; idem, *On Obligations* 1.93–151 (where Cicero redescribes temperance as "the fitting"); Thomas Aquinas, *Summa theologiae*, II-II, Q. 141–70.

[136] I.e., *temperantia*.

[137] *temperando*.

[138] *moderando*.

according to Aristotle, one should say σώζουσα τὴν φρόνησιν, that is, "the preserver of prudence."[139] According to Plato, it is used as if one should say σωτηρία τῆς φρονήσεως, "the preservation of prudence."[140] Each etymology pertains to the same thing—namely, that temperance makes prudence safe, that is, that it ensures that nothing happens contrary to prudence, whose guiding rule is right reason. And since the impulses of the mind often rise up against this guiding rule, temperance is added in order to restrain them, so that nothing may be done unbecomingly and prudence may remain safe. The praises of this virtue are deservedly very many among ancient authors; concerning it, someone said in Greek:

τῆς δὲ σαοφροσύνης οὐδὲν τιμιώτερον ἄλλο.

That is: "Nothing is more precious than temperance,"[141] for without it other things have no value. But when they are moderated by it, they are most sweet and precious. Menander calls temperance "the treasury of virtue," when he says, ταμιεῖον ἐστὶν ἀρετῆς ἡ σωφροσύνη [temperance is the treasury of virtue].[142] Xenophon calls the same thing θεμέλιον σοφίας, "the foundation of wisdom." And he adds: "Nothing evil can be found in the man who has laid this foundation."[143] And one of the Seven Wise Men of Greece advises thus: "Be temperate in adolescence,

---

[139] Aristotle, *Nicomachean Ethics* 6.5 (1140b12).

[140] Plato, *Cratylus* 411e4–5. Cf. also Stobaeus, *Anthology* 3.5.44 (a passage attributed to Hierax's lost work *On Justice*).

[141] I have been unable to find a source for this line of Greek dactylic hexameter.

[142] An alternative reading of Menander, *Sentences* 744, found in Stobaeus, *Anthology* 3.5.5.

[143] Xenophon, *Memorabilia* 1.5.4 (Xenophon refers to "self-control" [ἐγράτεια] rather than "temperance" [σωφροσύνη], and refers to the "foundation/groundwork of virtue" [ἀρετῆς κρηπῖδα] rather than the "foundation of wisdom" [θεμέλιον σοφίας]). The passage is also found in Stobaeus, *Anthology* 3.5.29; Stobaeus refers to both "temperance" and "self-control" and also uses the term θεμέλια, and thus it is plausible that he is Hemmingsen's source.

just in middle age, and prudent in old age, in order that you may die without sadness."[144] Cicero asserts that temperance makes us to follow reason; he says that it also brings peace to our minds, and calms and soothes them with, as it were, a sort of concord.[145] It stays between the extremes of intemperance and lack of feeling.

Bayerische Staatsbibliothek München, 940490 Ph.pr. 629, fol. N2r, urn:nbn:de:bvb:12-bsb00032962-5

Intemperance,[146] ἀκολασία, is an unbridled deviation from all understanding and from right reason, turning away from the limit imposed by reason so that the desires of the mind can in no way be ruled or contained. In Greek it is called ἀκολασία, from a combination

---

[144] I have been unable to find a source for this quotation. There is a similar saying attributed to Bias in Stobaeus, *Anthology* 3.1.172 (from a work attributed to the fourth/third-century Peripatetic philosopher Demetrius of Phalerum).

[145] Cicero, *On Ends* 1.47.

[146] Cf. Thomas Aquinas, *Summa theologiae*, II-II, Q. 142.

of an alpha privative and the word κολάζω, which means "to bridle" and "to moderate." For he who labors under this vice rushes wherever the impulses of his mind carry him, as though the reins have been shaken off. Cicero speaks about it: "Just as temperance checks all desires, and makes them to obey right reason and preserve the considered judgments of the understanding, so intemperance is hostile to it, and inflames, disturbs, and excites every state of mind."[147] Aristotle enumerates the vices that are connected to intemperance in the following words: ἀκολασίαν comitantur ἀταξία, ἀναίδεια, ἀκοσμία, τρυφὴ, ῥαθυμία, ἀμέλεια, ὀλιγωρία, ἔκλυσις.[148] That is, "Disruption of order, shamelessness, confusion, allurements, sloth, carelessness, heedlessness, and dissoluteness accompany intemperance."[149] The same writer affirms that the evil of intemperance is similar to that of dropsy and consumption, because once it has put down roots the evil is incurable.

Lack of feeling, ἀναισθησία, is stupor, the effect of which is that one takes no thought for mind or body. One does not find very many who labor under this vice. It was for that reason that Aristotle said that those who suffered from it did not even have a name.[150] However, they are called ἀναίσθητοι, that is, "those that are devoid of all feeling." The word ἀναισθησία occurs in Plato's *Philebus*, when he says that the soul is ἀπαθής [without feeling] of movements, calling such a condition the ἀναισθησία of the body.[151]

Temperance has many parts, such as: a sense of shame, honesty, continence, sobriety, chastity, modesty, humility, clemency or gentleness, propriety, εὐταξία [good order], decorum, αὐτάρκεια [self-sufficiency], and moderation.

---

[147] Cicero, *Tusculan Disputations* 4.9.22. Hemmingsen's text differs slightly from modern editions.

[148] Hemmingsen gives the verb in Latin, while the rest of the sentence is in Greek.

[149] The quotation is from the pseudo-Aristotelian *On Virtues and Vices* 6.8 (1251a22–23). The entire (brief) treatise is quoted in Stobaeus, *Anthology* 3.1.194.

[150] Aristotle, *Nicomachean Ethics* 3.11 (1119a10–11).

[151] Plato, *Philebus* 33e10–34a1.

A sense of shame,[152] αἰδώς, that is, when one observes the proper limit, is numbered among the virtues, and is called by Cicero a sort of "tincture of virtue,"[153] who also names it "the guardian of all the virtues"[154] because it avoids shame. It should especially be praised in virgins and young men, according to a remark of Plautus: "It is fitting that a young man have a sense of shame."[155] And it is said of a young man in Terence's *Brothers*: "He blushed, the matter is safe."[156] Pythagoras handed down the following commandment concerning the sense of shame:

πρήξεις δ' αἰσχρόν ποτε μήτε μετ' ἄλλου, μήτ' ἰδίη· πάντων δὲ μάλιστ' αἰσχύνεο σαυτόν.

[Never do anything shameful either with another or by yourself. Above all have a sense of shame for yourself.][157]

This sense of shame, moreover, stays between a vicious scrupulousness and shamelessness. Vicious scrupulousness is δυσωπία—a scrupulous modesty that is excessive, and therefore vicious and disgraceful.

Shamelessness, ἀναίδεια, is clearly the worst vice, because a person dares whatever he pleases with an icy demeanor and without any scrupulousness. Those who labor under this vice Homer calls κυνῶπες if they are men, κυνώπιδες if they are women [dog-eyed, i.e., shame-

---

152 Cf. Thomas Aquinas, *Summa theologiae*, II-II, Q. 144.

153 This expression is not found in Cicero, to my knowledge. It seems to be a Latin translation of a remark attributed to Diogenes the Cynic in Diogenes Laertius, *Lives of Eminent Philosophers* 6.54. The same expression (correctly attributed) is found in the commentary of Cornelius a Lapide (1567–1637) on Ecclesiasticus 7.21; see Cornelius a Lapide, *Commentaria in Sacram Scripturam* (Naples: I. Nagar, 1855), 165.

154 Cicero, *Classification of Oratory* 23.79.

155 Plautus, *The Comedy of Asses* 833.

156 Terence, *The Brothers* 643.

157 *Golden Verses* 11–12. The passage is quoted, with some differences in modern editions, in Stobaeus, *Anthology* 3.1.11.

less], since they are endowed with a canine aspect and lack all sense of shame. Menander laments about it in the following way:

> Ὦ μεγίστη τῶν θεῶν
> νῦν οὖσ' ἀναίδει', εἰ θεὸν καλεῖν σε δεῖ,
> Δεῖ δέ, τὸ κρατοῦν γὰρ νῦν νομίζεται θεός.
> Ἐφ' ὅσον βαδίζεις; ἐφ' ὅσον ἥξειν μοι δοκεῖς;

That is:

> O greatest of the gods,
> you who now are shamelessness—if it is permitted to call
>   you a god;
> but it is right, for that which gives commands is now held to
>   be a god—
> how far will you progress? How far will I see you to
>   reach?[158]

He also says:

> κακὴ ἡ αἰδὼς ἔνθαγε ἀναιδὲς κρατεῖ.

Where shamelessness conquers, shame is considered evil.[159]

Pollux says: "He who is excessively shameless is said to have a dog's eye; if you should also add rudeness to him, you would make him a κυνόμυιαν [dogfly]."[160] By this word is signified a person most shameless, in whom is obviously joined the character of a fly with that of a dog.

---

[158] Preserved in Stobaeus, *Anthology* 3.32.11.

[159] This quotation is preserved in Stobaeus, *Anthology* 3.32.13 (the text differs slightly in modern editions), but Stobaeus' editors identify it as a fragment of a tragedian, not of Menander.

[160] This quotation must come from the *Onomasticon* of Julius Pollux, a second-century Greek grammarian, but Hemmingsen quotes it in a Latin version (except for one Greek term) that is found elsewhere, and so he presumably has an intermediary. Cf. Pierio Valeriano (1477–1558), *Hieroglyphica, seu de sacris Aegyptiorum aliarumque gentium literis commentarii* (Lyon: Frelon, 1602), 55; Valeriano also includes the one Greek term (but with cor-

Euripides speaks about this vice in the following way: ἡ μεγίστη τῶν ἐν ἀνθρώποισιν νόσων ἡ ἀναίδεια. That is, "Of all the vices there are in men, the greatest is shamelessness."[161] Xenophon bears witness that it is the chief guide on the path to every disgrace. The complaint of Theognis about it is as follows:

ἤδη νῦν αἰδὼς μὲν ἐν ἀνθρώποισιν ὄλωλεν,
αὐτὰρ ἀναιδείη γαῖαν ἐπιστρέφεται.

Among mortals all sense of shame has perished,
and shamelessness looks out over all the earth.[162]

Honor,[163] σεμνότης, watches out lest anything be done or thought about unbecomingly, effeminately, lustfully, and disgracefully. But here let us recall that that is called "honor" which deserves the name from the wise and good, not that which is observed among the masses under a fictive name: αἰσχρὸν γὰρ κρίνειν τὰ καλὰ τῷ πολλῷ ψόφῳ [for it is shameful to judge noble things by empty sound].[164] Cicero says: "When what is useful in friendship is compared with what is honorable, let the appearance of utility be of no account, and let honor have great

---

rect accent), and it is possible that he is Hemmingsen's source. There was a Latin version available in Hemmingsen's day (*Iulii Pollucis Onomasticon* [Basil: Winter, 1541) translated by Rudolphus Gualtherus, but I am unable to find this quotation in it. Pollux's work does not survive complete: "Like his other works, the *Onomasticon* in its original form has perished: the extant manuscripts are derived from four incomplete, and interpolated, copies, all descending from an early epitome possessed (and interpolated) by Arethas, archbishop of Caesarea, *c.* AD 900" (*OCD*, s.v. "Pollux, Iulius").

[161] Euripides, *Medea* 471–72 (Euripides writes νόσων πασῶν).

[162] Theognis 647–48, also preserved, in slightly different form, in Stobaeus, *Anthology* 3.32.8.

[163] Cf. Thomas Aquinas, *Summa theologiae*, II-II, Q. 145.

[164] Clement of Alexandria, *Miscellanies* 5.3 (Clement is citing the *Poetics* of the Stoic Cleanthes; modern editions of his text differ slightly from Hemmingsen's).

value."[165] He also says: "Utility must be directed by honor."[166] Again: "The honorable (something I have often spoken of), even when we see it in another, still moves us, and makes us friends with the one in whom it is seen to be present."[167] Again: "All honor depends upon attending to one's obligation, and all disgrace comes from neglecting it."[168] Therefore disgrace is opposed to honor.

Self-control,[169] ἐγκράτεια, is the virtue by which desire is ruled by the governance of deliberation. For this virtue especially moderates the pleasure of the body: food and drink and sexual pleasure. Moreover, it has the name "self-control" for the following reason: because it holds back the desires for food and drink and sexual pleasure under the rule of reason so that one does not allow himself to be conquered by them. Pythagoras' command is relevant to this:

κρατεῖν δ' ἐθίζεο τῶνδε,
γαστρὸς μὲν πρώτιστα καὶ ὕπνου λαγνείης τε
καὶ θυμοῦ.

That is:

First accustom yourself to ruling the stomach, sleep, sensual desire, and anger.[170]

---

[165] Cicero, *On Obligations* 3.46.

[166] Cicero, *On Obligations* 3.83.

[167] Cicero, *On Obligations* 1.55. Hemmingsen's text differs slightly from modern editions of Cicero.

[168] Cicero, *On Obligations* 1.4.

[169] Or "continence." Cf. Thomas Aquinas, *Summa theologiae*, II-II, Q. 155.

[170] Pythagoras, *Golden Verses* 9–11.

And Anacharsis says: γλώσσης, γαστρὸς, αἰδοίων κρατεῖν.[171] That is: "Control the tongue, the stomach, and the sexual urge."[172] And Menander: γαστρὸς πειρῶ πᾶσαν ἡνίαν κρατεῖν. That is: "Try with every bridle to control the stomach."[173] It seems right to add to this Vergil's verses as well:

Be seized by love of neither sex nor wine:
for in one and the same way wine and sex are harmful.[174]

And again:

Restrain sexual pleasure with shackles and wine with chains,
lest either injure you with its own gifts.
Wine assuages thirst; fruitful sex is serviceable
for the procreation of children; it is harmful to transgress
these intended ends.[175]

---

[171] The Greek term αἰδοίον/αἰδοῖα actually means "genitals," though Hemmingsen translates it as Venus. Hemmingsen presumably takes this saying from Diogenes Laertius, Lives of Eminent Philosophers 1.8.104, who reports that it was inscribed on Anacharsis' statue (for usage of the term, cf. 8.1.34). Anacharsis, a Scythian prince about whom our information is historically dubious, was sometimes listed as one of the Seven Wise Men. For this inscription and similar anecdotes about Anacharsis and others, see Jeremy F. Hultin, The Ethics of Obscene Speech in Early Christianity and Its Environment (Leiden: Brill, 2008), 78–81.

[172] The name Venus is often used as a euphemism for sex or sexual pleasure, and is frequently translated accordingly in this section.

[173] Menander, Sentences 81.

[174] These lines are not by Vergil; their author is unknown. The Lutheran poet Helius Eobanus Hessus (1488–1540) quotes them as well in The Species of Drunkards 26.3, but is more guarded in saying that "certain people attribute" them to Vergil. See Helius Eobanus Hessus, The Poetic Works of Helius Eobanus Hessus, vol. 3, King of Poets, 1514–17, ed. and trans. Harry Vredeveld (Leiden: Brill, 2014), 318–19.

[175] The poem from which this comes, De libidine et vino 13–16, is number 633 in the Latin Anthology (Alexander Riese, ed., Anthologia latina sive poesis

Therefore let us follow the advice of Cicero, who says: "So much food and drink should be used as refreshes the strength, not oppresses it."[176]

Lack of self-control,[177] ἀκράτεια, which is when someone does not rule over pleasures but is overcome by them and makes himself their servant, is opposed to self-control.

Sobriety,[178] νηφαλιότης, is a more specific word than self-control. For it is moderation in drinking, and is opposed to drunkenness.[179] A rational account of the Latin term is as follows: it is called "sobriety"[180] as though formed from the words "without inebriation."[181] Horace very beautifully describes the advantages of sobriety:

> Learn now what and how great are the benefits a meager diet brings; in the first place you will be healthy.[182]

He also says:

> The other man (namely, a sober man), when he has cared for his body and yielded to sleep more swiftly than speech, rises refreshed for his prescribed duties.[183]

But sobriety's praises cannot be given their due from any other source more correctly than from the disgrace and disadvantages that belong to drunkenness. "We are not able," says Cicero, "to use our

Latinae supplementum, pars prior, fasciculus II [Leipzig: Teubner, 1906]), where it is attributed to a "Vitalis." Elsewhere one finds it attributed to a "Basilius."

[176] Cicero, *On Friendship* 11.36.

[177] Cf. Thomas Aquinas, *Summa theologiae*, II-II, Q. 156.

[178] Cf. Thomas Aquinas, *Summa theologiae*, II-II, Q. 149.

[179] Cf. Thomas Aquinas, *Summa theologiae*, II-II, Q. 150.

[180] *sobrietas.*

[181] *sine ebrietate.*

[182] Horace, *Satires* 2.2.70–71. This is obviously a rather odd proof text, given that Hemmingsen has just restricted the term to drinking.

[183] Horace, *Satires* 2.2.80–81. The parenthetical clarification is Hemmingsen's.

minds correctly when filled full with much food and drink."[184] And a Greek poet says:

οἰνωθεὶς ἀνὴρ ἥσσων μὲν ὀργῆς ἐστὶ, τοῦ δὲ νοῦ κενός, φιλεῖ τε πολλὴν γλῶτταν ἐκχέας μάτην ἄκων ἀκούειν, ἄπερ ἑκὼν εἰπεῖν κακῶς.

That is:

The lover of wine is overcome by anger, but he has an empty mind, and is accustomed, when he has poured forth many words rashly, to be unwilling to hear what he was willing to say.[185]

Relevant to this is the proverb πολλάκις ἐν οἴνου κύμασι τὶς ναυαγεῖ. That is: "Often on the waves of wine a person is shipwrecked."

Aristophanes said that wine was the milk of Venus in the following words: ἡδύς τε πινεῖν οἶνος Ἀφροδίτης γάλα: "It is pleasant to drink wine, the milk of Venus."[186] And for that reason Plato established a law that no one taste wine before the completion of his eighteenth year. Next, it must be tasted only in moderation up to one's twenty-third year. He adds the following reasoning for the law: οὐ γὰρ χρὴ

---

[184] Cicero, *Tusculan Disputations* 5.35.100.

[185] Sophocles, frag. 929. Hemmingsen cites this fragment as though it were prose (that is, with no line breaks). The play from which this fragment comes is unknown. It is cited, in slightly different form, in Stobaeus, *Anthology* 3.18.1; Clement of Alexandria, *The Instructor* 2.2.4; and Plutarch, *How to Profit from Your Enemies* 5.89A. For the citations, see Hugh Lloyd-Jones, ed. and trans., *Sophocles: Fragments* (Cambridge, MA: Harvard University Press, 1996), 398. Where Stobaeus and Clement differ, Hemmingsen's text matches that of Clement, suggesting that he rather than Stobaeus is Hemmingsen's source.

[186] Aristophanes, frag. 613. The play from which this fragment comes is unknown; it is cited in Athenaeus, *The Learned Banqueters* 10.444D. See Jeffrey Henderson, ed. and trans., *Aristophanes: Fragments* (Cambridge, MA: Harvard University Press, 2008), 418.

πῦρ ὀχετεύειν, that is, "It is not right to go through fire."[187] There are also the following verses in Clement of Alexandria:

οἶνος θ' ὃς πυρὶ ἴσον ἔχει μένος εὖτ' ἂν εἰς ἄνδρας
ἔλθῃ· κυμαίνει δ' οἷα λίβυσσαν ἅλα,
βορέης ἦε νότος, τὰ δὲ πάντα κεκρυμμένα φαίνει.

[And, when it comes to men, wine has strength equal to fire;
it tosses them on the waves, as the north or south wind
   swells the Libyan sea,
and it reveals all things hidden.][188]

And Ausonius says:

Many fall by the sword, but intoxication kills more.[189]

This verse of Propertius should also be noted:

Because of wine beauty perishes; by wine is youth corrupted.[190]

Also pertinent is the following line of Menander:

πολὺς γὰρ οἶνος πολλὰ ἁμαρτάνειν ποιεῖ.

Much wine makes for many sins.[191]

---

[187] Plato, *Laws* 2.666a–b, though Plato says that it is those under *thirty* who ought to take wine only in moderation. The particular Greek phrase Hemmingsen quotes (which differs slightly from what is found in Plato's *Laws*) is also quoted in Athenaeus, *The Learned Banqueters* 10.440C.

[188] Clement of Alexandria, *The Instructor* 2.2; Hemmingsen's text differs slightly from modern editions of Clement. The passage is also cited in Athenaeus, *The Learned Banqueters* 2.36F, where it is attributed to "the Cyrenean poet."

[189] I have been unable to find this line in Ausonius. It is a commonly quoted and conventional proverb, but is unattributed in every other instance I have consulted.

[190] Propertius, *Elegies* 2.3.33.

[191] The line is found in Athenaeus, *The Learned Banqueters* 10.443F, where it is attributed not to Menander, but to the lost play *The Guardian* by the comic poet Alexis (c. 375–c. 275 BC).

And a Latin poet says:

Venus rages in *vino*,[192] fire in fire.[193]

Bayerische Staatsbibliothek München, 940490 Ph.pr. 629, fol. N7v, urn:nbn:de:bvb:12-bsb00032962-5

Chastity,[194] ἁγνία, is a religious cleanness and purity by which both the mind is clean of impure lust and the body is preserved pure. Even Aristotle considered cleanness of body without purity of mind of little account. He, when he saw Xenocrates urinating and not moving his

---

[192] I attempt to preserve the wordplay *Venus in vinis*.

[193] Ovid, *Art of Love* 1.244; Hemmingsen's text differs slightly from modern editions of Ovid. The line is quoted in the same form by Melanchthon in his commentary on book 2 of Aristotle's *Nicomachean Ethics* (CR 16:323).

[194] *castitas*. Cf. Thomas Aquinas, *Summa theologiae*, II-II, Q. 151. Hemmingsen's contrast with Aquinas, who makes virginity superior to chastity just as magnificence is superior to liberality, is instructive of a key difference between Roman Catholic and emerging Protestant sexual ethics.

hand τῷ αἰδοίῳ [to his genitals], laughingly said, χεῖρες μὲν ἀγναὶ, φρὴν δ' ἔχει μιάσματα: "His hands are chaste, but his mind is stained."[195] Nor is the chastity about which I am speaking found only in virgins, but also in honorable spouses. For that reason, Horace says, "Chastity is parents' great dowry and what keeps one back from another's husband by a sure compact."[196]

Ausonius says:

What is a matron's most beautiful dowry? A chaste life.

Who is chaste? She about whom rumor is afraid to lie.[197]

Modesty,[198] ἀγνεία,[199] is the virtue by which one abstains not only from illicit sex, but also from the signs of sex. For it is not right for only the body to be chaste, but the eyes should be as well. And for that reason it was customary for the Romans to paint and sculpt Modesty with veiled face. And by others it was likened to a tortoise shell, because it belonged to modest women to keep themselves at home and to avoid all crowded places.

To modesty is opposed ἀσέλγεια [licentiousness], which uses external signs to bear witness to a lustful mind. Hence it is that virgins and women who desire excessive ornamentation reveal the lust of their minds. For that reason, Tibullus forbids that beauty be polluted by gold, for he speaks thus:

---

[195] The anecdote is preserved in Athenaeus, *The Learned Banqueters* 12.530D. Aristotle is, in turn, quoting Euripides, *Hippolytus* 316.

[196] Horace, *Odes* 3.24.21–23. Hemmingsen's citation is elliptical and differs slightly from modern editions of Horace's text, thus requiring a modified translation.

[197] [Ausonius], *Sayings of the Sages* 1.4–5. This work, not actually by Ausonius, is part of the *Appendix Ausoniana*.

[198] *pudicicia*. Cf. Thomas Aquinas, *Summa theologiae*, II-II, Q. 160.

[199] Hemmingsen spells the word ἀγνία, which he has just used above to render the term *castitas* ("chastity").

How often have I warned, "Don't pollute beauty with gold;
often many evils are accustomed to follow close behind
gold!"[200]

A certain writer quite charmingly[201] handled womanly καινοσπουδίαν [fondness for style] via the following dilemma: "If women are beautiful, nature is sufficient; let not art contend against nature, that is, let not pretense strive with the truth. If they are shameful by nature, what they add serves to prove their ugliness the more."[202] Therefore it is right to embrace simplicity. And the painter Apelles[203] justly rebuked his pupil who was painting Helen adorned with gold. "Young man," he said, "because you were not able to paint her as beautiful, you made her rich."[204]

Humility,[205] ταπεινοφροσύνη, holds back and restrains overbold impulses, lest we promise ourselves more than is proper. Concerning this virtue, the following verses of Menander should be noted:

ἄνθρωπον ὄντα σαυτὸν ἀναμίμνησκ' ἀεί.
βούλου δὲ ἀρέσκειν πᾶσι, μὴ σαυτῷ μόνον.
εἰ θνητὸς εἶ, βέλτιστε, θνητὰ καὶ φρόνει,
θνητὸς πεφυκὼς μὴ φρονῇς ὑπέρθεα.
ἐν δὲ εὐπροσηγόροισιν ἐστί τις χάρις.
ἴσος μὲν ἴσθι πᾶσι, κἂν πρόυχῃς βίῳ.

---

[200] Tibullus, *Elegies* 1.9.17–18.

[201] There is a play on words here: "charmingly" renders *venuste*, which is related to *Venus*, the name of the goddess of love and Hemmingsen's term for sexual pleasure.

[202] Clement of Alexandria, *The Instructor* 2.13.

[203] Apelles of Colophon (afterwards of Ephesus), the most famous of ancient Greek painters, flourished in the fourth century BC.

[204] The anecdote is preserved in Clement of Alexandria, *The Instructor* 2.13.

[205] Cf. Thomas Aquinas, *Summa theologiae*, II-II, Q. 161.

That is:

> Always remember that you are a man;
> desire to please all, not yourself alone.
> If you are mortal, dear friend, then think on mortal things.
> Born a mortal, be not wiser than the divine power;
> a certain grace is present in those who pay reverence in a
>   comely way.
> Show yourself to be like to all, though you excel them in
>   life.[206]

Ovid commends humility in the same way in the following verses:

> If in anything you believe a friend who has been taught by
>   experience,
> live for yourself, and keep great names at a distance.
> Live for yourself and, as much as you are able, avoid all
>   that gleams;
> a cruel thunderbolt comes from the gleaming citadel.
> The lowered sail yard escapes the winter's gales,
> and wide sails harbor more fear than small ones.
> You see how the light bark floats on the top of the wave
> when the heavy load plunges the woven nets underwater
>   with itself.[207]

And again:

> Why was it that Daedalus mounted safely on his wings
> while Icarus marks a huge sea with his name?
> Because, of course, the latter was flying high, the former at
>   a lower altitude,
> for neither had wings that were really their own.

---

[206] Menander, *Sentences* 18, 102, 246, 346, 265, 358. Hemmingsen's text differs slightly from modern editions of the *Sentences*.

[207] Ovid, *Tristia* 3.4.3–6, 9–12. Hemmingsen's text differs slightly from modern editions of Ovid.

Believe me, he who has hidden well has lived well, and
each one ought to remain where Fortune has placed him.[208]

Ausonius gives a beautiful example in the case of Agathocles, the
Syracusan king:

> The story is that King Agathocles dined from earthen
>   vessels,
> and that he often loaded his sideboard with Samian
>   clay.[209]
> To one who asked the reason he answered, "I who am now
>   king
> of Sicily was born of a father who was a potter.
> Hold your good fortune with modesty, if you suddenly
> rise to riches from a place of poverty."[210]

Propertius says:

> Mind you that one oar graze the water, the other the shore;
> you will be safe—the greatest tumult occurs in the midst of
>   the sea.[211]

Opposed to humility is pride, ὑπερηφανία: pride is a vice that causes
blindness, and it is the worst of all, for it makes it so that no one looks
to the injunction "Know yourself,"[212] and it is the cause of many evils;
finally it brings destruction upon itself. Greek and Latin authors wrote
many things against this beast; I shall include a few from their records.

---

[208] Ovid, *Tristia* 3.4.21–26. Hemmingsen's text differs slightly from modern editions of Ovid.

[209] The "sideboard" referred to by this word (*abacus*) was normally made of marble or precious metals and was used to display vessels made of precious metals; see LS, s.v. "abacus" I.

[210] Ausonius, *Epigrams on Various Matters* 2.1–2, 5–8.

[211] Propertius, *Elegies* 3.3.23–24.

[212] Note Hemmingsen's use of the Delphic Oracle earlier in the Preface to the Reader (p. 19–21).

In the first place let me bring forward Menander, who speaks as follows:

> ὦ τρισάθλιοι
> ἄπαντες οἱ φθσῶντες ἐφ᾽ ἑαυτοῖς μέγα,
> αὐτοὶ γὰρ οὐκ ἴσασιν ἀνθρώπου φύσιν.

> Thrice wretched
> are all those who are puffed up and think highly
> of themselves, for they do not know the nature of man.[213]

He also says:

> ἀλαζονίας οὔτις ἐκφεύγει δίκην.

That is:

> No one will escape the punishment owed to arrogance.[214]

And again:

> ἐφ᾽ ᾧ φρονεῖς μέγιστον, ἀπολεῖ τοῦτό σε.

> What you are most prideful about will destroy you.[215]

Another Greek comic poet says:

> εἰ καὶ βασιλεὺς πέφυκας, ὡς θνητὸς ἄκοθσον,
> ἂν μακρὰ πτύῃς, φλέγματι ᾧ κρατῇ περισσῷ,
> ἂν εὐματῇς, ταῦτα, πρό σοῦ προβάτιον εἶχεν,
> ἂν χρυσοφορῇς, τοῦτο τύχης ἐστὶν ἔπαρμα,
> ἂν πλούσιος ᾖς, τοῦτο χρόνου ἄδικος ἰσχὺς,
> ἂν ἀλαζονῇς, τοῦτο ἀνοίας ἐστὶ φρύαγμα.

---

[213] Menander, frag. 251 (Körte-Thierfelder) 1–3, preserved in Stobaeus, *Anthology* 3.22.11.

[214] Menander, *Sentences* 35. Hemmingsen's text differs slightly from modern editions of the *Sentences*.

[215] Menander, frag. 144 (Körte-Thierfelder) 1, preserved in Stobaeus, *Anthology* 3.22.28.

That is:

> Although you are a king, hear that you are mortal.
> If you train for a long time, you generate too much
>   phlegm, which hinders you.
> If you wear good clothing, a little sheep wore it before.
> If you wear gold, it is the haughtiness of fortune.
> If you are rich, it is the unjust violence of time.
> If you are proud, it is the din of madness.[216]

This foul beast is the most unwelcome companion of the virtues, and whatever it touches it basely befouls, according to the familiar verses:

> Although abundance, wisdom, and beauty be given to you,
> pride alone, if it should be your companion, destroys all
>   things.[217]

And Claudian says:

> When pride is present, it defiles good morals.[218]

And again:

>   because pride has departed
> far from you, a common vice when affairs are favorable
> and an unpleasant companion of the virtues.[219]

---

[216] These lines, attributed to the poet Sotades, are preserved in Stobaeus, *Anthology* 3.22.26. Hemmingsen's text differs slightly from modern editions of the *Anthology*.

[217] A frequently cited piece of proverbial wisdom, found, for example, in Albertano of Brescia's *Ars loquendi et tacendi*.

[218] Claudian, *Panegyric on the Fourth Consulship of the Emperor Honorius* 305.

[219] Claudian, *On Stilicho's Consulship* 2.161–63. Hemmingsen's text differs slightly from modern editions of Claudian.

Seneca says:

> Rule fearfully, raise your spirits high!
> God the avenger follows the prideful from behind.[220]

Clemency or gentleness, πραότης, is the virtue by which minds that have been rashly stirred up toward hatred of someone are restrained by kindness. About this virtue Cicero says: "Nothing is more praiseworthy, nothing is more worthy of a great and illustrious man, than readiness to forgive and clemency; yet we should approve of clemency in such a way that, for the sake of the commonwealth, severity (without which the state cannot be governed) can still be applied."[221] And again, "Cruelty is an object of hatred to everyone; piety and clemency are objects of love."[222] Terence says: "Truly, I have found that nothing is better for man than affability and clemency."[223]

Ovid writes:

> It is a royal thing, believe me, to help those who have
> fallen.[224]

In book 3 of the *Tristia* he also says:

> The greater a man is, the more can he be soothed from his
> anger,

---

[220] Seneca, *Hercules* 384–85. Hemmingsen inexplicably reads *timidus* ("fearful") in every edition I have consulted instead of Seneca's *tumidus* ("swollen [with pride]"), which ruins the sense. One might just catch Seneca's original meaning (which would have cohered better with Hemmingsen's discussion) by reading "fearfully" in the sense of "as an object of fear [to your subjects]," though the Latin adjective cannot bear that meaning.

[221] Cicero, *On Obligations* 1.88. I read *adhibeatur* with the *Opuscula theologica*, rather than *adbibeatur*, found in the 1564 edition.

[222] Cicero, *Letters to Friends* 216.2 (15.19).

[223] Terence, *The Brothers* 860–61. Hemmingsen's text differs slightly from modern editions of Terence.

[224] Ovid, *Letters from Pontus* 2.9.11.

and a noble mind can be easily moved.
It is enough for the courageous lion to have laid bodies low;
his fight has its end when his enemy lies defeated.
But the wolf and disgraceful bears, and any savage beast
of lesser nobility, pursue the dying.[225]

Claudian commends this virtue to the consul Honorius in the following words:

First of all be pious. For although we should be
surpassed in every
duty, clemency alone makes us equal to the gods.[226]

He also recites the advantages of this virtue in the following verses:

She[227] also strengthens friendships to last long into the
future,
and binds them with adamant that will endure, nor does
she change her nature
as though it were fickle, nor does she allow bonds to be
loosened
by trivial murmurings of injury, nor is she persuaded to
scorn an old friend
when a new one comes; she is ready to keep kindnesses
in mind and to cast off offenses,
and equally mindful of favors small and great she labors
to outdo them;
and as she conquers enemies with arms, so does she
conquer friends
by her services. She cherishes the absent, she alone takes
thought

---

225 Ovid, *Tristia* 3.5.31–36.

226 Claudian, *Panegyric on the Fourth Consulship of the Emperor Honorius*, 276–77.

227 Hemmingsen clearly means *Clementia*, "Clemency," but Claudian is writing of a personified *Fides*, "Good Faith" or "Trustworthiness."

for those far off, she does not open an ear eager for
    rumors,
in order that treacherous grumblings that would harm a
    weak client
may not make your feelings averse to him.
Her love that is joined to the living does not allow her to
    forget the dead;
the kindness shown by fathers she passes on to their
    offspring.[228]

To clemency is opposed inclemency, ἀπήνεια, a cruelty and savagery against either the conquered, or the subject, or the accused.

Propriety, κοσμιότης, is the virtue by which an honorable sense of good manners acquires an evident and stable authority. It maintains the harmony of things in opinion, speech, gesture, and action. With it conflict boastful pride,[229] vanity or bragging, talkativeness, empty triviality, buffoonery, impudence, obscenity, and lewdness; likewise luxury and tastelessness in dress, and more especially meddlesomeness or πολυπραγμοσύνη, about which the following verse speaks:

τῆς πολυπραγμοσύνης οὐδὲν χερεώτερον ἄλλο.

That is:

Nothing is worse than meddlesomeness.[230]

Εὐταξία [good order] preserves order in actions, without which nothing is agreeable; nothing is pleasing; nothing, finally, is worthy of praise. To this is opposed ἀταξία [disorder].

---

[228] Claudian, *On Stilicho's Consulship* 2.38–52. Hemmingsen's text differs slightly from modern editions of Claudian.

[229] The word Hemmingsen uses for "boastful," *Thrasonica*, is a reference to the character Thraso in Terence's *Eunuch*.

[230] This (unattributed) line was also cited above where Hemmingsen discussed πολυπραγμοσύνη in connection with idleness.

Decorum, τὸ πρεπὸν,[231] is united to εὐταξία [good order]—except that, just as the latter properly belongs to things, so decorum belongs to persons, although this difference does not always hold. To it is opposed indecorum, ἀπρέπεια [unfittingness].

Αὐτάρκεια [self-sufficiency] is the virtue by which someone is content with what is his own and does not desire anything from elsewhere. It is a virtue that is really quite rare, but it is particularly to be praised. It is the enemy of greed, wastefulness, luxury, pride, and many other vices.

Moderation, μετριότης, is the handmaid of self-sufficiency. For it prevents anyone from requiring excessively fancy things. He who is αὐτάρκης [self-sufficient] moderates all things so that he satisfies nature rather than lust.

Let these stand as my brief remarks about the four kinds of virtues and their parts and duties—virtues whose seeds (as the Stoics used to say) are conferred on us by nature, greater in some, lesser in others. They affirmed, moreover, that they should be cultivated, increased, and perfected by instruction, training, and practice, which I judge that I have clearly shown. I have spoken, too, about the vices that are opposed to them,[232] in order that the glory of the virtues may be better perceived by comparison. My remarks, however, find their conclusion in the following demonstration:

Whatever is appropriate for a man according to right reason must be sought out, and what conflicts with reason must be avoided. The virtues are appropriate, and the vices are not. Therefore, as the former must be sought out, so the latter must be avoided.

The major premise is the principle declared above. The minor premise is inferred from the enumeration of effects. For the effects preserve the state and dignity of man, and likewise they render house-

---

[231] The Greek phrase means "the fitting" (cf. the Latin verb *decet*, "it is fitting," to which the Latin noun *decorum*, whence we have the English *decorum*, is related).

[232] I read *oppositis* with the 1564 edition rather than *expositis* with, for example, the *Opuscula theologica*.

holds and commonwealths stable; whereas the vices that are contrary to them not only conflict with the dignity of man, but also overturn houses and commonwealths, as experience shows.

Here it can rightly be asked whether all the things that are concluded from the principles of the law of nature are necessary or not. To this question I answer that they are all necessary, but some are necessary as to species, others as to genus. The conclusions that are constructed correctly from the principles are necessary and immovable, such that whatever is established by any man contrary to the conclusions that have been constructed correctly is contrary to the law of nature. A law was passed by Semiramis that people can take their relatives as wives, which a most shameful woman did in order to enjoy the embraces of her son, by whom she was also killed.[233] Those who married relatives (such as mothers, sisters, etc.) in accordance with this law are not excused by this tyrannical and impious law—nay, rather, they are condemned by the law of nature. And for that reason whatever is concluded as honorable from the axioms of the law of nature is honorable, and whatever is concluded as shameful must always be considered shameful.

Other conclusions are necessary as to genus, not species. These can be changed as to species while the genus remains. Very many laws of emperors and princes who consistently have regard for the integrity of the commonwealth and ordain their laws in order to strengthen it are of this kind. Let the following law serve as an example: "Let no foreigner climb the wall of the city." This law is necessary as to genus, not species. As to genus, it is necessary insofar as it contributes to the common good and to preserving the integrity of the commonwealth. As to species, however, it is not necessary, because this determination is not directly concluded from the axioms of nature. It could also happen that a law is passed by which a foreigner is obligated to climb the wall, which obviously conflicts with the first law, but as to species and not genus.

---

[233] The Assyrian queen Semiramis was both a historical figure (i.e., Sammu-ramat) and a figure of Greek legend. Among ancient sources, she is discussed by Diodorus Siculus, *Library of History* 2.4–20.

Let me add another example. There was formerly a law that said: "Let no one charge any interest." This law is necessary as to genus, not species. As to genus, insofar as it is in service to the integrity of the commonwealth and is advantageous to the citizens, it is necessary. But as to species it is not necessary, because it can happen that, due to men's vice, it does not obtain its purposed end, that is, that it is neither useful for the commonwealth nor advantageous to the citizens. If, therefore, in order to head off a greater disadvantage the magistrate permits the taking of moderate interest, such as 5 percent, in order that the citizens may be aided by this system and in order that he himself may be mindful of the health of the commonwealth, he does not overturn the previous law as to genus,[234] although he allows permission as to species. For this reason, it must be carefully observed which hypotheses are necessary as to species or ἁπλῶς [simply], and which are necessary only as to genus or κατά τι [in a qualified sense]. This distinction can resolve many questions, and shows that, although all honorable laws are constructed from the axioms of the law of nature, it is nevertheless not necessary that we have the same laws as the Gauls, or the Italians, or the Germans as to species.

For even an ἀνυπεύθυνος [unaccountable][235] magistrate will be able to establish useful laws for his own commonwealth, provided that he does nothing against the norm of nature—even more than that, the same magistrate can have some laws in some jurisdictions under his dominion, and other laws in other jurisdictions, if either the condition of the people or the consideration of regional peculiarities[236] seems to demand it. These different laws, although they vary from each other as to species, nevertheless agree most beautifully as to genus, and are not opposed to each other. Therefore the magistrate should apply himself with care to passing laws that are both agreeable to the law of nature and useful for the health of the commonwealth. I mean this to be understood, however, in such a way that it does not result in a rash

---

[234] I.e., the previous law forbidding the charging of interest.

[235] For the term, the equivalent of the Latin *dictator*, cf. Aristotle, *Politics* 4.10 (1295a20) and LSJ, s.v. ἀνυπεύθυνος.

[236] *ratio proprietatum.*

change of the laws in commonwealths that have been constituted well. For laws confirmed by the long duration of time and the authority of the ancients ought now to be considered sacrosanct, such that it is wicked to change them.

It is also possible to respond to the proposed question in the following way. Nature dictates that certain things must necessarily be done; similarly, it judges that certain things must necessarily be avoided; and certain things it leaves in the middle between the two.

The things that nature dictates as necessarily having to be done are, when they are done, just everywhere and among all, and this by nature, not by opinion. The proper actions of all the virtues that[237] are constructed from the axioms of nature by demonstration are of this type.

The things that nature judges as necessarily having to be avoided are, when they are done, unjust everywhere and among all, and this by nature, and not by opinion. All actions that deviate even the least bit from the proper actions of the virtues are of this kind.

The things that are left in the middle between the two are free, in such a way that the one who either does them or omits them is called neither just nor unjust. To this category pertain the actions that are placed neither among the vices nor among the virtues. The law of nature leaves it free as to either climbing or not climbing the wall of the city. But when, in a matter that the law of nature has left free, a decree of the magistrate has been added by which it is forbidden that anyone climb the wall, he who, having scorned the decree of the magistrate, climbs the wall anyway must be considered a transgressor of justice and the law; and, on the other hand, he who refrains on account of the magistrate's edict must be considered just in this part of the law.

It can be asked about this third type whether, once a law has been passed, it is unjust by nature to climb the wall. If it is not unjust by nature, it seems to be unjust only by opinion. I say that it was free by nature, and for that reason was neither just nor unjust, but after the word of the magistrate was added, which, looking to the end of nature—that is, to the integrity of the commonwealth—forbade what

---

[237] The antecedent is "actions," not "virtues."

was free, whoever violates this law transgresses the bounds of nature, and I pronounce the deed unjust by nature, not indeed ἁπλῶς [simply], but κατὰ τι [in a qualified sense], that is, on account of the end that nature looks to in actions pertaining to the preservation of the integrity of human society.

6

The Conscience

But because the conscience is the witness and judge of things done badly and well, it remains to say a few words about it. The conscience, which, according to the proverb, is like a thousand witnesses, is truly a wondrous creation of God in men. It not only bears witness concerning the law of nature, which commands honorable things and prohibits their opposites, as I have thus far explained. It also sets us before the tribunal of God, as it were, accusing us of some things, praising us for others, punishing at one time, excusing at another.[1]

Moreover, although sometimes the conscience lies hid as though asleep, it nevertheless is frequently aroused by adversities as if by a whip, according to the remark of Sophocles:

παθόντες ἂν ξυγγνοῖμεν ἡμαρτηκότες.

That is:

> When we are afflicted, consciousness of our crimes is
> aroused.[2]

---

[1] Cf. Rom. 2:15.

[2] Sophocles, *Antigone* 926.

And Lucretius says:

> But in the present life there is fear of punishments for evil
> deeds—
> fear that is extraordinary for deeds that are extraordinary—
> and an expiation for crimes:
> prison, and the horrible hurling from the rock,[3]
> lashes, executioners, the Tullian jail,[4] pitch, red-hot plates,[5]
> torture torches.
> Nevertheless, even if these are absent, yet the mind,
> conscious of what has been done,
> fears before it has been punished, and applies the goads
> and sears itself with whips.[6]

And Pindar in the *Pythian Odes* says:

> ἐντὶ μὲν θνατῶν φρένες ὠκύτεραι
> κέρος αἰνῆσαι πρὸ δίκας δόλιον,
> τραχεῖαν ἑρπόντων πρὸς ἐπίβδαν δ᾽ ὅμως.[7]

That is, in Philip Melanchthon's translation: "The minds of men are too swift to praise deceitful gain rather than justice, although they are creeping toward a harsh outcome after the festival."[8] Ἐπίβδη [the day after a festival], which Philip calls *postfestum* [after the festival], is the day that follows some festival filled with banquets, at which men

---

[3] I.e., the Tarpeian Rock on the Capitoline Hill in Rome, from which murderers and traitors were hurled to their deaths.

[4] I.e., the *Tullianum*, "the underground execution cell of the prison at Rome"; prisoners of state were killed here (*OCD*, s.v. "Tullianum").

[5] These *laminae ardentes* were "instruments of torture for slaves" (see LS, s.v. "lamina" II.A).

[6] Lucretius, *On the Nature of Things* 3.1014–19.

[7] Pindar, *Pythian Odes* 4.139–41. Hemmingsen's text differs slightly from modern editions of Pindar.

[8] The remark is found in Philip Melanchthon, *Interpretatio Pythiorum Pindari* (CR 19:223).

have made themselves merry and given themselves too liberally to drinking. When he says that this will be harsh—namely, because of drunkenness—he signifies that the result will be that those who have done badly will, at some point after the doing of their deeds, be tormented by the consciousness of their crimes, and will pay the penalty.

But in order that young men may be correctly advised about this creation of God, it must first of all be maintained that its seat is in the mind. In the mind, moreover, there are three faculties that are relevant to this matter.

In the first place is the understanding that they call "contemplative," whose duty consists in contemplation; and this is the better part of the mind, which Aristotle says always exhorts and provokes to better things. Συντήρησις [synteresis][9]—that which supplies propositions—is placed in it. For, since this συντήρησις [synteresis] is the guardian and preserver of the notions[10] that are innate in us concerning things done in the correct way and in the opposite way, it always attends to what is advantageous or disadvantageous; and for that reason it is said to supply the propositions for practical syllogisms, which are of the following kind: honorable things must be done; shameful things must not be done. These, moreover, are the two primary axioms that the συντήρησις [synteresis] discloses concerning actions in accordance with the law of nature. From these, very many hypotheses are constructed afterwards that provide propositions for the practical syllogism. I constructed many propositions of this kind from those primary axioms in the earlier part of this work.

In the second place in the mind is the practical understanding, whose duty consists in acting. The conscience, which discloses the minor premises that are in service to the practical syllogism in accordance with the specific differences of actions, is located in it. In the case of Hector,[11] the συντήρησις [synteresis] supplies the major premise: honorable things must be done. The conscience discloses the following

<hr>

[9] I.e., "preservation." See LSJ, s.v. συντήρησις.

[10] *noticiarum*, the plural of the noun translated as "knowledge" (*noticia*) in Hemmingsen's definition of the law of nature.

[11] The chief defender of Troy in Homer's *Iliad*.

minor premise: to defend one's country and to die bravely on its behalf is honorable. The συντήρησις [synteresis] furnished the following major premise to Oedipus:[12] shameful deeds must be avoided, and especially the worst of them must be avoided. His conscience, however, brought forth the following minor premise: incestuous intercourse with one's mother and parricide are most shameful deeds. And likewise in other actions the συντήρησις [synteresis] supplies the major premise and the conscience supplies the minor premise for the practical syllogism.

In the third place in the mind is τὸ κριτήριον, that is, the faculty of judging. This is what judges whether deeds are worthy of praise or punishment. It judges honorable deeds to be worthy of praise and reward in accordance with their degree of honor and, in contrast, it condemns shameful deeds and pronounces them worthy of penalty in accordance with their degree of shamefulness. This κριτήριον [faculty of judging] therefore adds a judgment to the major premise that the συντήρησις [synteresis] supplies. Next, the conscience adds a minor premise regarding the deed about which the judge makes pronouncement in the conclusion, in the following way. In the case of Hector, the συντήρησις [synteresis], when the κριτήριον [faculty of judging] has been applied, supplies the following premise: honorable deeds are worthy of praise. The conscience adds as a minor premise: to defend one's country and to die bravely on its behalf is an honorable deed. Τὸ κριτήριον, or the judge, concludes: therefore, to defend one's country and to die bravely on its behalf is worthy of praise.

And again, in the case of Oedipus, the συντήρησις [synteresis], when the faculty of judging has been applied, supplies the following major premise: the most shameful deeds are worthy of the most weighty punishments. The same one's conscience adds a minor premise: incestuous intercourse with one's mother and parricide are most shameful deeds. Τὸ κριτήριον [the faculty of judging] concludes: therefore, incestuous intercourse with one's mother and parricide are most worthy of the most weighty punishments.

---

[12] In the Theban cycle of Greek myth, Oedipus unwittingly killed his father and (again, unwittingly) married his mother. When the truth was discovered, his wife, Jocasta, killed herself and Oedipus gouged out his eyes (see below).

Happiness followed the former syllogism in the mind of Hector, which greatly soothed his heart in the midst of the most weighty dangers—nay, rather, it so freed it that he was no longer afraid to die on behalf of his country. For when Polydamas was advising him not to wage war against the Greeks, he answered: εἷς οἰωνὸς ἄριστος ἀμύνεσθαι περὶ πάτρης [One auspice is best: to fight for one's country].[13] To such a degree that outstanding hero, relying on his good conscience concerning his deed, fortified himself against the troubles present in the dangers he had undertaken for the sake of defending his country. For when the augur was announcing that the flight of the birds signified a gloomy outcome, Hector courageously answered: "Whether the birds should fly to the right toward the east or to the left toward the west, ἡμεῖς δὲ μεγαλοῖο Διὸς πειθώμεθα βουλῇ," that is, "we are prepared to obey the plan of great Jupiter"[14]—calling the heroic impulse of his mind, by which he was driven toward the illustrious and honorable accomplishing of his task, the "plan of Jupiter." Nor, indeed, did he think that there was any time at which the things that are honorable ought not to be done, especially when the safety of one's country was the matter at hand. For this is in accordance with the maxim of Euripides: ὅ τι καλὸν φίλον ἀεί, "What is honorable is always pleasing."[15]

Such great grief followed the latter syllogism in the mind of Oedipus, king of the Thebans, that he, not enduring the shame perpetrated by himself on himself, himself[16] gouged out his eyes when confronted with his grief.

Indeed, Oedipus was a heroic man, who, although he scorned the prophet Tiresias without hesitation when he confronted him with his incestuous marriage, nevertheless was so overcome by the witness of his conscience alone that he recognized himself to be guilty and ruined. For Menander truly says:

ὁ συνιστορῶν αὑτῷ τι, κἂν ᾖ θρασύτατος,
ἡ σύνεσις αὐτὸν δειλότατον εἶναι ποιεῖ.

---

[13] Homer, *Iliad* 12.243.

[14] Homer, *Iliad* 12.239–41.

[15] Euripides, *Bacchae* 881, 901.

[16] I preserve Hemmingsen's emphasis with the threefold "himself."

That is:

> If someone is conscious of some evil, although he be very bold, conscience nevertheless makes him very fearful.[17]

Therefore the state of the conscience varies according to the nature of one's deeds. For a good conscience follows deeds done rightly, as in the case of Hector, but, as in the case of Oedipus, a bad conscience follows shameful deeds. Plato discusses both of these things most elegantly in the first book of the *Republic*. He says:

> When someone seems near to death, dread and anxiety over things he had not previously thought about suddenly attacks him. And the accounts that are given of the Underworld—namely, that it is right that those who have harmed others here pay the penalty there—up to this point had seemed laughable fairy tales, but now they torment the mind of the one who is sick, and he himself, now much nearer to the Underworld, whether from the weakness of old age or from some other cause, considers what occurs there. Therefore, full of suspicion and dread, he reflects and ponders in his mind whether he has harmed anyone. But if he realizes that he has done many things unjustly in his life, he, roused again and again from the sleep as children are, is in dread and lives with apprehension. But for the one who is conscious of no injustice, ἡδεῖα ἐλπὶς ἀεὶ πάρεστι καὶ ἀγαθὴ γηροτρόφος [hope that is sweet and a fine nourisher of old age is ever present], as Pindar also says.[18]

---

[17] Menander, frag. 522 (Körte-Thierfelder) 1–2, preserved in Stobaeus, *Anthology* 3.24.3.

[18] Plato, *Republic* 1.330d5–331a3, quoting Pindar, frag. 214.

And just afterwards he says:

> And for the one who has passed his life justly and piously,
> sweet hope is his companion, nourisher of his heart and nurse
> of his old age.[19]

In the ninth *Nemean Ode*, Pindar also says:

> ἐκ πόνων δ' οἱ σὺν νεότατι γένωνται, σύν τε δίκᾳ τελέθει πρὸς
> γήρας αἰὼν ἀμέρα.

That is:

> From just labors in one's youth comes a pleasing time of old
> age.[20]

The tragedian Sophocles writes that Oedipus, when he had been blinded, arrived at Athens by the leading of his daughter Antigone, and there was buried in the temple of the Erinyes.[21] By this story, he signifies that those who have lived a shameful life will finally die with a bad conscience. The Erinyes, moreover, are nothing other than the disturbances of the mind due to a bad conscience that always accompany shameful deeds. And for this reason the Erinyes are called μνήμονες, that is, mindful, because they never forget just punishment for the crimes that have been committed. Although it is inflicted rather slowly, nevertheless the Erinyes always ensure that punishment is felt when it is least expected.

Moreover, the Erinys is named ἀπὸ τῆς ἔριδος καὶ νοῦ, that is, as if from the strife and contention of the mind, which Vergil mentions in *Aeneid*, book 2: "whither the gloomy Erinys, whither the roar of war calls."[22] Hence it is that those who have committed grave crimes, although they promise security to themselves for a time, nevertheless

---

[19] Plato, *Republic* 1.331a4–8, quoting Pindar, frag. 214.

[20] Pindar, *Nemean Odes* 9.44.

[21] I.e., the Furies.

[22] Vergil, *Aeneid* 2.337–38.

are thrown into turmoil when the smallest danger has been put before them. On the other hand, those who are conscious of no evil have good hope even in the greatest dangers. To this pertains that saying of Menander:

βροντῆς ἀκούσας μηδαμῶς πόρρω φύγῃς,
μηδὲν συνειδὼς αὐτὸς ἑαυτῷ.

That is:

You who are conscious of no evil, there is no reason why you should run away when you have heard thunder.[23]

The Latin poets too have handed down memorable maxims about the conscience. Ovid, in the *Fasti*, writes:

As is the state of each person's conscience, so it conceives in the heart either hope or dread in keeping with his deed.[24]

Here the poet beautifully distinguishes between the conscience and its effect.

The conscience, which refers to a mind with knowledge of itself, means the faculty that adjusts the deed to the rule—a thing that occurs in the minor premise of the practical syllogism. It makes hope and dread the effects of this faculty: hope, which is the expectation of future good and which follows the consciousness of deeds done rightly; and dread, which fears future evil or punishment. For this latter accompanies the consciousness of evil deeds. Horace, in the first book of the *Epistles*, says:

---

[23] Pseudo-Justin, *On the Sole Government of God* 4. In fact, Pseudo-Justin is quoting Philemon, not Menander.

[24] Ovid, *Fasti* 1.486–87. Hemmingsen has already cited these lines as part of a much longer quotation in chapter 5, on endurance.

But boys when they are playing say, "You will be king,
if you should do right. Let this be a bronze wall:
to be conscious of no evil, to grow pale at no fault."[25]

Ausonius says:

What is the supreme good? A mind that is conscious of having
done right.[26]

Ovid again:

The conscience, aware of being in the right, laughs at rumor's
lies.
But we, the masses, are gullible to believe a vicious report.[27]

Here the poet clearly distinguishes between cause and effect. The same
one, in the first book of the *Letters from Pontus*, writes:

My mind is eaten away as a ship infected with secret rot,
as salt water hollows out the cliffs by the sea,
as stored iron is corroded by scurfy rust,
as a book in a cabinet is grazed on by the worm's mouth:
so my heart has the continual biting of anxieties,
by which it is consumed without end.
Nor will these goads leave my mind before my very life does,
and the one who is in pain will die more quickly than the pain
itself.[28]

---

[25] Horace, *Epistles* 1.1.59–61.

[26] Pseudo-Ausonius, *Sayings of the Seven Wise Men* 1. (The author of this poem, long attributed to Ausonius, is unknown.)

[27] Ovid, *Fasti* 4.311–12.

[28] Ovid, *Letters from Pontus* 1.69–76. Hemmingsen's text differs slightly from modern editions of Ovid.

And Juvenal says:

> Why, nevertheless, would you think
> that these have escaped, whom the mind, conscious of the awful
>   deed,
> holds in terror? And it strikes them with noiseless lash,
> while the heart as torturer shakes a hidden whip.
> It is, moreover, a terrible punishment, much more savage than
>   those
> that either grave Caeditius or Rhadamanthus have discovered,
> night and day to carry around one's own prosecuting witness in
>   one's heart.[29]

And Lucan says:

> Alas, how great a punishment the mind conscious of evil gives to
> a wretched man.[30]

Plautus, in *The Braggart Soldier*, writes:

> But this deed vexes me, wretched,
> and it torments my heart and body.[31]

---

[29] Juvenal, *Satires* 13.192–98. The identity of Caeditius ("Caedicius" in modern editions) is unknown. Rhadamanthus appears regularly as a judge in the Underworld (as, e.g., in Plato's *Gorgias* 523e, referred to in Justin Martyr, *First Apology* 8).

[30] Lucan, *Civil War* 7.784. This is Hemmingsen's meaning, though it is the opposite of Lucan's, for whom *donat*, here translated as "gives," means "forgives" or "excuses" in this context. This provides good evidence that Hemmingsen at least sometimes, and quite probably often, is citing his sources at second hand. Likewise, the next citation, from Plautus, is much more lighthearted in its context than one might gather from the way in which Hemmingsen quotes it.

[31] Plautus, *The Braggart Soldier* 616–17.

He also says:

> Nothing is more wretched than a mind
> conscious of having done evil.[32]

The poets' sentiments of this kind concerning the good and evil conscience should be more carefully observed and committed to memory in order that we, when we have been warned by them, might more carefully take heed to ourselves lest we stain our conscience with any crime, since, when once it has been been stained, it grows more filthy by the day. Consequently, let us remember the words of Seneca: "It profits nothing to have our conscience shut up inside; we lie open to God; there is no place for a lie, no place for dissimulation."[33]

Here it can deservedly be asked, especially by those ignorant of church teaching, how it comes about that, although man's συντήρησις [synteresis] always prompts him toward the things that are honorable and warns away from their opposites, the majority are carried off into vices and do, against the judgment of the mind, those things that they will later have to repent of. Here some bring forward some causes, others bring forward others, as regularly happens in obscure matters. I shall mention these briefly, although I touched on them at the beginning of the work.

Some are of the opinion that the necessity of fate is the cause of all motions in men, and that it is administered by the three Fates and the accompanying Furies, whose minds are endowed with good memory. Thus the chorus in Aeschylus' *Prometheus Bound* asks: τὶς οὖν ἀνάγκης οἰακοστρόφος; That is: "Who, then, is the governor of necessity?" Prometheus answers: Μοῖραι τρίμορφοι καὶ μνήμονες ἐρίννυες, "The

---

[32] Plautus, *The Ghost* 544. Hemmingsen's text differs from modern editions of Plautus.

[33] Lactantius, *Divine Institutes* 6.24. Lactantius quotes this passage from Seneca (which does not survive elsewhere) twice in this section; the latter part ("there is no place for a lie, no place for dissimulation") appears to belong to Lactantius, and only occurs the second time.

three Fates and the mindful Furies."[34] The Stoics are of the opinion that even God is bound by the necessity of fate. But since this opinion clearly conflicts with experience and with laws both divine and human, and makes God himself the slave of fate, it deserves to be hissed off stage[35] and detested.

Some, although they exempt God from the laws of fate, are nevertheless of the opinion that he himself is the author of all things, both good and evil. They say that he gives two evils to men when he bestows one good. From this belief comes the saying of Pindar: ἓν παρ' ἐσθλὸν πήματα σὺν δύο δαίονται βροτοῖς ἀθάνατοι: "Alongside one good the gods allot two troubles to men."[36] The description of Homer about the two urns placed on the threshold of Jove, of which the one is said to be full of good things, the other of evils, pertains to this belief.[37] The story of Pandora in Hesiod also pertains to it.[38] But Homer himself elegantly refutes this opinion as most false in the first book of the *Odyssey*. He says that men have summoned evils upon themselves by their own ἀτασθαλίῃσιν, that is, by their own foolishness, as Aegisthus did, who committed adultery with the wife of Agamemnon when he was away—driven to do so not, indeed, by God, but by his own lust. For it has been rightly said, "If the gods have done any evil, they are not gods."[39] And Plato, at the end of book 2 of the *Republic*, says with utmost seriousness: "We must fight with all of our strength in order that no one in the city that we wish to be ruled well, whether old man

---

[34] Aeschylus, *Prometheus Bound* 515–16. Hemmingsen's reading differs slightly from that of modern editions.

[35] The word he uses is *explodenda*, whose primary meaning is theatrical—perhaps due to the reference earlier in the paragraph to Aeschylus' play.

[36] Pindar, *Pythian Odes* 3.81–82.

[37] Homer, *Iliad* 24.527–28.

[38] Hesiod tells the story of Pandora twice (with significant variations): *Theogony* 570–616 and *Works and Days* 53–105.

[39] I have been unable to find a source for this quotation, but the sentiment is found in, for example, Plato's works *passim*.

or young man, whether in a poem or in another kind of story, either say or hear that God is the cause of evils for anyone."[40]

And elsewhere he says: ὁ θεὸς αἴτιος μὲν ἐστὶ καλῶν, ἀναίτιος δὲ κακῶν. That is, "God is the author of good things, but not of evils."[41]

Some pretend that the goddess Ate[42] incites evils, and that she, being strong and swift, runs over gentler and more moderate affections. But that fiction, correctly understood, signifies nothing other than that men's rashness and thoughtlessness is the cause of evils. This rashness is Ate, who always harms men, from which fact she also has her name, because she always ἀᾶται [harms].

Again, there are those who ascribe goods and evils, both in morals and in other matters, to men's fortunes, in accordance with the following saying of the poet:

ὥσπερ κυαθίζουσα ἡμῖν ἐνιοθ᾽ ἡ τύχη,
ἓν ἀγαθὸν ἐπιχέουσα τρί᾽ ἐπανθλεῖ κακά.

That is:

Fortune is for us a cupbearer, which, when it pours out one good, draws a draught of three evils alongside it.[43]

I omit the opinion of those who think that both morals and events among men depend on the stars, and of those who affirm that morals generally follow the nature of a region, for which reason Hippocrates says that those who live in northern climes, that is, in Europe, or in mountainous places, are endowed with rustic morals; but that Asia is far more clement than other regions, and in it all things are found to be much better and more charming; and likewise, that men's morals are both gentler and readier for action on account of the ideal tem-

---

[40] Plato, *Republic* 2.380b6–c4.

[41] Cf. Plato, *Republic* 2.379c2–7.

[42] The personified goddess of reckless infatuation or impulse.

[43] A fragment of the fourth-century-BC New Comic poet Diphilus (frag. 107 Kassel-Austin) preserved in Stobaeus, *Anthology* 4.40.16. Hemmingsen's text differs slightly from modern editions of Stobaeus.

perateness of the Asian weather—but that nevertheless the men there are considered less warlike than in Europe.[44]

Those who say that natural ἰδιοκρασίαν [peculiar temperament] is the reason why some are more given to virtues, others to vices, come very close to the opinions just discussed. These, although I grant that they say something, do not say enough. For temperament is not a sufficient cause of evil actions; it is rather only a passionate and enticing partisan that can be overcome by the command of reason.

Some, in whose number are Plato, Aristotle, and Plutarch, and very many of the chief philosophers, attribute the fact that some are upright, others wicked, to rearing and their initial education. For just as fields that have been neglected produce useless plants, so the characters of men, when they have been neglected, are made liable to evil morals, in accordance with that proverbial verse of Horace:

> A fern fit for burning grows in fields that have been
> neglected.[45]

In contrast, as a field that has been cultivated produces good fruit, so the characters of men, when they have been cultivated, make their morals more agreeable, wherefore Plato rightly said: παιδείας κεφάλαιον ὀρθὴ τροφὴ [Proper rearing is the chief part of education].[46]

It is also for this reason that Plutarch advises that children should be kept away from fellowship and familiarity with evil men. To this pertains the creed of Pythagoras: "Do not taste those things whose tail is black," that is, do not be on terms of friendship with those who are thought loathsome on account of the condition of their morals.

Euripides says in the *Medea* that τὸν θυμὸν [the irascible power] is the author of evils, for he speaks thus in the character of Medea:

> θυμὸς δὲ κρείσσων τῶν ἐμῶν βουλευμάτων·
> ὅπερ μεγίστων αἴτιος κακῶν βροτῖς.

---

[44] See Hippocrates, *Airs Waters Places*, 12–24.

[45] Horace, *Satires* 1.3.37.

[46] Plato, *Laws* 643d1–2. Hemmingsen's word order differs from Plato's.

That is:

> The irascible power of my soul,[47] which is the author of the greatest evils for mortals, overcomes the judgments of my mind.[48]

Pindar seems to divine the true cause most correctly of all, although obscurely, when he says:

> καὶ χάρματ᾽ ἀνθρώποισι προμαθέος αἰδώς, ἐπὶ μὰν βαίνει τε
> καὶ λάθας ἀτέκμαρτον νέφος, καὶ παρέλκει πραγμάτων ὀρθὰν
> ὁδὸν γ᾽ ἔξω φρενῶν.

That is:

> Prometheus brings virtue and happiness to men, but nevertheless the dark cloud of forgetfulness is added and takes the right course of conducting one's affairs away from their minds.[49]

The poet here seems to signify the fall of Adam, whom many assert is signified by Prometheus. For his fall is the true cause of errors in life and morals, and of the fact that men do not so obey their λόγῳ [reason] as they do their erring ἐπιθυμίαις [desires].

Furthermore, because the word *conscience* is not always used in its proper sense, as I just now explained it, but sometimes in a figurative sense, I have decided here at the end to add some remarks about the various uses of the word.

Sometimes, then, *conscience* is used for the whole practical syllogism and the motion of the heart that follows the syllogism, and this by synecdoche, by which the whole often receives the name of

[47] Hemmingsen's phrase is *impetus animi*.

[48] Euripides, *Medea* 1079–80, also preserved in Stobaeus, *Anthology* 3.20.37. Hemmingsen has already cited this passage in chapter 2.

[49] Pindar, *Olympian Odes* 7.44–47. Hemmingsen's text differs slightly from modern editions of Pindar. Furthermore, Pindar is speaking of the gifts of a personified Shame or Reverence, the daughter of Forethought (which is the meaning of "Prometheus").

the part. Sometimes it is used in its proper sense for the faculty of the mind that supplies minor premises for the practical syllogism and adjusts the deed to the rule. Third, it is used by metonymy for the practical syllogism's conclusion itself, that is, for the judgment of the mind about the fact, as it is used by Paul in Romans 2.[50] Finally, it is sometimes used by metalepsis[51] for the motion that is aroused in the heart from thinking about the practical syllogism, that is, for the pain or happiness that accompanies the practical syllogism. By reason of this use in particular, the general category "conscience" embraces different specific types, so that one conscience is called good, another one bad: the one is called good because the recollection of a life led honorably, together with the hope and expectation of its outcome, is pleasant; the other is called bad because the recollection of a life led shamefully, conjoined with the dread of impending punishment, is sad and a cause of torment.

Here one can see that there are two συζυγίας [pairs] of affections in men: in the one συζυγίᾳ [pair] are happiness and hope; in the other are grief and dread. Each is preserved by means of the memory, but each has different causes. For a life spent honorably joins happiness and hope, but a life led shamefully is the cause of the latter συζυγία [pair], grief and dread. Therefore, as the recollection of a life well led is happy and has pleasant hope for the future, so the recollection of a life badly led is troublesome and suffers dread, which is the mind's fear for future danger. These affections are, as it were, witnesses given to men by God, which bear witness concerning the law of nature and seal it on the hearts of men.

It is sufficient to have noted these considerations concerning the law of nature in order to point out in some way that some sparks of it still remain in men, which, if they are aroused by good rearing and

---

[50] Rom. 2:15.

[51] "The rhetorical figure consisting in the metonymical substitution of one word for another which is itself a metonym; (more generally) any metaphorical usage resulting from a series or succession of figurative substitutions" (*Oxford English Dictionary*, s.v. "metalepsis").

honorable training, will be more open to view. These sparks—that is, the natural notions[52] about honorable and shameful things—are the sources of all honorable laws. Whoever rightly knows the things that I have noted will not find it toilsome to trace these honorable laws back to the rule of philosophy, which is demonstration. For I have not only demonstrated the first axioms and principles of the law of nature, which are immovable and infallible, and how hypotheses ought to be constructed from them κατὰ σύνθεσιν [by synthesis], but I have also pointed out how one can return by analysis from the last hypotheses to the principles, so that the truth and certainty of even the smallest hypotheses may be established. Nor do I doubt that those who know these things well will usefully read the *Ethics* of Aristotle and other writings about morals, to say nothing for the time being of the fact that it is useful for beginners in theology and jurisprudence to see and understand these sources of morals in nature.

But as to the fact that I have adduced no maxims from theology in this entire treatise, I did it so that I might show how far reason is able to progress without the prophetic and apostolic word. As to what remains, I beseech the eternal God and Father of our Lord Jesus Christ both to kindle the sparks of nature in a higher degree and to illuminate our minds by his own true light, and to give us such grace for living our lives while we tarry here that we may be able happily and with a good conscience, when the trumpet has proclaimed the last day, to pass over into the company of the most chaste spirits and saints of God.

---

[52] *noticiae.*

Selected Bibliography

Given Hemmingsen's extensive use of classical sources, I have not attempted to provide specific editions for every source. Most of Hemmingsen's classical sources are available in standard modern editions, such as the Loeb Classical Library series. This bibliography therefore contains only early modern and modern sources, as well as those modern editions of classical works to which specific reference is made in the footnotes of the translation. —EJH

Adam, Melchior. *Decades duae continentes vitas theologorum exterorum principum, qui ecclesiam Christi superiori seculo propagarunt et propugnarunt.* Frankfurt am Main: J. Rosae, 1618.

Allgemeine Deutsche Biographie. 56 vols. Leipzig and Berlin: Duncker & Humblot, 1875–1912.

Andersen, Carl Christian Thorwald. *The Chronological Collection of the Kings of Denmark.* Copenhagen: Forlagsbureauet, 1878.

Aristophanes. *Fragments.* Edited and translated by Jeffrey Henderson. Cambridge, MA: Harvard University Press, 2008.

Aristotle. *The Ethics of Aristotle.* Edited by John Burnet. New York: Arno Press, 1973.

———. *Eudemian Ethics.* Translated by B. Inwood and R. Woolf. Cambridge: Cambridge University Press, 2013.

———. *The Nicomachean Ethics.* Edited and translated by Horace Rackham. Cambridge, MA: Harvard University Press, 1934.

———. *The Nicomachean Ethics of Aristotle*. Translated by David Ross. Oxford: Oxford University Press, 1954.

Augustine. *City of God*. Translated by Marcus Dods. In *A Select Library of Nicene and Post-Nicene Fathers of the Christian Church*, edited by Philip Schaff, first series, vol. 2, 1–511. Reprint, Grand Rapids, MI: Eerdmans, 1952.

Baker, Robert C., and Roland Cap Ehlke, eds. *Natural Law: A Lutheran Reappraisal*. St. Louis, MO: Concordia, 2011.

Berman, Harold J. *Law and Revolution II: The Impact of the Protestant Reformations on the Western Legal Tradition*. Cambridge, MA: Harvard University Press, 2006.

Binder, Wilhelm. *Novus Thesaurus Adagiorum Latinorum*. Stuttgart: Eduard Fischhaber, 1861.

Blaise, Albert. *Lexicon Latinitatis Medii Aevi: praesertim ad res ecclesiasticas investigandas pertinens*. Turnhout: Brepols, 1975.

Bretschneider, C. G., H. E. Bindseil et al., eds. *Corpus Reformatorum*. 101 vols. Halle a. Salle and Brunsvigae: Schwetschke, 1834–1959.

Calvin, John. *Institutio Christianae Religionis* [1559]. In *Ioannis Calvini opera quae supersunt omnia*, edited by G. Baum, E. Cunitz, and E. Reuss, vol. 2, 1–1118. Brunsvigae: C. A. Schwetschke, 1864. ET: *Institutes of the Christian Religion*. Translated by Henry Beveridge. 3 vols. Edinburgh: Calvin Translation Society, 1845–46.

Campbell, Gordon, ed. *The Oxford Dictionary of the Renaissance*. Oxford: Oxford University Press, 2003.

Cancik, Hubert, Helmuth Schneider, Christine F. Salazar et al., eds. *Brill's New Pauly*. First series. 15 vols. Leiden: Brill, 2002–2008.

Cicero. *Academics*. Translated by Charles Brittain. Indianapolis: Hackett, 2006.

———. *On Obligations*. Translated by P. G. Walsh. Oxford: Oxford University Press, 2000.

———. *The Republic* and *The Laws*. Translated by Niall Rudd. Oxford: Oxford University Press, 1998.

Danstrup, John. *History of Denmark*. Copenhagen: Wivel, 1949.

Deferrari, Roy J., M. Inviolata Barry, and Ignatius McGuiness. *A Lexicon of St. Thomas Aquinas based on the Summa theologica and Selected Passages of His Other Works.* Washington, D.C.: Catholic University of America Press, 1948–49.

Diels, Hermann. *Die Fragmente der Vorsokratiker.* Edited by Walther Kranz. Hamburg: Rowohlt, 1964.

Dindorf, Wilhelm, ed. *Poetae scenici graeci: accedunt perditarum fabularum fragmenta.* London: Black, Young and Young, 1830.

Ennius, Quintus. *The Annals of Quintus Ennius.* Edited by Otto Skutsch. New York: Oxford University Press, 1985.

Erasmus. *Adagia.* Part 2. Edited by M. L. van Poll-van de Lisdonk and M. Cytowska. Part 2, vol. 2 of *Opera omnia Desiderii Erasmi Roterodami,* edited by Jan Hendrik Waszink. Amsterdam: North Holland, 1998.

Erdmann, Johann Eduard. *A History of Philosophy.* 3 vols. New York: Macmillan, 1890–92.

Finnis, John. *Collected Essays.* 5 vols. Oxford: Oxford University Press, 2013.

———. *Natural Law and Natural Rights.* 2nd ed. Oxford: Oxford University Press, 2011.

Garstein, Oskar. *Jesuit Educational Strategy, 1553–1622.* Vol. 3 of *Rome and the Counter-Reformation in Scandinavia.* Leiden: Brill, 1992.

George, Robert P. *The Clash of Orthodoxies: Law, Religion, and Morality in Crisis.* Wilmington, DE: Intercollegiate Studies Institute, 2002.

———. *In Defense of Natural Law.* Oxford: Oxford University Press, 1999.

———, ed. *Natural Law, Liberalism, and Morality: Contemporary Essays.* Oxford: Oxford University Press, 2001.

Gerhard, Johann. *Loci theologici.* Edited by F. Frank. 9 vols. Leipzig: J. C. Hinrichs, 1885.

Gilbert, Neal Ward. *Renaissance Concepts of Method.* New York: Columbia University Press, 1960.

Glare, P. G. W., ed. *Oxford Latin Dictionary.* 2nd ed. 2 vols. Oxford: Oxford University Press, 2012.

Grabill, Stephen J. *Rediscovering the Natural Law in Reformed Theological Ethics.* Grand Rapids, MI: Eerdmans, 2006.

Grane, Leif. "Teaching the People—The Education of the Clergy and the Instruction of the People in the Danish Reformation Church." In *The Danish Reformation against Its International Background*, edited by Leif Grane and Kai Hørby, 164–84. Göttingen: Vandenhoeck & Ruprecht, 1990.

Gregory, Brad S. *Rebel in the Ranks: Martin Luther, the Reformation, and the Conflicts That Continue to Shape Our World.* New York: HarperCollins, 2017.

———. *The Unintended Reformation: How a Religious Revolution Secularized Society.* Cambridge: Belknap Press, 2012.

Grell, Ole Peter. "The Emergence of Two Cities: The Reformation in Malmø and Copenhagent." In *The Danish Reformation against Its International Background*, edited by Leif Grane and Kai Hørby, 129–45. Göttingen: Vandenhoeck & Ruprecht, 1990.

Grendler, Paul F., ed. *Encyclopedia of the Renaissance.* 6 vols. New York: Scribner's, 1999.

Grotius, Hugo. *The Rights of War and Peace.* Edited by Richard Tuck. 3 vols. Indianapolis, IN: Liberty Fund, 2005.

Hagen, Kenneth. "*De Exegetica Methodo*: Niels Hemmingsen's *De Methodis* (1555)." In *The Bible in the Sixteenth Century*, edited by David C. Steinmetz, 181–96. Durham, NC: Duke University Press, 1990.

Haines, David, and Andrew Fulford. *Natural Law: A Brief Introduction and Biblical Defense.* Moscow, ID: Davenant, 2017.

Hauck, Albert, ed. *Realencyclopädie für protestantische theologie und kirche.* 3rd ed. 24 vols. Leipzig: J. C. Hinrichs, 1896–1913.

Hazeltine, Harold Dexter. Introduction to *The Medieval Idea of Law*, by Walter Ullmann, xv–xxxix. London: Methuen, 1969.

Hemmingsen, Niels. *Admonitio de supserstitionibus magicis vitandis, in gratiam sincerae religionis amantium.* Copenhagen: Iohannes Stockelman & Andreas Gutterwitz, 1575.

————. *Commentaria in omnes Epistolas Apostolorum*. Leipzig: Andreas Schneider and Ernst Vögelin, 1572.

————. *D. Nicolai Hemmingii, sacrarum literarum in Haffniensi schola professoris celeberrimi opuscula theologica*. Edited by Simon Goulart. Geneva: Eustathius Vignon, 1586.

————. *De lege naturae apodictica methodus*. Wittenberg: Rhaw, 1562.

————. *De methodis*. 1555. In *D. Nicolai Hemmingii, sacrarum literarum in Haffniensi schola professoris celeberrimi opuscula theologica*, edited by Simon Goulart, 1–90. Geneva: Eustathius Vignon, 1586.

————. *Demonstratio indubitatae veritatis de Domino Jesu vero Deo et vero homine unico Christo, Mediatore atque Redemtore nostro unico*. Copenhagen: Balthasar Kaus, 1571.

————. *Enchiridion theologicum*. Wittenberg: Iohannes Crato, 1557.

————. *Om naturens lov 1562*. Translated by Richard Mott. 4 vols. Copenhagen: Øresund, 1991–95.

————. "On the Law of Nature in the Three States of Life, and the Proofs That This Law Is Summarized in the Decalogue." Translated by E. J. Hutchinson. *Journal of Markets & Morality* 17, no. 2 (2014): 619–46.

————. *Syntagma institutionum christianarum perspicuis assertionibus ex doctrina prophetica et apostolica congestis (plerisque propositis et disputatis in Academia Hafniensi)*. Copenhagen: Vinitor, 1574.

Herzog, Johann Jakob, ed. *Realencyclopädie für protestantische theologie und kirche*. 22 vols. Stuttgart and Hamburg: R. Besser, 1854–68.

Hessus, Helius Eobanus. *King of Poets, 1514–17*. Vol. 3 of *The Poetic Works of Helius Eobanus Hessus*. Edited and translated by Harry Vredeveld. Leiden: Brill, 2014.

Hillerbrand, Hans J., ed. *Oxford Encyclopedia of the Reformation*. 4 vols. New York: Oxford University Press, 1996.

Høffding, Harald. *A History of Modern Philosophy*. Translated by B. E. Meyer. 2 vols. London: Macmillan, 1908.

Hørby, Kai. "Humanist Profiles in the Danish Reform Movement." In *The Danish Reformation against Its International Background*, edited by Leif Grane and Kai Hørby, 28–38. Göttingen: Vandenhoeck & Ruprecht, 1990.

Hornblower, Simon, and Anthony Spawforth, eds. *The Oxford Classical Dictionary*. 3rd ed. New York: Oxford University Press, 1996.

Hultin, Jeremy F. *The Ethics of Obscene Speech in Early Christianity and Its Environment*. Leiden: Brill, 2008.

Hutchinson, E. J. "Divine Law, Naturally: *Lex naturae* and the Decalogue in Two Works of Niels Hemmingsen." In *For Law and for Liberty: Essays on the Trans-Atlantic Legacy of Protestant Political Thought*, edited by W. Bradford Littlejohn, 1–19. Moscow, ID: Davenant, 2016.

———. "Nature and the Wound of Nature: A Pauline View of the Testimony of the Ancients in Niels Hemmingsen's *De Lege Naturae*." In *Ad Fontes Witebergenses: Select Proceedings of Lutheranism and the Classics III: Lutherans Read History*, edited by James A. Kellerman, E. J. Hutchinson, and Joshua J. Hayes, 58–75. Minneapolis, MN: Lutheran Press, 2017.

———. "Pagans and Theologians: An Examination of the Use of Classical Sources in Niels Hemmingsen's *De lege naturae*." *Perichoresis*, forthcoming.

———. "The Poets as Philosophers of Practical Action." In *Acta Conventus Neo-Latini Vindobonensis*, edited by Astrid Steiner-Weber. Leiden: Brill, forthcoming.

Jansen, F. J. Billeskov. "From the Reformation to the Baroque." In *A History of Danish Literature*, edited by Sven Hakon Rossel, 71–119. Lincoln: University of Nebraska Press, 1992.

Jensen, Janus Møller. *Denmark and the Crusades: 1400–1650*. Leiden: Brill, 2007.

Kaltenborn, Carl von. *Die Vorläufer des Hugo Grotius*. Leipzig: Gustav Mayer, 1848.

Kassel, Rudolf, and Colin Austin, ed. *Poetae comici Graeci*. 8 vols. Berlin: De Gruyter, 1983–2001.

Keen, Ralph. "The Moral World of Philip Melanchthon." PhD dissertation, University of Chicago, 1990.

Kühlmann, Wilhelm. "Neo-Latin Literature in Early Modern Germany." In *Early Modern German Literature 1350–1700*, edited by Max Reinhart, 281–329. Vol. 4 of *Camden House History of German Literature*, edited by James Hardin. Rochester, NY: Camden House, 2007.

Landfester, Manfred, with Brigitte Egger, eds. *Dictionary of Greek and Latin Authors and Texts.* Translated and edited by Tina Jerke and Volker Dallman. Vol. 2 of *Brill's New Pauly: Supplements*, edited by Hubert Cancik, Manfred Landfester, and Helmuth Schneider. Leiden: Brill, 2009.

Lapide, Cornelius a. *Commentaria in Sacram Scripturam*. Naples: I. Nagar, 1855.

Larson, James L. *Reforming the North: The Kingdoms and Churches of Scandinavia, 1520–1545.* New York: Cambridge University Press, 2010.

Lausten, Martin Schwarz. "The Early Reformation in Denmark and Norway, 1520–59." In *The Scandinavian Reformation: From Evangelical Movement to Institutionalisation of Reform*, edited by Ole Peter Grell, 12–41. Cambridge: Cambridge University Press, 1995.

Lewis, Charlton T., and Charles Short, eds. *A Latin Dictionary founded on Andrews' edition of Freund's Latin Dictionary*. Oxford: Clarendon Press, 1879.

Liddell, Henry G., Robert Scott, and Henry Stuart Jones, eds. *A Greek-English Lexicon*. 9th ed. Oxford: Clarendon Press, 1996.

Littlejohn, W. Bradford. *The Peril and Promise of Christian Liberty: Richard Hooker, the Puritans, and Protestant Political Theology*. Grand Rapids, MI: Eerdmans, 2017.

Lockhart, Paul Douglas. *Frederick II and the Protestant Cause: Denmark's Role in the Wars of Religion, 1559–1596.* Leiden: Brill, 2004.

Lund, Eric. "Nordic and Baltic Lutheranism." In *Lutheran Ecclesiastical Culture, 1550–1675*, edited by Robert Kolb, 411–54. Boston: Brill, 2008.

Luther, Martin. *Against the Heavenly Prophets in the Matter of Images and Sacraments.* Translated by Bernhard Erling and Conrad Bergendoff. In *Luther's Works*, edited by Jaroslav Pelikan, Helmut Lehman, and Christopher Brown, vol. 40, 73–223. Philadelphia: Fortress; St. Louis, MO: Concordia, 1955–.

————. *How Christians Should Regard Moses.* Translated by E. Theodore Bachmann. In *Luther's Works,* vol. 35, 155–74.

Lyby, Thorkild, and Ole Peter Grell. "The Consolidation of Lutheranism in Denmark and Norway." In *The Scandinavian Reformation: From Evangelical Movement to Institutionalisation of Reform,* edited by Ole Peter Grell, 114–43. Cambridge: Cambridge University Press, 1995.

Malling, Ove. *Great and Good Deeds of Danes, Norwegians, and Holstenians.* London: C. and R. Butler, 1807.

Meister, Christian Friedrich Georg. *Bibliotheca iuris naturae et gentium. Pars prima.* Göttingen: Vandenhoeck, 1749.

Melanchthon, Philip. *Corpus doctrinae Christianae.* Leipzig: Rhamba, 1572.

————. *De restituendis scholis.* 1540. In *Corpus Reformatorum,* vol. 11, 487–95.

————. *Enarrationes aliquot librorum Ethicorum Aristotelis.* In *Corpus Reformatorum,* vol. 16, 278–416.

————. *Enarratio Symboli Niceni.* 1550. In *Corpus Reformatorum,* vol. 23, 198–346.

————. *Ethicae doctrinae elementorum libri duo.* 1550. In *Corpus Reformatorum,* vol. 16, 165–276.

————. *In Ethica Aristotelis Commentarius.* Wittenberg: Josef Klug, 1529.

————. *Interpretatio Pythiorum Pindari.* 1558. In *Corpus Reformatorum,* vol. 19, 213–238.

————. *Loci praecipui theologici.* 1559. In *Corpus Reformatorum,* vol. 21, 601–1106. ET: *The Chief Theological Topics:* Loci Praecipui Theologici *1559.* Translated by J. A. O. Preus. 2nd ed. St. Louis, MO: Concordia, 2011.

————. *Loci Theologici Germanice.* 1558. In *Corpus Reformatorum,* vol. 22, 45–636.

————. *Oratio de Legibus.* 1550. In *Corpus Reformatorum,* vol. 11, 908–16.

————. *Oratio de Legum Fontibus et Causis.* In *Corpus Reformatorum,* vol. 11, 916–24.

————. *Philosophiae moralis epitome.* In *Corpus Reformatorum,* vol. 16, 21–164.

————. *Postilla Melanthoniana*. 1594. In *Corpus Reformatorum*, vol. 24, 1–966; vol. 25, 1–992.

Menander. *Menandri quae supersunt*. Edited by Alfred Körte and Andreas Thierfelder. 2nd ed. 2 vols. Leipzig: Teubner, 1957–59.

Migne, J.-P., ed. *Patrologiae cursus completus: Series Graeca*. 161 vols. Paris: Migne, 1857–1866.

Nettleship, Henry. *Contributions to Latin Lexicography*. Oxford: Clarendon Press, 1889.

Oakley, Francis. *Natural Law, Laws of Nature, Natural Rights: Continuity and Discontinuity in the History of Ideas*. New York: Continuum, 2005.

Olden-Jørgensen, Sebastian. "Scandinavia." In *European Political Thought, 1450–1700: Religion, Law and Philosophy*, edited by Howell A. Lloyd, Glenn Burgess, and Simon Hodson, 300–31. New Haven, CT: Yale University Press, 2007.

Orfield, Lester B. *The Growth of Scandinavian Law*. Philadelphia: University of Pennsylvania Press, 1953.

Plato. *The* Timaeus *of Plato*. Edited by R. D. Archer-Hind. New York: Arno Press, 1973.

Pollux, Julius. *Iulii Pollucis Onomasticon*. Basel: R. Winter, 1541.

Pound, Roscoe. *The Ideal Element in Law*. Indianapolis, IN: Liberty Fund, 2002.

Prodi, Paolo. *Eine Geschichte der Gerechtigkeit: Vom Recht Gottes zum modernen Rechtstaat*. Munich: Beck, 2003.

————. *The Papal Prince: One Body and Two Souls: The Papal Monarchy in Early Modern Europe*. Cambridge: Cambridge University Press, 1987.

Raunio, Antti. "Divine and Natural Law in Luther and Melanchthon." In *Lutheran Reformation and the Law*, edited by Virpi Mäkinen, 21–61. Leiden: Brill, 2006.

Reimmann, Jakob Friedrich. *Versuch einer Einleitung in die Historiam literariam derer Teutschen*. Halle im Magedeburg: Renger, 1713.

Reuchlin, Johannes. *On the Art of the Kabbalah*. Translated by Martin Goodman and Sarah Goodman. Lincoln: University of Nebraska Press, 1993.

Riese, Alexander, ed. *Anthologia latina sive poesis Latinae supplementum, pars prior, fasciculus II*. Leipzig: Teubner, 1906.

Robertson, Teresa, and Philip Atkins. "Essential vs. Accidental Properties." *Stanford Encyclopedia of Philosophy* 2008/2013. http://plato.stanford. edu/entries/essential-accidental/.

Rommen, Heinrich A. *The Natural Law: A Study in Legal and Social History and Philosophy*. Indianapolis, IN: Liberty Fund, 1998.

Rørdam, Holger Frederik. *Kjøbenhavns Universitets Historie fra 1537 til 1621*. Vol. 2 of *Kjøbenhavns Universitets Historie*. Copenhagen: B. Lunos, 1872.

Roth, Andreas. "Crimen contra naturam." In *Natural Law and the Laws of Nature in Early Modern Europe: Jurisprudence, Theology, Moral and Natural Philosophy*, edited by Lorraine Daston and Michael Stolleis, 89–103. Abingdon, UK: Ashgate, 2008.

Sandys, John Edwin. *A History of Classical Scholarship*. 3 vols. Cambridge: Cambridge University Press, 1908–21.

Scattola, Merio. *Das naturrecht vor dem Naturrecht*. Tübingen: Max Niemeyer, 1999.

———. "Models in History of Natural Law." *Ius Commune: Zeitschrift für Europäische Rechtsgeschichte* 28 (2001): 91–159.

Scharpius, Johannes. *Cursus theologicus*. Geneva: Chouet, 1620.

Schmauss, Johann Jacob. *Neues "Systema" des Rechts der Natur*. Göttingen: Vandenhoeck, 1754.

Schröder, Jan. "The Concept of (Natural) Law in the Doctrine of Law and Natural Law of the Early Modern Era." In *Natural Law and the Laws of Nature in Early Modern Europe: Jurisprudence, Theology, Moral and Natural Philosophy*, edited by Lorraine Daston and Michael Stolleis, 57–71. Abingdon, UK: Ashgate, 2008.

Seybold, Johann Georg. *Selectiora Adagia Latino-Germanica*. Nuremburg: Johann Andreas Endter, 1669.

Sophocles. *Fragments*. Edited and translated by Hugh Lloyd-Jones. Cambridge, MA: Harvard University Press, 1996.

St. Leger, James. *The "Etiamsi Daremus" of Hugo Grotius: A Study in the Origins of International Law.* Rome: Pontificum Athenaeum Internationale "Angelicum," 1962.

Stigel, Johann. *Poematum liber I.* Jena: Donatus Ritzenhayn and Thomas Rebart, 1566.

Stobaeus, Johannes. *Joannis Stobaei Anthologium.* Edited by Kurt Wachsmuth and Otto Hense. 4 vols. Berlin: Weidmann, 1884.

Tamm, Ditlev. *"Nolo falcem in alienam messem mittere:* Der dänische Theologe Niels Hemmingsen (1513–1600) aus juristischer Sicht." In *Gerichtslauben-Vorträge: Freiburger Festkolloquium zum fünfundsiebzigsten Geburtstag von Hans Thieme,* edited by Karl Kroeschell, 47–56. Sigmaringen, Germany: Jan Thorbecke, 1983.

Tucker, George Hugo. Homo Viator: *Itineraries of Exile, Displacement and Writing in Renaissance Europe.* Geneva: Droz, 2003.

Turretin, Francis. *Institutio theologiae elencticae.* 3 vols. Geneva: S. de Tournes, 1688–89.

Valeriano, Pierio. *Hieroglyphica, seu de sacris Aegyptiorum aliarumque gentium literis commentarii.* Lyon: Frelon, 1602.

VanDrunen, David. *A Biblical Case for Natural Law.* Grand Rapids, MI: Acton Institute, [2006].

———. *Divine Covenants and Moral Order: A Biblical Theology of Natural Law.* Grand Rapids, MI: Eerdmans, 2014.

———. *Natural Law and the Two Kingdoms: A Study in the Development of Reformed Social Thought.* Grand Rapids, MI: Eerdmans, 2009.

Williams, Steven J. *The* Secret of Secrets: *The Scholarly Career of a Pseudo-Aristotelian Text in the Latin Middle Ages.* Ann Arbor: University of Michigan Press, 2003.

Witte, John, Jr. *Law and Protestantism: The Legal Teachings of the Lutheran Reformation.* Cambridge: Cambridge University Press, 2002.

Xenophon. *Memorabilia.* Edited by Josiah Renick Smith. Boston: Ginn, 1903.

INDEX